Constitutional
Underclass

The Constitutional Underclass

Gays, Lesbians, and the Failure of Class-Based Equal Protection

Evan Gerstmann

The University of Chicago Press
Chicago and London

EVAN GERSTMANN is assistant professor of political science
at Loyola Marymount University.

The University of Chicago Press, Chicago 60637
The University of Chicago Press, Ltd., London
© 1999 by The University of Chicago
All rights reserved. Published 1999
08 07 06 05 04 03 02 01 00 99   1 2 3 4 5

ISBN: 0-226-28859-5 (cloth)
ISBN: 0-226-28860-9 (paper)

Library of Congress Cataloging-in-Publication Data

Gerstmann, Evan.
    The constitutional underclass : gays, lesbians, and the failure of
class-based equal protection / Evan Gerstmann.
        p.   cm.
    Includes bibliographical references and index.
    ISBN 0-226-28859-5 (cloth : alk. paper).—ISBN 0-226-28860-9
(pbk. : alk. paper)
        1. Gays—Legal status, laws, etc.—United States.   2. Lesbians—
Legal status, laws, etc.—United States.   3. Homosexuality—Law and
legislation—United States.   4. Equality before the law—United
States.   I. Title.
KF4754.5.G47   1999   98-11679
342.73'087—dc21   CIP

For my mother, who died too young, but still taught me the love of learning.

CONTENTS

A C K N O W L E D G M E N T S

First and foremost, I am indebted to Professor Donald A. Downs, my committee chair for the dissertation that launched the research used in this book. I could not have asked for a better advisor, teacher, or friend than Don Downs, who encouraged, inspired, and incited me throughout my time in graduate school.

I am also indebted to Professors Joel Grossman, R. Booth Fowler, James Baughman, Gordon Baldwin, David Canon, Herbert Kritzer, and Jane Schacter, all of whom are with the University of Wisconsin, Madison. Their input much improved this project at the dissertation stage. Also, Beloit College, the Wisconsin Alumni Research Fellowship, and the Institute for Legal Studies at the University of Wisconsin, Madison, provided support in various important ways while I was a graduate student.

The empirical part of this book could not have been accomplished without the generous help of the men and women I interviewed in Colorado and elsewhere. They gave me the benefit of their time and insight and often went out of their way to provide me with important documents. Talmey-Drake Research & Strategy, Inc., generously gave me access to results of their polling data; Equality Colorado provided me with numerous useful documents, including the reports of their focus group research conducted by Miller Research Group, Inc.; and several other interviewees also provided me with useful information and documents.

I would also like to thank Loyola Marymount University for its support, financial and otherwise, of my work. Special thanks are due to Professors Seth Thompson and Michael Genovese for their help and support and to my research assistants, Aimee Hamoy, Bethany Albertson, and Christopher Shortell.

I thank the faculties of the law schools of UCLA and the University of Wisconsin for inviting me to present my ideas at their faculty colloquia and for their helpful comments and insights. I am also indebted to Professors Arthur Leonard, Kenneth Sherrill, and Jethro Lieberman, all of whom read drafts of the manuscript and suggested revisions that made the book's arguments stronger. Professor Sherrill also gave me access to data that proved important to the concluding chapter of this book. Professor Bernard Schwartz of the University of Tulsa also generously shared his insights with me.

Finally, I would like to thank my father, Kurt Gerstmann, and my friends Matthew Bosworth, Robert Schwoch, Jillian Savage, Robert Knopf, and especially Michael Gauger. Their patient ears and helpful insights helped me throughout this project.

PART ONE

The Conundrum of Class-Based Equal Protection

The Failure of Equal Protection

On one level, this book is about the equal protection clause of the United States Constitution and how it has been used to carve the American people into separate legal classes. Since the 1970s the United States Supreme Court has held that the equal protection clause protects different groups differently—an approach that has denied many citizens the equal protection of the laws. Some groups are "suspect classes" that receive strong judicial protection against discriminatory laws. Other groups are "quasi-suspect classes" that receive an intermediate level of protection. Courts rarely tolerate laws that discriminate against these classes. Still other groups, such as gays, lesbians, the elderly, and the poor, constitute neither suspect nor quasi-suspect classes and therefore receive very little protection under the equal protection clause; laws that discriminate against them will be tolerated so long as there is any "rational basis" for those measures. But the Supreme Court cannot adequately explain why groups are frozen in this hierarchy. Why, for example, do women receive greater protection than the elderly? Why are illegitimate children and their parents protected more than gays and lesbians?[1] Part 1 of this book addresses these issues.

On another level, this book is about how this class-based approach has denied justice to gays and lesbians in particular, whom the courts have always treated as a minimally protected class. I pay special attention to how this status shaped the recent battle over gay rights in Colorado, which was the subject of the most recent Supreme Court decision on gay rights, *Romer v. Evans.*[2] Part 2 of the book is organized around the political and legal issues posed by that case. Although *Romer* is widely perceived as a victory

1. Throughout this book, I will refer to gays, lesbians, and bisexuals as either "gays and lesbians" or "homosexuals," depending on the context. This is done for the sake of brevity, or in the case of "homosexuals," to match the language used in certain statutes or regulations. I do not intend to imply by this that bisexuals are excluded from the analysis contained in this book. Also, I will sometimes refer to the issue of gay and lesbian rights as "gay rights." This is also merely for the sake of brevity.
2. 517 U.S. 620 (1996).

for gay and lesbian rights, the decision does nothing to alter the place of gays and lesbians in the equal protection hierarchy. Why they remain at its bottom is a central question of this book.

The issue of gay and lesbian rights is, of course, important in and of itself, for the government discriminates against gays and lesbians in a number of very significant ways. But gay and lesbian rights cannot be analyzed separately from the overall structure of equal protection jurisprudence. While the courts have generally been unreceptive to gay and lesbian equal protection claims, they have been no more receptive to claims from other groups such as the elderly and the poor. To understand the place of gays and lesbians within equal protection jurisprudence we must take a fresh look at the overall structure of that jurisprudence. Thus, this book is aimed at those generally interested in constitutional law as well as those especially interested in gay and lesbian rights.

The Origins of the Class-Based System

The class-based system of equal protection has its origins in Justice Harlan Fiske Stone's famous footnote 4 in the 1938 decision *United States v. Carolene Products*.[3] Although Stone, writing for the Court, deferred to legislative intent in upholding a law that related to commercial transactions, he suggested that the Court should engage in a "more searching judicial inquiry" of legislation that targets unpopular "discrete and insular minorities."[4] In Stone's view, majority prejudice against unpopular and powerless minorities poisons the political process, and the Court must intervene to protect these groups. The idea that the Court should protect minorities who cannot protect themselves through the normal political process is widely popular among jurists and scholars. According to Laurence Tribe, this "political process" theory "was anticipated by John Marshall; it assumed a central role for Harlan Fiske Stone; it signally motivated Earl Warren and it has been elaborated by numerous scholars, most powerfully in the work of John Ely."[5] Although African Americans are the prototypical example of a discrete and insular minority to be protected under this theory, the same logic can be used to protect the rights of women, illegitimate children, aliens, and ethnic minorities. Indeed, the Supreme Court has declared each of these groups to be a suspect or quasi-suspect class.

3. 304 U.S. 144 (1938).

4. *Carolene Products*, 304 U.S. at 152 n. 4.

5. Laurence H. Tribe, *Constitutional Choices* (Cambridge: Harvard University Press, 1985), 14 (citations omitted).

How the political-process theory came to assume a central place in the Court's equal protection doctrine is widely misunderstood. The conventional view associates this theory with the liberal Warren Court and the expansion of the equal protection clause to protect groups other than racial minorities. In his seminal book *Democracy and Distrust*, John Hart Ely wrote, "During the Warren era, the Supreme Court was quite adventurous in expanding the set of suspect classifications beyond race. Laws classifying to the comparative disadvantage of aliens, persons of illegitimate birth, even poor people, were all at one time or another approached as suspect."[6]

In fact, the very opposite is true: the Warren Court meticulously avoided applying the political-process theory to the equal protection clause. Even more important, the Warren Court never claimed that it was subjecting laws that classified according to gender, alienage, or illegitimacy to heightened scrutiny. It was the far more conservative Burger Court that began holding in the 1970s that the purpose of the equal protection clause was to protect those minorities who need "extraordinary protection from the political process."[7] *The current three-tiered framework of suspect, quasi-suspect, and minimally protected classes is purely a creation of the Burger Court, and it was created to sharply limit the scope of the equal protection clause in the wake of the Warren Court's and early Burger Court's adventurous expansion of equal protection doctrine.*

To understand the placement of gays, lesbians, and other groups in the equal protection hierarchy, we must understand both why the Warren Court avoided the political-process model of equal protection and why the Burger Court conservatives embraced it. These questions will be addressed in chapters 2 and 3, respectively.

A "Constitutional Underclass"?

The argument that gays and lesbians remain a "constitutional underclass" within the class-based framework may surprise readers who are familiar with recent decisions that have ruled in favor of gay and lesbian litigants. In *Romer v. Evans*, the Supreme Court struck down "Amendment 2"—the voter-approved amendment to the Constitution of the State of Colorado that would have voided all state and local gay rights laws. In *Gay Rights Coalition v. Georgetown University*,[8] the District of Columbia Court of Ap-

---

6. John Hart Ely, *Democracy and Distrust: A Theory of Judicial Review* (Cambridge: Harvard University Press, 1980), 148.

7. *San Antonio Independent School District v. Rodriguez*, 411 U.S. 1, 28 (1973).

8. 536 A.2d 1 (D.C. 1987).

peals held that Georgetown University could not claim a religious free-dom exemption from a Washington, D.C., civil rights law that prohibited universities from denying access to their facilities on the basis of a student's sexual orientation. In *Watkins v. United States*,[9] the U.S. Court of Appeals for the Ninth Circuit (en banc) held that the Army was equitably estopped from discharging an openly gay soldier who had served in the military for over fourteen years. In *Nabozny v. Podlesny*,[10] the Seventh Circuit held that a school had no rational basis for refusing to protect a gay student who was being physically abused by his classmates.

While the importance of these cases should not be dismissed, neither should it be exaggerated. Neither *Romer* nor *Georgetown* grants gays and lesbians any affirmative constitutional protection against discrimination. *Romer* held that, when gays and lesbians manage to convince state and local legislatures to pass protective laws, these protections cannot be voided wholesale via a state constitutional amendment. Although *Georgetown* rejected a claim that religious institutions are *automatically* exempt from gay rights laws, *Romer* suggests that explicit exclusions for religious institutions might be upheld. *Watkins* also has limited precedential value, because it rests on an out-of-date policy and unusual facts: Watkins joined the Army in 1967, and "in filling out the Army's pre-induction medical form, he marked 'yes' in response to a question about whether he had homosexual tendencies."[11] The Army admitted him anyway, and he never tried to hide his sexual orientation. The Ninth Circuit (en banc) held that the Army's sudden effort to discharge Watkins after fourteen years of exemplary service violated the doctrine of equitable estoppel.[12] In *Nabozny*, as well, the victory is a narrow one. Outside of its effect on the parties involved, perhaps *Nabozny*'s greatest value is its demonstration that gays and lesbians are still forced to go to court to get school officials to offer them the same protection against violence that other students receive.

Meanwhile, courts have rejected equal protection challenges to a vast array of discriminatory policies against gays and lesbians.[13] Courts have

9. 875 F.2d 699 (9th Cir. 1989).

10. 92 F.3d 446 (7th Cir. 1996).

11. *Watkins*, 875 F.2d at 701.

12. Judge Norris's concurring opinion in the en banc decision argued that gays and lesbians should be considered a suspect class under the equal protection clause. The three-judge panel had made the same argument. But this reasoning did not make it into the majority en banc opinion.

13. Some would argue that at least some of these policies do not constitute discrimination in the usual sense of the word—that exclusion of gays from the realm of national defense, for example, is a rational response to the possibility that homosexuals are vulnerable to black-

upheld federal laws and government policies that prohibit homosexuals from immigrating to the United States[14] and that ban them from FBI jobs and from any positions in the civilian defense industry requiring high-level security clearance.[15] While many of these policies have been recently reformed, the position of gays and lesbians at the bottom of the equal protection hierarchy denies them constitutional protection against the reinstatement of any of these policies should the political climate change.

Further, the military's "don't ask, don't tell" policy has been upheld by every federal appellate court that has considered it,[16] and the Supreme Court has let each of these decisions stand. The military remains extraordinarily aggressive about tracking down and discharging even the most exemplary service members, including those who have never voluntarily disclosed their homosexuality. The case of Timothy McVeigh (no relation to the man convicted of the Oklahoma City bombing) illustrates the tenuous position of homosexuals in the military. In 1997 McVeigh exchanged America Online (AOL) E-mail with a civilian Navy volunteer regarding a Christmas toy drive for children. She looked up his AOL profile and saw that he had listed his marital status as "gay," although the profile did not include his last name or any other identifying information about him other than the fact that he lived in Honolulu. She forwarded the profile to her husband, a Navy enlisted man, who reported it to the military authorities. Although McVeigh had served for seventeen years with an exemplary record, receiving four Good Conduct Medals, the Navy Commendation Medal, and performance reviews that rated him as an "outstanding role model," the Navy went to AOL for evidence and sought to discharge McVeigh three years short of pension eligibility. At this writing, the situation is in the early stages of litigation: a federal judge has halted disciplinary action against McVeigh on grounds unrelated to the Constitution or

---

mail or that homosexuals in the military might be disruptive. As we will see in chapter 4, this is a difficult issue to discuss because there is no generally accepted definition of what it means to discriminate. For now, I define practices as discriminatory if they would be so considered if they were applied to groups such as African Americans or women. The question of whether discrimination against gays and lesbians should be considered *legally* equivalent to discrimination against these other groups is discussed throughout this book, and especially in chapter 4.

14. *Boutilier v. INS*, 387 U.S. 118 (1967).

15. These cases are discussed in chapter 4.

16. *Phillips v. Perry*, 106 F.3d 1420 (9th Cir. 1997); *Richenberg v. Perry*, 97 F.3d 256 (8th Cir. 1996); *Thomasson v. Perry*, 80 F.3d 915 (4th Cir. 1996). The district courts have split on the issue, but those that have struck down the policy have been reversed by the appellate courts.

equal protection,[17] and the Navy has announced its intention to appeal. Regardless of the outcome, the situation demonstrates the extraordinary aggressiveness with which the military continues to pursue gay and lesbian service members.

At the state level, gays and lesbians face perhaps even greater legal disadvantages. State courts have issued orders revoking a mother's custody of her child largely because she is a lesbian, imprisoning gays and lesbians for consensual private sexual acts, and placing restrictions on divorced gay fathers that effectively make visitation with their own children impossible.[18] Meanwhile the federal courts at the highest level continue to tolerate overt job discrimination against gays and lesbians, even by public employers. In January 1998 the Supreme Court let stand an Eleventh Circuit decision upholding the right of Georgia's attorney general to rescind a job offer to a top-ranked Emory law school graduate solely because she planned to celebrate her commitment to her female partner in a Jewish ceremony performed by a rabbi.[19] In 1985 the Supreme Court let stand a decision upholding a public school's right to suspend a guidance counselor solely because she had told some teachers she was bisexual, despite the jury's express finding that the counselor's statements did not "in any way interfere" with her job performance or the regular operation of the school.[20] As these cases show, gays and lesbians are indeed members of a constitutional underclass.

The Incoherence of Equal Protection Jurisprudence

This is not to say that gays and lesbians can never win an equal protection case. *Romer* shows that they can. The argument is that they can win only by appealing to judicial sympathy and intuitions about fairness rather than by invoking any coherent legal principle. Equal protection doctrine has become so amorphous and so full of contradictions and ambiguities that it is impossible for gays and lesbians to appeal to any *legal* standard to protect them from discrimination. If a law discriminates against racial minorities, the standard is clear: the law will be struck down unless it is narrowly tailored to further a compelling governmental interest.[21] If a law discriminates against women, it will be struck down unless it serves important

17. *McVeigh v. Cohen*, 1998 U.S. Dist. LEXIS 3007 (D.D.C. Jan. 26, 1998) (Judge Stanley Sporkin).

18. See chapter 4, notes 17–24 and accompanying text.

19. *Shahar v. Bowers*, 1998 U.S. LEXIS 83, *denying cert. to* 120 F.3d 211 (1997).

20. *Rowland v. Mad River School District*, 470 U.S. 1009 (1985) (Brennan, J., dissenting), *denying cert. to* 730 F.2d 444 (6th Cir. 1984).

21. *Batson v. Kentucky*, 476 U.S. 79 (1986).

governmental objectives and is substantially related to the achievement of those objectives.[22] But gays and lesbians cannot rely on such clear legal standards. For gays and lesbians, and for other groups at the bottom of the equal protection hierarchy, the law has become so malformed that it is no exaggeration to say that there is literally no actual law there. The many incoherences of equal protection law are laid out later in the book, but two in particular are worth briefly highlighting at this juncture.

The Class/Classification Switch

The Supreme Court has held that, to qualify as a suspect or quasi-suspect class, a group must show that it lacks political power.[23] On this basis, the courts have granted enhanced protection to racial minorities and women but have denied such protection to gays, lesbians, the elderly, and other groups. Yet the Supreme Court has also granted enhanced protection to whites and to men in a variety of contexts. The idea that gays and lesbians are too politically powerful to qualify for enhanced protection but whites and men are not is, to use Justice John Marshall's familiar phrase, "too extravagant to be maintained."[24]

The Court has been oscillating between two terms that are deceptively similar: "suspect class" and "suspect classification." Every suspect class implies a corresponding suspect classification. If racial minorities are a suspect class, then race is a suspect classification. Women are a quasi-suspect class, but gender is a quasi-suspect classification.

When gays seek to move up in the equal protection hierarchy, the courts tell them they are not a *suspect class* because they are not politically powerless. But when whites seek protection against affirmative action programs, courts do not ask them to prove that they are politically powerless (obviously they are not). Instead, courts subtly switch terminology; they hold that race is a *suspect classification* and thereby protect whites from racial preferences. Similarly, the courts protect men from discrimination by holding that gender is a quasi-suspect classification.

By switching between the terms *suspect class* and *suspect classification,* the Supreme Court can require some groups to show that they are politically powerless but allow other, far more politically powerful groups to benefit from strong constitutional protection. The Court has never explicitly recognized that it does this, and it has never attempted to justify it. Indeed, all the criteria the courts use to decide where different groups belong in the equal

22. *Craig v. Boren,* 429 U.S. 190 (1976).
23. *Massachusetts Board of Retirement v. Murgia,* 427 U.S. 307, 313 (1975).
24. *Marbury v. Madison,* 5 U.S. (1 Cranch) 137, 179 (1803).

protection hierarchy are so loaded with contradictions, double standards, and unresolvable ambiguities that principled decision making in this area is virtually impossible. These points are discussed at length in chapter 4.

Rational-Basis Duality

Groups at the bottom of the equal protection hierarchy are protected only by "rational basis" scrutiny. Courts will uphold laws that burden groups such as gays and lesbians so long as there is any rational basis whatsoever for such laws. This standard is intended to give very minimal protection to groups that are not suspect or quasi-suspect classes. But sometimes the Supreme Court silently changes the rules and applies heightened scrutiny in these cases without acknowledging that it is doing so. Justice Thurgood Marshall referred to this type of analysis as "second order" rational-basis scrutiny and denounced the practice for its complete lack of accountability and its failure to give guidance to lower courts.[25]

I argue in chapter 6 that the Supreme Court applied second-order rational-basis scrutiny in *Romer*. While this produced a narrow victory for gay and lesbian rights, it produced no principle to be relied on in future litigation. Because the Court does not acknowledge that second-order rational-basis scrutiny exists, it is impossible to make a principled argument that it should be applied to any particular case. This leaves gays and lesbians (as well as opponents of gay rights) at the mercy of judicial intuitions about the substantive fairness of laws that burden gays and lesbians.

The Importance of Constitutional Doctrine

It has been argued that judges' *attitudes*, not legal doctrine, are the best predictors of how courts will decide cases.[26] Jeffrey Segal and Harold Spaeth make this argument in connection with the Supreme Court, and other scholars have concluded that the lower courts also have substantial discretion to render decisions based on their own policy preferences.[27] But the experience of gays and lesbians in First Amendment cases shows that strong, clear constitutional doctrine from the Supreme Court can protect unpopular groups regardless of judicial attitudes. In many cases public

25. *City of Cleburne v. Cleburne Living Center*, 473 U.S. 432, 459–60 (1985) (Marshall, J., concurring).

26. Jeffrey A. Segal and Harold J. Spaeth, *The Supreme Court and the Attitudinal Model* (New York: Cambridge University Press, 1993).

27. McNollgast, "Politics and the Courts: A Positive Theory of Judicial Doctrine and the Rule of Law," *Southern California Law Review* 68 (1995): 1631–89; Donald R. Songer, Jeffrey A.

universities have sought to ban gay student organizations, claiming that such groups advocate illegal sexual activity. The Supreme Court, however, has held that a person cannot be punished for advocating illegal action unless his or her speech is directed to inciting imminent lawless action that is likely to occur.[28] Lower courts (including five federal appellate courts) have ruled in favor of gay student groups based on this doctrine, without regard to the popularity of the groups' message.[29] In one case a judge concurred to express his distaste for the result but acknowledged that the law required it.[30] In another case, the federal district court judge stated, "It is of no moment, in First Amendment jurisprudence, that ideas advocated by an association may to some or most of us be abhorrent, even sickening,"[31] but he ruled in favor of the gay and lesbian plaintiffs. These cases show how strong, clear doctrine can protect unpopular groups irrespective of judicial attitudes.

In contrast, equal protection doctrine is so incoherent that judges have no choice but to rely on their own values and instincts when they face equal protection claims brought by gays and lesbians. Without a substantial revamping and clarification of legal principle, the promise of equal protection of the laws is a hollow one for groups not deemed to be suspect or quasi-suspect classes.

Equal Protection and the Politics of Amendment 2

Constitutional doctrines are important outside the courtroom as well, for they can serve as potent symbols in political debates. Chapter 5 examines how class-based constitutional doctrine created problems for gays and lesbians in 1992 in the political debate over Amendment 2 to the Colorado constitution. That measure, which would have nullified all state and local gay rights laws[32] and would have prohibited the creation of new gay rights laws, read as follows:

Segal, and Charles M. Cameron, "The Hierarchy of Justice: Testing a Principal-Agent Perspective on Supreme Court–Circuit Court Interactions," *American Journal of Political Science* 38 (1994): 673.

28. *Brandenburg v. Ohio*, 395 U.S. 444 (1969).

29. For a list and discussion of such cases (as of 1992), see William B. Rubenstein, "Since When Is the 14th Amendment Our Route to Equality: Some Reflections on the Construction of the Hate Speech Debate from a Lesbian / Gay Perspective," *Law and Sexuality* 2 (1992): 23.

30. *Gay Student Alliance v. Blanton*, 544 F.2d 162, 168 (4th Cir. 1976) (Markey, J., concurring).

31. *Cyr v. Walls*, 439 F. Supp. 697, 701 n. 3 (N.D. Tex. 1977).

32. At the time, several Colorado cities and the University of Colorado had a variety of laws and policies prohibiting discrimination on the basis of sexual orientation.

> *No protected status based on homosexual, lesbian or bisexual orienta-*
> *tion.* Neither the State of Colorado through any of its branches or
> departments, nor any of its agencies, political subdivisions, mu-
> nicipalities or school districts, shall enact, adopt or enforce any
> statute, regulation, ordinance or policy whereby homosexual, les-
> bian or bisexual orientation, conduct, practices or relationships
> shall constitute or otherwise be the basis of, or entitle any person
> or class of persons to have or claim any minority status, quota
> preferences, protected status or claim of discrimination. This Sec-
> tion of the Constitution shall be in all respects self-executing.

Voters approved Amendment 2 by a narrow margin—53.4 percent voted
for the amendment, and 46.6 percent voted against it. The amendment
never took effect, however, due to a series of injunctions issued by state
courts. It was eventually struck down by the United States Supreme Court.

The impact of constitutional doctrine on the public debate over Amendment 2 has not been explored or duly appreciated. This might be due to the
belief among many political scientists that the general public is ignorant of,
or indifferent to, Supreme Court decisions.[33] But the notion that the world
can be divided into classes of people, some more deserving than others of
protection against discrimination, has penetrated the public consciousness. Hence, the class-based equal protection doctrine had a substantial
impact on the political battle over Amendment 2.

Both advocates and opponents of Amendment 2 were well aware that
most Colorado voters had no desire to pass any law they perceived as discriminatory against gays and lesbians. Colorado was one of the first states
to abolish its antisodomy laws.[34] Further, public opinion in Colorado,
even after the passage of Amendment 2, remains clearly tolerant toward
gays and lesbians. For example, as of March 1993, only 16 percent of Coloradans polled agreed with the statement, "Homosexual behavior should
be against the law, even if it occurs between consenting adults."[35] Seventy-
seven percent agreed with the statement, "Except for their choice of sexual
partners, homosexuals are not really different from anyone else." Only 8
percent strongly disagreed with that statement. Further, most Coloradans
actually supported the very laws that Amendment 2 nullified. Seventy
percent of those polled believe that an employer should not have the right
to refuse to hire someone because of sexual orientation. Over 80 percent

33. The literature in this area is discussed in chapter 5.
34. Stephen Bransford, *Gay Politics vs. Colorado: The Inside Story of Amendment 2* (Cascade,
Colo.: Sardis Press, 1994), 2.
35. These statistics are based on polls by Talmey-Drake Research & Strategy, Inc. These
polls and the data are discussed in greater detail in chapter 5.

believe that a landlord should not be allowed to evict a tenant because that tenant is gay.

Because most Colorado voters clearly did not want to allow discrimination against gays and lesbians, proponents of Amendment 2 had to frame the issue very carefully. The Court's class-based jurisprudence allowed them to argue that what was really at issue was whether gays and lesbians should be treated as a special class. Proponents argued that Amendment 2 merely confirmed politically what the Court had decided as a matter of constitutional law: gays and lesbians as a class are not deserving of the same protections against discrimination as are groups such as racial minorities. In this way, supporters of the amendment were able to shift the debate away from the issue of discrimination against gays and lesbians and focus the public on the question of whether gays and lesbians are similar enough to racial minorities to deserve "special" rights against discrimination.

Also, by focusing the public's attention on whether gays and lesbians are a special class, Amendment 2's proponents were able to tap into public hostility toward affirmative action programs. Focus group research showed that, while Coloradans did not want to discriminate, they were extremely sensitive to the question of whether gays and lesbians, like racial minorities, might qualify for affirmative action. (As will be discussed in chapter 5, class-based analysis blurs the line between traditional civil rights protection and affirmative action.) Thus, using the courts' class-based framework proved to be politically advantageous for supporters of Amendment 2.

Equal Protection and Litigating Amendment 2

Once Amendment 2 passed, a variety of plaintiffs immediately challenged it under the equal protection clause; chapter 6 examines in detail the long legal battle that ensued. There is no better demonstration of the incoherence of the three-tiered framework of equal protection doctrine than the judicial attempts to respond to the issues posed by the amendment. Three different courts ruled on its constitutionality: a Colorado trial court,[36] the Colorado Supreme Court, and the United States Supreme Court. All appeared to share the intuition that the amendment treated gays and lesbians unfairly. All three courts concluded that the amendment violated the equal protection clause, yet they had no idea *why* it was unconstitutional. Each court created its own rationale, and each rationale raised more questions than it answered.

36. The state trial court referred to here is the District Court for the City and County of Denver. Colorado district courts are the lowest state courts of general jurisdiction.

The United States Supreme Court ruled that the amendment violated the equal protection clause because there was no rational basis for such a law. Justice Anthony Kennedy's majority opinion asserted that Coloradans voted for Amendment 2 out of "animus" toward gays, but it offered no empirical basis for this assertion and ignored a great deal of evidence suggesting otherwise. The dissenting opinion, written by Justice Antonin Scalia, is equally problematic. Scalia accused Kennedy, a fellow Reagan appointee, of spearheading a liberal offensive in a "Kulturkampf" over sexual morality. The dissent also characterized gays as a "politically powerful minority" seeking "special protection." As we will see, the issue of whether gays are seeking rights or protections that can be fairly characterized as "special" is extremely complex. The dissent does nothing to shed light on this issue.

Neither the majority opinion nor the dissent was able to put together a coherent argument about how to evaluate the constitutionality of Amendment 2. Without significantly revamping equal protection law, the Court had few alternatives. It could have held that gays, like racial minorities, have suffered from such a history of discrimination that they merit enhanced constitutional protection. But such a ruling would have eventually pulled the courts into countless controversial areas of social policy, such as laws limiting adoption and marriage by gay couples. The Court could have upheld Amendment 2 by ruling that gays are not as oppressed as racial minorities and therefore do not deserve the same constitutional protections. If a history of oppression were the key variable, however, the Court might have to explain why affirmative action policies that burden white males are unconstitutional. It would be a tough sell indeed to argue that gays are not an oppressed minority but whites and men are.[37] Thus, it is easy to understand why the Court fell back on a second-order rational-basis test.

Reforming Equal Protection Doctrine

The last chapter of the book looks to the future. How can equal protection doctrine be made more coherent, less rigid, and more even-handed? Chapter 7 looks at numerous proposals to break away from the tiered approach. Various jurists and scholars have suggested that the Court should use the equal protection clause to strike down laws that are "arbitrary," "irrational," or "prejudiced." None of these terms are particularly helpful. Are

37. Some have argued that white men deserve greater protection than gays because race and gender are immutable characteristics. The problems with this argument are discussed in chapter 4.

laws that seek to discourage homosexual relationships (or the bearing of illegitimate children) arbitrary? Irrational? Prejudiced? Even to state such questions explicitly highlights their subjective nature.

The last chapter also lays out my suggestions for reform. Building on the work of J. Harvie Wilkinson, I suggest that the level of constitutional protection against a challenged law should be based on the right involved rather than the group affected. Instead of asking *who* has been denied equality, the Court would ask *what kind* of equality has been denied. Under the proposed approach, the right to political equality would receive the most protection. Current equal protection jurisprudence protects the right to vote, but under the suggested reforms, political equality would be defined more broadly: it would also include the right to run for office, to serve on juries, to receive a fair trial, and to have access to the legal system.

The difference between the class-based system and the rights-based system would be significant. For example, under the current system for choosing juries, the state is prohibited from using its "free strikes" to exclude a prospective juror from a given trial on account of his or her race or gender since these are, respectively, suspect and quasi-suspect classifications. Yet the state is free to attempt to keep gays, lesbians, the elderly, or poor people off juries without regard to how this would affect the fairness of the trial, because these groups are not suspect or quasi-suspect classes.[38] This is equally true in civil cases. So, for example, if a Latino pride group and a gay and lesbian pride group were both suing for the right to march in a town parade, it would be unconstitutional for the town's lawyers to attempt to keep Latinos and Latinas off the jury, but they could, without constitutional impediment, try to keep gays and lesbians off the jury. It is hard to understand how this is "equal" protection. The system ignores the crucial issue of the right to a fair trial.

Under the proposed approach to reforming equal protection analysis, the equal protection clause would also protect "economic opportunity" rights. Again, these rights would be equally protected for every person, not just for members of suspect or quasi-suspect classes. These rights would include the right to access to education and the right to pursue a lawful occupation.

Access to education is the most indispensable requirement for genuine equality of opportunity. Justice Thurgood Marshall often argued that this right should be strongly protected under the equal protection clause. Dissenting from a decision that rejected an equal protection challenge to un-

---

38. Discrimination in the use of "peremptory challenges" is discussed in greater detail in chapter 7.

equal funding of school districts, he wrote that "the majority's holding can only be seen as a retreat from our historic commitment to equality of educational opportunity. . . . In my judgment, the right of every American . . . to an equal start in life . . . is far too vital to permit state discrimination on grounds as tenuous as those presented by this record."[39] Indeed, as we will see in chapter 2, the Warren Court based its decision in *Brown v. Board of Education* on the premise that education is "a right which must be made available to all on equal terms."[40] Of course, race was hardly irrelevant to *Brown:* the badge of inferiority that segregation imposed was an important aspect of the injury to African American children. Even if the Court moves away from class-based analysis, there is no need for it to be blind to the historical or social context of race in our society or to the especially grave injury that racial discrimination can cause. The special context of race, however, should not blind the Court to the importance of the underlying right involved. For example, if a school district, in a paranoid reaction to AIDS, were to segregate gay high school students, this would profoundly violate their right to educational opportunity. Yet under the current system, the segregation of gay students would be subjected to the same lax level of judicial review as would a run-of-the-mill administrative regulation. A rights-based analysis, on the other hand, would recognize the importance of equality of educational opportunity.

As for the right to pursue a lawful occupation, I argue that it has been seriously shortchanged in contemporary equal protection jurisprudence. Justice Marshall referred to the right to work as "of the very essence of the personal freedom and opportunity it was the purpose of the [Fourteenth] Amendment to secure."[41] Indeed, there is strong evidence that the framers of the Fourteenth Amendment were greatly concerned about protecting the right to pursue the occupation of one's choice. Under the proposed reforms, such a right would not require the Court to become an arbiter of every government regulation regarding employment; chapter 7 suggests a balancing test that would respect the legitimate interests of the state in regulating employment and recognize the inherent limitations of judicial intervention in this area. I argue as well that this test provides a much more defensible ground for invalidating Colorado's Amendment 2—one that would not require the Court to level unsupported accusations that Col-

---

39. *San Antonio Independent School District v. Rodriguez,* 411 U.S. 1, 70–71 (1973) (Marshall, J., dissenting).

40. *Brown v. Board of Education,* 347 U.S. 483, 493 (1954).

41. *Massachusetts Board of Retirement v. Murgia,* 427 U.S. 307, 317 (1975) (quoting *Truax v. Raich,* 239 U.S. 33, 41 (1915)).

orado voters acted solely out of bigotry in approving the amendment.

Finally, a rights-based approach to equal protection would not require a return to the *Lochner* era of judicial intrusion in economic matters. I endorse Wilkinson's proposal that matters of "economic equality"—entitlement to welfare benefits, for example—are best left to the legislature and should received only minimal review by the courts.

The purpose of the last chapter is not, of course, to lay out a fully formed scheme of equal protection jurisprudence. The chapter is merely an outline of a possible approach, and the goal is only to suggest that future debate about the direction of equal protection doctrine need not slavishly adhere to the limits of class- or classification-based law. I believe that the current approach is so deeply flawed that a fundamental shift should at least be considered. But if my argument merely leads to sharpening the debate over how the current classes and classifications can be made fairer and more coherent, this would be major progress.

In sum, this book addresses three basic questions: (1) how and why the class-based system of equal protection developed; (2) what its impact has been, especially on gays and lesbians; and (3) how the law can be reformed to be more intellectually coherent and fair while respecting the democratic process and the limits of judicial capacity.

The Issue of Judicial Behavior

Finally, a word about my assumptions regarding judicial behavior at the Supreme Court level is in order. I accept the overwhelming view of judicial scholars that justices act, at least in part, to advance their conceptions of good law or good policy. I also assume that justices are sometimes willing to engage in "strategic" or "sophisticated" behavior to achieve these ends—drafting opinions, for example, with a view to getting the support of other justices or legitimating the Court's authority rather than expressing their own ideal preferences.[42]

Regarding the direct or indirect influence of public opinion on the Court, I make no assumptions.[43] In the final chapter I argue that the Court should adopt a balancing test to address certain equal protection ques-

42. For an excellent recent review and treatment of the literature in this area, see Lawrence Baum, *The Puzzle of Judicial Behavior* (Ann Arbor: University of Michigan Press, 1997).

43. For a good example of the debate on this issue, see William Mishler and Reginald S. Sheehan, "Response: Popular Influence on Supreme Court Decisions," *American Political Science Review* 88 (1994): 716–24, reporting evidence of direct and indirect impact of public opinion on Court decisions; and Helmut Norpath and Jeffrey Segal, "Comment: Popular Influence on Supreme Court Decisions," *American Political Science Review* 88 (1994): 711–16, which comments on Mishler and Sheehan's article.

tions. Since balancing tests inherently allow for some degree of judicial discretion, one concern might be that public hostility toward gays and lesbians could influence the Court to give a cold shoulder to gay and lesbian rights claims. I argue in the final chapter that, even *if* the Court is influenced by public opinion toward gays and lesbians, public opinion is actually quite supportive of gay and lesbian rights (while remaining hostile to gays and lesbians as a group) and that a balancing test would allow the Court to protect gay and lesbian rights without having to assert that gays and lesbians are a group that deserves some type of special protection.

The purpose of this book is to persuade people to look at old issues in a new light. The promise of "the equal protection of the laws" is majestic but it is also vague, as majestic phrases tend to be. To understand how we have come to today's class-based understanding of what this promise means, we have to look back at the specifics of how this doctrine developed and why. The next chapter looks at the origins of class-based analysis in the 1930s and follows its development through the 1950s, when the Court rejected class-based analysis in its famous desegregation cases.

Equal Protection and the Development of the Tiered Framework of Judicial Scrutiny

Never before in American history has the equal protection clause meant so much to so many. During the past several decades, the clause has evolved from "the usual last resort of constitutional arguments" into "the Court's chief instrument for invalidating state laws" and "a vital tool for effecting social change."[1] Therefore, it is crucial for the legal and academic communities to continually reexamine the logic and structure of equal protection jurisprudence to see if it is still capable of responding in a fair and principled way to those who believe they are being denied equal protection of the laws.

This chapter examines the beginning and initial evolution of the "three-tiered framework," a judicially constructed set of rules the courts use to apply the equal protection clause. Under this framework, different groups receive different levels of judicial protection. Laws that discriminate on the basis of characteristics such as race or national origin are almost never tolerated by the courts, while laws that discriminate against groups such as the elderly, the poor, or gays and lesbians are generally tolerated. Laws that discriminate on the basis of gender and illegitimacy are generally not tolerated, but are somewhat more likely to survive judicial scrutiny than are laws that discriminate on the basis of race or national origin. Thus, courts use the equal protection clause to apply three distinctly different levels of review, depending on the type of law the court is examining. State and federal courts have consistently held that gays and lesbians are entitled to only the lowest level of judicial protection under the three-tiered framework. This means that the courts will uphold laws that discriminate against gays and lesbians even if those laws would have been struck down if they discriminated on the basis of race or gender.[2] As Amendment 2 af-

---

1. Respectively, *Buck v. Bell*, 274 U.S. 200, 208 (1927); *Zablocki v. Redhail*, 434 U.S. 374, 395 (1975) (Stewart, J., concurring); *Coburn v. Agustin*, 627 F. Supp. 983, 986 (D. Kan. 1985).

2. There is much confusion about whether the courts are protecting women and racial minorities, or whether they are protecting both genders and all races equally. This is a complex

fected only gays and lesbians, the Supreme Court had to assume that the law served no rational basis in order to strike it down.

The Three-Tiered Framework

The equal protection clause commands that no state shall "deny to any person within its jurisdiction the equal protection of the laws." The Supreme Court has construed this to mean that "all persons similarly situated should be treated alike."[3] Unfortunately, how this broad principle should be applied to particular situations is not self-evident.[4] Therefore, "the courts have themselves devised standards for determining the validity of state legislation or other official action that is challenged as denying equal protection."[5] The three-tiered framework is the principal method created by the Supreme Court for this purpose. In the following discussion, I lay out the three-tiered framework in a straightforward and uncritical fashion, so as to clearly define what I am critiquing. Discussion of the three-tiered framework's many ambiguities and contradictions is reserved for later.

Under the three-tiered framework, the general rule is that legislation is presumed to be valid and "will be sustained if the classification drawn by the statute is rationally related to a legitimate state interest."[6] This standard is called the "rational basis" test. It is designed to allow even unwise legislation to pass muster easily, because the democratic process, rather than the courts, is supposed to be the usual means for repealing even foolish legislation. "The Constitution presumes that even improvident decisions will be rectified by the democratic processes."[7]

The Court applies a very different test when the law in question classifies by race, national origin, or alienage (i.e., noncitizen status). Such laws

---

question that will be addressed in detail in the following chapters. For the moment it suffices to say that African Americans are considered to be the paradigm group that is entitled to the highest level of judicial protection. As will be discussed in the following chapters, much of the legal and public debate over gay and lesbian rights centers on the question of how closely the situation of gays and lesbians resembles the situation of African Americans.

3. *City of Cleburne v. Cleburne Living Center,* 473 U.S. 432, 439 (1985); *Plyler v. Doe,* 457 U.S. 202, 216 (1982). My description of the three-tiered framework relies mainly on the Court's own elucidation in *Cleburne* because it is an unusually clear and methodical explanation. Also, coming from the Supreme Court itself, it is the most authoritative description available. Ironically, as will be discussed in chapter 6, after nicely stating the framework, the Court reaches a holding entirely unreconcilable with it.

4. Indeed, it has been argued that this statement actually has no real meaning. Peter Westen, "The Empty Idea of Equality," *Harvard Law Review* 95 (1982): 537–96.

5. *Cleburne,* 473 U.S. at 439–40.

6. *Id.*

7. *Id.*

are subjected to "strict scrutiny" rather than mere "rational basis" scrutiny. They will be sustained "only if they are suitably tailored to serve a compelling state interest."[8] The Court uses this much stricter test for laws involving race, alienage, and national origin because "such discrimination is unlikely to be soon rectified by legislative means."[9] The reasoning is that some minorities are so lacking in political power that they cannot effectively use the legislative process to protect their rights. Strict scrutiny is also applied because race, national origin, and alienage "are so seldom relevant to the achievement of any legitimate state interest that laws grounded in such considerations are deemed to reflect prejudice and antipathy—a view that those in the burdened class are not as worthy or deserving as others."[10] Race, alienage, and national origin are therefore referred to as "suspect" classifications.

Legislative classifications based on gender are subjected to a standard of review that is greater than rational-basis scrutiny, yet not so exacting as strict scrutiny. Courts generally refer to this standard as "heightened"[11] or "intermediate"[12] scrutiny. The courts will strike down laws that classify according to gender unless those laws are "substantially related to a sufficiently important governmental interest."[13] Gender classifications are subjected to heightened scrutiny because they "very likely reflect outmoded notions of the relative capabilities of men and women."[14] Statutes that classify according the characteristic of illegitimacy are also subject to heightened scrutiny. This is because "illegitimacy is beyond the individual's control and 'bears no relation to the individual's ability to participate in and contribute to society.'"[15] Since laws based on gender and illegitimacy attract the intermediate form of scrutiny, gender and illegitimacy are often called "quasi-suspect classifications."

---

8. *Cleburne*, 473 U.S. at 440. Although the Court used the phrase "suitably tailored" in *Cleburne*, it usually uses the phrase "narrowly tailored." See *Miller v. Johnson*, 515 U.S. 900 (1995); *Adarand Constructors v. Pena*, 515 U.S. 200 (1995).

9. *Cleburne*, 473 U.S. at 440.

10. *Id.*

11. *Id.* at 441.

12. *Brown v. Cohen*, 101 F.3d 155, 182 (1st Cir. 1996); *Navarro v. Block*, 72 F.3d 712, 716 (9th Cir. 1995).

13. *Cleburne*, 473 U.S. at 441.

14. *Id.*

15. *Id.* (quoting in part *Mathews v. Lucas*, 427 U.S. 495, 505 (1976)). It is still not completely clear whether classifications based on legitimacy are subjected to precisely the same test as gender classifications, although it is clear that they are subjected to greater than rational-basis scrutiny. Further, it is not completely settled whether gender-based classifications will be subjected to strict scrutiny in the future. See *J. E. B. v. Alabama ex rel. T. B.*, 511 U.S. 127 (1994).

In sum, the courts apply different standards to different laws depending on what group is affected by those laws. Most laws—including laws that classify people according to sexual orientation, age, or wealth—will be upheld so long as they are rationally related to any legitimate governmental purpose. Laws that create classifications based on gender or illegitimacy are subjected to heightened (or "intermediate") scrutiny and will be upheld by the courts only if they are substantially related to a significant governmental purpose. Laws that classify according to race, alienage, or national origin are subjected to strict scrutiny and will be upheld only if they are narrowly tailored to further a compelling governmental purpose. So, for example, one law banning African Americans from the military, another law banning women, and another banning gays and lesbians would all be subject to different levels of judicial review.

When state actors intentionally discriminate against suspect and quasi-suspect classes, the courts apply the same stringent level of review that they would apply to laws that are discriminatory on their face.[16] For example, the courts would apply strict scrutiny to a law that is neutral on its face but is actually enforced only against racial minorities. However, because gays and lesbians are not a suspect class, it is permissible to enforce a law only against them even if the law applies to both homosexuals and heterosexuals.[17]

Finally, the Courts will also apply strict scrutiny to laws that violate certain "fundamental rights," even if no suspect classification is involved. There are only a small number of such rights. These rights are not found within the text of the Constitution and should not be confused with explicitly protected rights such as freedom of speech and assembly. They include the right to vote, to travel between states, and to make reproductive choices.[18] This is often referred to as the "fundamental-rights branch" of equal protection. The concept of fundamental rights is analytically independent from the concept of suspect classes and is not the central focus of this book. The fundamental-rights branch of equal protection is discussed briefly in chapter 3 and in greater detail in chapter 6.

Gays, Lesbians, and the Three-Tiered Framework

As will be discussed in chapter 4, a broad array of laws and governmental policies classify people according to sexual orientation. Gays and lesbians

16. *J. E. B.*, 511 U.S. at 127; *Batson v. Kentucky*, 476 U.S. 79 (1986).

17. *Bowers v. Hardwick*, 478 U.S. 186 (1986).

18. Respectively, *Kramer v. Union Free School District No. 15*, 395 U.S. 621 (1969); *Shapiro v. Thompson*, 394 U.S. 618 (1969); and *Skinner v. Oklahoma*, 316 U.S. 535 (1942).

face serious legal obstacles when they seek to serve in the armed forces, adopt children, or—in some cases—even retain custody of their own children. When gays and lesbians challenge these laws under the equal protection clause, the outcome will largely be determined by the level of scrutiny applied by the courts. If the Supreme Court were to decide that gays and lesbians are a suspect class and direct all courts to apply strict scrutiny to laws that classify according to sexual orientation, virtually all these laws would likely be struck down. Indeed, strict scrutiny has been famously referred to as "'strict' in theory and fatal in fact."[19]

However, courts have been unwilling to apply strict or even intermediate scrutiny to laws that burden gays and lesbians. The courts apply only rational-basis scrutiny to these laws. Other than Amendment 2, laws that classify according to sexual orientation have passed rational-basis scrutiny. These laws include not only the ban on gays and lesbians in the military, but also the government's policy of denying security clearance even to "out" gays and lesbians.[20]

Rational-basis scrutiny has been described as "minimal scrutiny in theory and virtually none in fact."[21] Therefore, gays and lesbians have actively sought judicial recognition as a suspect or quasi-suspect class. Gays and lesbians have argued that the history of discrimination and current laws disadvantaging them are sufficient predicates for suspect-class status. This argument has not been successful. The Supreme Court has never directly addressed whether gays and lesbians are a suspect class,[22] but lower courts consistently apply only rational-basis scrutiny to laws that burden gays and lesbians.

Why have the courts been so reluctant to find that gays and lesbians are a suspect class that should be protected against discrimination the same way that racial and ethnic minorities are? To answer this question, we must take a closer look at the structure of equal protection jurisprudence itself, particularly the three-tiered framework.

19. Gerald Gunther, "Foreword: In Search of Evolving Doctrine on a Changing Court: A Model for a Newer Equal Protection," *Harvard Law Review* 86 (1972): 8.

20. *High Tech Gays v. Defense Industrial Security Clearance Office*, 895 F.2d 563 (9th. Cir. 1990).

21. Gunther, "Foreword," 8. There have been discrete instances where the Court has claimed to be applying the rational-basis test and actually has applied a test more akin to strict scrutiny. These cases are discussed in chapter 6.

22. In *Romer v. Evans*, the Colorado trial court had ruled that gays and lesbians are too politically powerful to be considered a suspect or quasi-suspect class. *Evans* (trial court opinion), at p. C-18 of Colorado's cert. petition. The attorneys challenging Amendment 2 decided that it was fruitless to appeal this issue since federal courts have so consistently refused to declare that gays and lesbians are a suspect or quasi-suspect class.

The Three-Tiered Framework Revisited

The courts' reluctance to hold that gays and lesbians are a suspect class is unsurprising when put in historical context. While it is true that the courts have been unwilling to grant this status to gays and lesbians, it is equally true that for the past twenty years courts have been unwilling to call *any* new group a suspect or quasi-suspect class. By "new group" I mean any group of people that was not already recognized as a suspect or quasi-suspect class by the mid-1970s. The list of protected classes has been in stasis since that time.

In fact, the judicial window for recognizing suspect and quasi-suspect classifications other than race and national ancestry was quite brief. In 1971 the Court explicitly stated for the first time that alienage is a suspect classification.[23] By 1977 the Court had held that gender and illegitimacy are quasi-suspect classifications.[24] No new suspect or quasi-suspect classifications have been found by the Court since 1977.

Thus, the question is why the courts have been so reluctant, after a brief, fitful period of expanding the number of suspect and quasi-suspect classes, to find any new suspect or quasi-suspect classes at all. As the Supreme Court has never explicitly acknowledged that it has closed the list of suspect classes, it has never sought to explain the reasons for this closure. To understand why the Court stopped creating new suspect and quasi-suspect classes, we must first look at the reasons the Court began holding that certain classifications are suspect in the first place. The modern formulation of suspect classifications emerged from a synthesis of perhaps the single most famous case and the single most famous footnote in constitutional history: *Brown v. Board of Education*[25] and footnote 4 of *United States v. Carolene Products Co.*[26]

23. *Graham v. Richardson*, 403 U.S. 365, 372 (1971), held that alienage is a suspect classification. It is not entirely clear when national ancestry was first recognized as a suspect classification. In *Graham*, the Court cites three cases from the 1940s involving discrimination against persons of Japanese ancestry for the proposition that national origin is a suspect classification. Since laws discriminating against persons of Japanese ancestry can be understood as discrimination both on the basis of race and national origin, the issue of national origin was not analyzed separately.

24. *Craig v. Boren*, 429 U.S. 190 (1976); *Trimble v. Gordon*, 430 U.S. 762 (1977). It should be noted that the Court did not use the term "quasi-suspect" at that time, but it did apply intermediate scrutiny to laws that discriminated on the basis of gender or illegitimacy.

25. 347 U.S. 483 (1954).

26. 304 U.S. 144 (1938).

Carolene Products and the "Political Process" Model

Carolene Products was decided in 1938, sixteen years before *Brown*. For the most part it is an unremarkable case, one of many cases in the late 1930s upholding federal economic regulations under the Constitution's commerce clause.[27] It was written at a time of "extraordinary vulnerability for the Supreme Court," a time when "the Court was just beginning to dig itself out of the constitutional debris left by its wholesale capitulation to the New Deal a year before."[28]

Before 1937, during what is known as the *"Lochner* era,"[29] the Supreme Court struck down many state and federal economic regulations. The justices' staunch defense of laissez-faire capitalism led them into a losing battle with President Franklin Roosevelt over the New Deal. By 1937 the Court had fully surrendered and no longer seriously questioned the constitutionality of New Deal programs.[30] This defeat was so spectacular that it even threw the basic concept of judicial review into question: "With the decisive triumph of the activist welfare state over the Old Court, an entire world of constitutional meanings, laboriously built up over two generations, had come crashing down upon the Justices' heads. Indeed, the Court had been so politically discredited by its constitutional defense of laissez-faire capitalism that it was hardly obvious whether *any* firm ground existed upon which to rebuild the institution of judicial review."[31]

Thus, by 1938 the Court was in the position of having to justify all over again why an unelected body of nine men should have any right at all to strike down democratically enacted laws. The famed *Carolene Products* footnote was an early hint at just such a justification. In the body of the opinion, the Court was at pains to assure that democratic processes would have a free hand in the area of economic regulation. The Court's constitutional defense of laissez-faire economics was over. But in footnote 4, the Court added a caveat:

27. In this case, the Court upheld the power of the federal government to regulate the sale of skim milk.

28. Bruce A. Ackerman, "Beyond *Carolene Products,*" *Harvard Law Review* 98 (1985): 713–14.

29. This name stems from the Supreme Court's decision in *Lochner v. New York*, 198 U.S. 45 (1905), in which the Court struck down a New York state law limiting the hours bakers could work to sixty per week.

30. For a more extended discussion of the battle between the Court and Roosevelt, see David P. Courrie's two-volume work, *The Constitution and the Supreme Court* (Chicago: University of Chicago Press, 1985, 1988).

31. Ackerman, "Beyond *Carolene Products,*" 714.

It is unnecessary to consider now whether legislation which restricts those political processes which can ordinarily be expected to bring about repeal of undesirable legislation, is to be subjected to more exacting judicial scrutiny under the general prohibitions of the Fourteenth Amendment than are most other types of legislation. . . . Nor need we inquire whether similar considerations enter into review of statutes directed at particular religious or racial minorities; whether prejudice against discrete and insular minorities may be a special condition which tends to seriously curtail the operation of those processes ordinarily to be relied upon to protect minorities, and which may call for a correspondingly more searching judicial inquiry.[32]

The Court was promising that it could be reborn as an ally of democracy, or more specifically, of pluralistic democracy. Pluralism, at its most optimistic, assumes that most minorities can protect their political interests via the pluralistic process, that is, forming coalitions with other minorities by making the necessary trade-offs to protect their vital interests.[33]

The gist of *Carolene Products* is that certain minorities, "discrete and insular minorities" who suffer from prejudice, are unable to form effective political coalitions and are often singled out for especially unfavorable treatment by the hostile majority. They will not be protected by the pluralistic process because of majority prejudice and their own lack of political power. *Carolene Products* says this prejudice and powerlessness are "a special condition which tends to seriously curtail the operation of those processes ordinarily relied upon to protect minorities."[34] Therefore the Court must take special care to protect these minorities. The Court, as promised in the *Carolene Products* footnote, will not completely defer to the democratic process when discrete and insular minorities are being targeted by the law. This lays the foundations for subjecting laws that target suspect classes to strict scrutiny.

The most famous modern exponent of this theory is John Hart Ely, whose *Democracy and Distrust* champions what he calls the "political process" model of constitutional interpretation. Ely notes that one of the purposes of the Bill of Rights is to protect minority interests. However, he argues that "the original Constitution's more pervasive strategy [for protecting minority rights] can be loosely styled as a strategy of pluralism, one

32. *Carolene Products,* 304 U.S. at 153 n. 4.
33. Ely, *Democracy and Distrust,* 151.
34. *Carolene Products,* 304 U.S. at 153 n. 4.

of structuring the government, and to a limited extent society generally, so that a variety of voices would be guaranteed their say and no majority coalition would dominate."[35]

Therefore, by subjecting laws that target discrete and insular minorities to heightened scrutiny, the Court is actually protecting the pluralistic political process. This is why Ely calls this approach the "political process" model: rather than undemocratically imposing its own values, the Court is merely protecting the pluralistic political process from the unwanted effects of prejudice against discrete and insular minorities.[36] The challenge, then, is for the Court to properly identify those groups that are so powerless or despised that they cannot effectively participate in the pluralistic political process. These groups are "suspect classes" and should be strongly protected by the courts.[37]

The beauty of the Carolene Products / political-process approach is that it answers so many questions at once. It provides a basis for deciding which groups are suspect classes. They are the groups that cannot effectively engage in the "sort of 'pluralist' wheeling and dealing by which the various minorities that make up our society typically interact to protect their interests."[38] This approach also explains why it is up to the courts to decide which groups are suspect classes. "The whole point of the approach is to identify those groups in society to whose needs and wishes elected officials have no apparent interest in attending. If the approach makes sense, it would not make sense to assign enforcement to anyone but the courts."[39] Finally, it justifies the whole concept of judicial review. If the drafters of the Constitution were counting on pluralism to protect minorities from the tyranny of democratic majorities, then it makes sense for a nondemocratic institution like the judiciary to step in when pluralism breaks down.

In this light, it is easy to see why the Supreme Court gravitated toward the concept of strict scrutiny of laws that involve suspect classifications. "[T]he equal protection technique of strict scrutiny operates in large part as

35. Ely, *Democracy and Distrust*, 80.

36. Of course not all jurists and scholars subscribe to this theory of pluralism or of the Court's role in monitoring the pluralistic process. However, the purpose of this section is merely to lay out the theory.

37. The applicability of the *Carolene Products* / political-process rationale to the equal protection clause and the concept of suspect classes is straightforward. Ely goes further, and argues that the primary goal of constitutional law should be protecting the political process rather than protecting substantive constitutional values.

38. Ely, *Democracy and Distrust*, 151.

39. *Ibid.*

an anti-majoritarian safe-guard which views with suspicion all public actions tending to burden 'discrete and insular' minorities."[40] The antimajoritarianism of judicial intervention is justified, because it is merely stepping in for the usual safeguard of pluralism. In a perfect world, one without the prejudice that keeps certain groups from forming coalitions to protect their interests, there would be no suspect classes.

The *Carolene Products* / political-process model seems so complete, in fact, that the only question left appears to be the specific identification of which groups should be regarded as suspect classes. The Court of Appeals for the Ninth Circuit has summarized the criteria used by the Supreme Court: "To be a 'suspect' or 'quasi-suspect' class, [a group] must 1) have suffered a history of discrimination; 2) exhibit obvious, immutable, or distinguishing characteristics that define them as a discrete group; and 3) show that they are a minority or politically powerless . . . ."[41]

These criteria can all plausibly be used to identify the kind of discrete and insular minorities referred to in *Carolene Products*. A group that has suffered from historical discrimination, has immutable or distinguishing characteristics that set it apart from the majority, and is a minority or lacks political power is probably a group that can use some extra judicial protection from the prejudice of the majority.

African Americans are the group that is most obviously identified as meeting these criteria. They have obviously suffered from historical prejudice, race is generally thought to be a clear example of an immutable characteristic,[42] and throughout most of American history they lacked political power. Indeed, as will be discussed in chapter 5, much of the debate in Colorado over Amendment 2 focused on whether gays and lesbians are sufficiently similar in status to African Americans to be a "real" minority.

By the mid-1970s, the political-process model came to dominate equal protection jurisprudence. The threshold question for any group seeking the protection of strict scrutiny today is whether they are "saddled with such disabilities, or subjected to such a history of purposeful unequal treatment, or relegated to such a position of political powerlessness as to command extraordinary protection from the majoritarian political process."[43] Thus,

40. Laurence H. Tribe, *American Constitutional Law* (Mineola, N.Y.: Foundation Press, 1978), 1077.

41. *High Tech Gays v. Defense Industrial Security Clearance Office*, 895 F.2d 563, 573 (9th Cir. 1990).

42. As will be discussed in chapter 4, there is actually a vigorous debate about whether race is truly an immutable characteristic.

43. *Massachusetts Board of Retirement v. Murgia*, 427 U.S. 307, 313 (1975) (quoting *San Antonio Independent School District v. Rodriguez*, 411 U.S. 1, 28 (1973)).

gays and lesbians will be considered a suspect class only if they can show they are a discrete and insular minority according to these criteria. When gays and lesbians challenged Amendment 2, the Colorado trial court held a lengthy trial to determine whether they met these criteria. It concluded that gays and lesbians do not lack political power and therefore were not a suspect class.

It is a major argument of this book that the game of "who is a discrete and insular minority?" is fixed. No group since the mid-1970s has been found to be a discrete and insular minority and it is unlikely that any new group ever will be. To understand why this is so, we must look at how the three-tiered framework developed. Its story begins just after *Carolene Products* in the 1940s and culminates in the 1970s, when the three-tiered framework was born.

We will see that the three-tiered framework and the *Carolene Products*/political-process rationale of equal protection have actually been tools for preventing groups from receiving protection from legal discrimination under the equal protection clause. This argument is taken up in the next section, which traces the political-process model from its rejection in *Brown* to its triumph in a case called *San Antonio Independent School District v. Rodriguez* in 1973.

Brown v. Board of Education and Fear of the Political-Process Model

This brings us to *Brown v. Board of Education*.[44] In 1954 the Supreme Court was asked to decide whether legally segregated schools violated equal protection. If the Court held that segregated schools were unconstitutional, it would, of course, have to explain why it was overruling the democratically enacted preferences of those states that had chosen to segregate their schools.

From a contemporary vantage point it would seem that the *Carolene Products*/political-process approach was ideal for this purpose. At the time of *Brown*, African Americans were the prototypical discrete and insular minority, since they lacked even the most basic civil rights and were far more politically powerless than they are today. Relying on *Carolene Products*, the Court could have ruled that the pluralistic political process is inadequate to protect the interests of African Americans, and therefore, the Courts will not tolerate racial classifications unless there is a compelling justification for them.

---

44. The following discussion of *Brown* draws largely on Michael Klarman's excellent article, "An Interpretive History of Modern Equal Protection," *Michigan Law Review* 90 (1991): 213–318.

Applying *Carolene Products* to the issues raised in *Brown* would have merely been an extension of what the Court had already been doing in other areas of constitutional law at that time. By 1954 the Court had enthusiastically embraced the political-process rationale for judicial review. For example, throughout the 1940s, the Court regularly invoked it in cases protecting freedom of speech under the First Amendment. The Court argued that legislatures have a vested interest in suppressing criticism and that the courts had to protect freedom of speech in order to safeguard the political process.[45] In 1945 the Court used the political-process rationale to strike down laws requiring labor organizers to register with the state, citing the importance of freedom of assembly to the political process.[46]

The Court even relied on the political-process model in justifying its decisions under the commerce clause. The Court struck down state economic regulations that discriminated against out-of-state businesses, arguing that, "when the regulation is of such a character that its burden falls principally upon those without the state, legislative action is not likely to be subjected to those political restraints which are normally exerted on legislation where it affects adversely some interests within the state."[47]

What then could be more obvious than to use the political-process rationale to decide *Brown?* African Americans epitomized a discrete and insular minority, a group in need of special judicial protection from a hostile majority. Seemingly, *Brown* provided the Court with a golden opportunity to apply the political-process rationale to the equal protection clause and declare that racial classifications are subject to strict scrutiny. In this way, the Court could have overturned the infamous "separate but equal" doctrine of *Plessy v. Ferguson*.[48]

However, the Court did no such thing. Rather, the Court chose to emphasize the importance of education. The unanimous opinion in *Brown,* written by Chief Justice Earl Warren, argued that *Plessy v. Ferguson* involved "not education but transportation."[49] Warren noted that the Court had earlier "reserved decision on the question whether *Plessy v. Ferguson* should be held inapplicable to public education."[50] The Court never stated

45. For a description of the Court's use of the political-process rationale in First Amendment cases during the 1940s, see Klarman, "Interpretive History," 224–25.

46. *Thomas v. Collins,* 323 U.S. 516 (1945).

47. *South Carolina Highway Department v. Barnwell Brothers, Inc.,* 303 U.S. 177, 184–85 n. 2 (1938). For a discussion of the Court's use of the political-process rationale in commerce clause cases, see Klarman, "Interpretive History," 225–26.

48. 163 U.S. 537 (1896).

49. *Brown,* 347 U.S. at 491.

50. *Id.* at 492.

that racial classifications are impermissible. The Court did not cite *Carolene Products*, nor did it use the term "discrete and insular minorities." It stated that the case turned on the importance of education: "We must consider public education in light of its full development and its present place in American life throughout the Nation. Only in this way can it be determined if segregation in public schools deprives these plaintiffs of the equal protection of the laws."[51] The Court held that the "separate but equal" doctrine had no place in public education:

> Today, education is perhaps the most important function of state and local governments. Compulsory school attendance laws and the great expenditures for education both demonstrate our recognition of the importance of education to our democratic society. It is required in the performance of our most basic public responsibilities, even service in the armed forces. It is the very foundation of good citizenship. Today it is a principal instrument in awakening the child to cultural values, in preparing him for later professional training, and helping him to adjust normally to his environment. In these days, it is doubtful that any child may reasonably be expected to succeed in life if he is denied the opportunity of an education. Such an opportunity, where the state has undertaken to provide it, is a right which must be made available to all on equal terms.[52]

As the constitutional scholar Herbert Wechsler has noted, many people who were following the case had hoped that the Court would take a bolder approach and forbid all racial line drawing in the law. Yet the Court carefully restricted its holding to the field of education: "The Court did not declare, as many wish it had, that the Fourteenth Amendment forbids all racial lines in legislation, though subsequent per curium opinions may, as I have said, now go that far. Rather, as Judge Hand observed, the separate-but-equal formula was not overruled "in form" but was held to have no place in public education."[53]

An important question to ask is why the *Brown* Court emphasized the importance of education rather than the evil of racial classifications. The Court could have relied on the political-process rationale, just as it had been doing in constitutional cases outside of equal protection. Also, the Court had previously stated that racial classifications are suspect. For ex-

51. *Id.* at 492–93.

52. *Id.* at 493.

53. Herbert Wechsler, "Toward Neutral Principles of Constitutional Law," *Harvard Law Review* 73 (1959): 32.

ample, in *Strauder v. West Virginia*,[54] the first post–Civil War race discrimination case to reach the Supreme Court, the Court held that states could not exclude African Americans from jury service.

Further, in the World War II Japanese curfew and exclusion cases, although not relying on the political-process rationale, the Court issued broad declarations that racial classifications are suspect and must be subjected to exacting judicial scrutiny. In *Korematsu v. United States*,[55] the Court stated, "all legal restrictions which curtail the civil rights of a single racial group are immediately suspect. . . . courts must subject them to the most rigid scrutiny."[56] In *Hirabayashi v. United States*, the Court stated, "Distinctions between citizens solely because of their ancestry are by their very nature odious to a free people whose institutions are founded upon the doctrine of equality."[57]

As history grimly recalls, there was a sharp disparity between the Court's rhetoric and its holdings in these cases. Given the World War II context, the Court was unwilling to protect persons of Japanese ancestry from government persecution.[58] Yet it is hardly unheard of for the Court to rely on prior bold declarations of constitutional principle even if those declarations are contained in decisions with toothless holdings. Most famously, John Marshall claimed that the Court had the power of judicial review in *Marbury v. Madison*[59] but went out of his way to give President Jefferson and his allies a victory in the case at hand. This did not stop the Court from returning to its heroic rhetoric in *Marbury*, years later, to strike down acts of Congress.

Thus, heading into *Brown*, the Court was armed with the rhetorical precedent of *Hirabayashi* and *Korematsu* and with the political-process rationale developed in *Carolene Products* and the Court's First Amendment and commerce clause cases. Yet up to this point the Court had never applied the political-process model to an equal protection case. In *Brown* the Court once again refused to do so. Although African Americans in the

54. 100 U.S. 303 (1880).

55. 323 U.S. 214 (1944).

56. *Korematsu*, 323 U.S. at 216.

57. 320 U.S. 81, 100 (1943).

58. Sadly, it now seems clear that the wartime persecutions of Japanese Americans cannot even be explained as overzealous attempts to counter possible Japanese espionage. The federal courts have found that secret War Department records show that the government was motivated by racial hostility rather than military concerns. See *Hirabayashi v. United States*, 828 F.2d 591 (9th Cir. 1987); *Korematsu v. United States*, 584 F. Supp. 1406 (N.D. Cal. 1984).

59. 5 U.S. (1 Cranch) 137 (1803).

1950s were a perfect example of a discrete and insular minority the Court chose instead to emphasize the importance of education.

This approach proved to be highly unsatisfactory. It failed to explain the Court's subsequent per curiam decisions declaring segregated facilities ranging from public golf courses to public beaches to be unconstitutional.[60] These decisions could hardly be explained by the Court's rationale in *Brown*. They could of course be easily explained by the political-process rationale. Since African Americans are discrete and insular minorities who cannot adequately fight for their rights in the pluralistic process, then decisions to segregate public facilities, be they schools, beaches, or golf courses, on the basis of race are not entitled to the same degree of judicial deference as other democratic decisions. Yet the Court's reliance on the special nature of education in *Brown* simply could not explain why segregated beaches and golf courses are unconstitutional.

Legal scholars did not fail to note that the Court's rationale in *Brown* did not explain the holdings of its per curiam progeny. Perhaps the most famous critic of the Court's approach in *Brown* is Herbert Wechsler, who argued that the Court was acting as a "naked power organ" because it failed to set forth the reasons for its post-*Brown* desegregation cases.[61] However, the attack on *Brown*'s rationale was hardly limited to Wechsler. The Supreme Court had to endure sharp criticism from such luminaries as Alexander Bickel, Harry Wellington, and Henry M. Hart.[62] Although many of these scholars approved of the Court's holding, they could not abide its reasoning. The education-oriented rationale of *Brown* simply could not justify the Court's subsequent desegregation decisions.

Given the stakes involved, however, the professoriat was not inclined to just sit back and lob bombshells at the *Brown* Court. Many of the day's most prominent legal scholars set out to save *Brown* from its critics by reconstructing it, post hoc, as a political-process decision protecting discrete and insular minorities. Charles Black argued that *Brown* was best understood as a decision striking down racial classifications generally. Louis Pollack wrote an article specifically responding to Wechsler's criticism of *Brown*, arguing that the *Carolene Products* rationale justified a general rule

60. See, respectively, *Holmes v. City of Atlanta*, 350 U.S. 879 (1955), and *Mayor of Baltimore City v. Dawson*, 350 U.S. 877 (1955).

61. Wechsler, "Toward Neutral Principles," 12, 33–35.

62. Alexander M. Bickel and Harry H. Wellington, "Legislative Purpose and the Judicial Process: The *Lincoln Mills* Case," *Harvard Law Review* 71 (1957): 1; and Henry M. Hart, "The Supreme Court, 1958 Term—Foreword: The Time Chart of the Justices," *Harvard Law Review* 73 (1959): 84; both cited in Klarman, "Interpretive History," 248 n. 162.

against racial classifications. Owen Fiss argued that *Brown* and its progeny were best understood as rejecting the results of a political process that effectively excluded African Americans.[63]

This post hoc reconstruction of *Brown* was so effective that it has now become the popular vision of what that decision stands for. Rather than being a decision whose rationale was specifically limited to the area of education, it is now perceived as "a revolutionary statement of race relations law"[64] and "nothing short of a reconsecration of American ideals."[65]

This is not to disparage the *Brown* Court. Quite the contrary, it seems beyond question that striking down segregated schools was a courageous and important decision by the Court.[66] However, the idealization of *Brown* as the decision that bravely and forthrightly announced that all racial classifications are impermissible, or at least highly suspect, has significant consequences. As will be discussed below, it has helped generate a set of unrealistic expectations on the part of gays and lesbians that someday "their *Brown*" will come. This point will be discussed shortly, but first, another question must be addressed. Given all the obvious problems with the Court's approach in *Brown*, the problems that subjected it to a storm of criticism, why didn't the Court simply rely on the *Carolene Products* / political-process rationale to begin with?

The answer can be found in the nature of the political-process rationale itself. The rationale, for all its benefits, has two significant, inherent problems, both of which made it unsuitable for application to the particular context of *Brown*. These two problems are separately discussed below.

The "Judicial Overkill" Problem with the Three-Tiered Framework

The political-process rationale is an exceedingly blunt instrument. Since it assumes that the political process cannot be trusted to deal fairly with

63. Charles L. Black, "The Lawfulness of the Segregation Decisions," *Yale Law Journal* 69 (1960): 421–30; Louis H. Pollack, "Racial Discrimination and Judicial Integrity: A Reply to Professor Wechsler," *University of Pennsylvania Law Review* 108 (1959): 1–34; and Owen Fiss, "Racial Imbalance in the Public Schools: The Constitutional Concepts," *Harvard Law Review* 78 (1965): 564–617; all cited in Klarman, "Interpretive History," 255 nn. 190, 191.

64. Robert L. Carter, "The Warren Court and Desegregation," *Michigan Law Review* 67 (1968): 237.

65. Richard Kluger, *Simple Justice: The History of* Brown v. Board of Education *and Black America's Struggle for Equality* (New York: Knopf, 1976), 710.

66. But see Gerald N. Rosenberg, *The Hollow Hope: Can Courts Bring About Social Change?* (Chicago: University of Chicago Press, 1991), which argues that *Brown*'s real world impact was actually quite limited.

"suspect classes," when a group is designated as a suspect class *all* laws regarding that group are, by definition, suspect. Therefore, if the *Brown* Court had held that African Americans are a suspect class, they would have been effectively deciding a vast array of racial issues all at once. The Court would be holding that all racial classifications are subject to strict scrutiny and therefore presumptively unconstitutional.

In fact, there was substantial support on the Court for just such a holding. During the Court's first conference on *Brown,* Justices Hugo Black, William Douglas, Harold Burton, and Sherman Minton all leaned toward the position that, in the words of Justice Minton, "classification by race is not reasonable."[67] But there was also significant opposition to this position. Justice Stanley Reed indicated at conference that he would vote to uphold the "separate but equal" doctrine. At the same conference, Justice Tom Clark stated, "we had led the states on to think segregation is ok and we should let them work it out."[68] Justice Felix Frankfurter stated that he would not accept a broad rule that "it's unconstitutional to treat a Negro differently from a white."[69] Given this diversity of viewpoints, the political-process rationale could never have produced the united front that Chief Justice Warren sought. Further, had the *Brown* Court relied on the political-process rationale to declare that African Americans are a discrete and insular minority in the *Carolene Products* mode, the consequences would have reached far beyond segregated schools. It would have even reached issues beyond segregated public facilities in general.

Perhaps most significantly, to declare African Americans a suspect class would throw the Court into the emotional thicket of miscegenation laws. If racial classifications are inherently suspect under the *Carolene Products* rationale, then it is difficult to see how laws that prohibited interracial marriage could be upheld. For the Court to call miscegenation laws into question at the same time that it desegregated the public schools would have been biting off far more than the Court was willing to chew. Justice Frankfurter warned his colleagues that the issue of interracial marriage raised such "deep feelings" that the Court should avoid the issue if at all possible.[70] He further warned that invalidating miscegenation laws

---

67. Bernard Schwartz, *A History of the Supreme Court* (New York: Oxford University Press, 1993), 287. The first conference was held on December 13, 1952. The case was subsequently held over for reargument due to the multiplicity of the justices' views and the likelihood that any opinion would be highly fractured. *Ibid.*

68. *Ibid.*

69. *Ibid.,* 288.

70. Memorandum of Justice Frankfurter (read at conference, 4 November 1955), as quoted in Klarman, "Interpretive History," 242.

would "seriously handicap" the enforcement of *Brown*.[71] In fact, the Court was doing everything it could to duck the miscegenation issue during this period. In the same year as *Brown*, the Court denied certiorari in a miscegenation case.[72] The next year, in 1955, the Court ducked another miscegenation case on its docket on the flimsy excuse that the domicile of the parties needed "clarification."[73] The Court was not ready to take on the miscegenation issue until thirteen years after *Brown*, in *Loving v. Virginia*.[74]

This is not to criticize the *Brown* Court for its timidity on the issue of miscegenation. Frankfurter was probably right that invalidating interracial marriage laws would compromise enforcement of *Brown*. Indeed, the Court had serious difficulty enforcing its desegregation decisions even without the further complications of the miscegenation issue.[75] Rather, the point is to show that, while the "discrete and insular minorities" approach has its benefits, it also has some serious drawbacks. It is no small step to declare that factors such as prejudice toward a particular group render democratic decisions regarding that group "suspect." It means putting on the judicial table all manner of laws regarding that group. If segregation in the schools is suspect under a *Carolene Products* rationale, then so must be segregation at the marriage altar.

The crucial point is this: if the underlying political process is flawed because African Americans are shut out of the pluralistic process by powerlessness and prejudice, then *all* laws implicating African American interests are suspect. There is no logical way to contain strict scrutiny to one substantive issue area. Under the political-process rationale, to decide one case is virtually to decide them all. Deciding *Brown* under the political-process rationale would have meant deciding *Loving*, thirteen years before the Court was ready to do so. While all constitutional cases require the Court to make decisions that have effects beyond the parties involved, the three-tiered framework is extreme in this regard. Deciding that a group is a suspect class judicializes vast areas of social policy that are far removed from the case at hand.

The same problems that kept the Warren Court from relying on the political-process approach in *Brown* currently create enormous problems for gays and lesbians who challenge discriminatory laws under the equal pro-

71. *Ibid.*

72. *Jackson v. Alabama*, 72 So. 2d 114 (Ala.), *cert. denied*, 348 U.S. 888 (1954).

73. *Naim v. Naim*, 350 U.S. 891 (1955).

74. 388 U.S. 1 (1967).

75. Rosenberg, *Hollow Hope*, 39–169.

tection clause. For example, if the Supreme Court had struck down the federal government's policy of denying high-level security clearance to gays and lesbians by deciding that gays and lesbians are a suspect class, this would have important implications for the issue of gay and lesbian marriage. States would have to allow same-sex marriage unless they could demonstrate that they have a compelling reason not to.[76] Therefore, the Court is constrained from finding gays and lesbians to be a suspect class today for exactly the same reason that constrained it from holding that African Americans were a suspect class in the 1950s: it would catapult the Court into highly controversial areas of social policy far removed from the case under review.

It is not surprising that the Court has no enthusiasm for creating new suspect classes. The three-tiered framework is the very opposite of incremental judicial policy making. Once the Court has decided that the democratic process cannot be trusted to make laws pertaining to gays and lesbians, or to any other groups, many varieties of laws are open to plausible judicial challenge. Justice Thurgood Marshall noted this problem when he wrote, "It should be no surprise, then, that the Court is hesitant to expand the number . . . of classes subject to strict scrutiny, when each expansion involves the invalidation of virtually every classification bearing upon a newly covered category."[77]

For this reason, the Court's power to declare that some groups are suspect classes is something like the constitutional equivalent of the atomic bomb. It is an instrument of theoretically great power, but it is so sweeping in effect that it can never be used. Even in the case of African Americans, the Court was unwilling to make a blanket statement that all racial classifications are suspect until 1967, after Congress had cleared the way by outlawing racial discrimination in vast areas of public life, including employment, housing, public accommodations, and voting practices.[78]

---

76. The possibility of a constitutional right to homosexual marriage is no mere academic speculation. The Supreme Court of Hawaii has gone so far as to hold that state prohibitions against homosexual marriage are subject to strict scrutiny under the equal protection clause of the State Constitution of Hawaii. *Baehr v. Lewin*, 852 P.2d 44 (Haw. 1993). The court held that prohibiting two persons of the same gender from marrying one another is *gender* discrimination. (If Ms. X can marry Mr. Y but Mr. Z cannot, then Mr. Z is being discriminated against on the basis of his gender.) Clearly, were sexual orientation considered a suspect classification, the creation of a constitutional right to same-sex marriage would be a serious possibility.

77. *Massachusetts Board of Retirement v. Murgia*, 427 U.S. 307, 319 (1975) (Marshall, J., dissenting).

78. See *Loving v. Virginia*, 388 U.S. 1 (1967).

The Accusation Problem

Another problem with the political-process rationale is that it is inherently accusatory in nature. As discussed above, it is premised on the belief that some groups have been so victimized and discriminated against that they require special protection from the normal majoritarian political process. This feature of the political-process rationale made it entirely unsuitable for Warren's plan to muster unanimous support for his opinion. It was crucial to Warren that his opinion "did not contain any accusations against the South (that would certainly have raised the hackles of Justices Reed and Clark... [two of the Court's southern members])."[79]

The political-process rationale creates the same problem of unnecessary accusation when it comes to gay rights cases. As noted above, when gays and lesbians challenge a law under the equal protection clause, the three-tiered framework means that the first issue will always be whether they are a suspect class. Whether the law being challenged is Amendment 2, the military ban on gays and lesbians, presumptions against the fitness of gay parents, or anything else, the three-tiered framework strongly encourages gays and lesbians to argue that they are a suspect class.

Thus, the issues before the courts are invariably framed as "gay rights" issues rather than issues about the limits of governmental power. Rather than arguing that they are simply seeking the same rights as everyone else, gays and lesbians are forced to argue that they are a suspect class, entitled to enhanced judicial protection. This requires gays and lesbians to portray themselves as an oppressed group because the courts have held that a group can only be a suspect class if it has suffered a history of discrimination, lacks political power, and/or is so victimized by societal prejudice that the democratic process is unfit to deal with gays and lesbians fairly. Thus, to hold that gays and lesbians are a suspect class, the courts would have to admonish society in a very broad way for society's past and present treatment of homosexuals. The courts would essentially have to condemn society for being prejudiced against gays and lesbians.

It is easy to see why the Court is reluctant to engage in this kind of broad denouncement of societal attitudes toward gays and lesbians. As noted, in drafting the Court's opinion in *Brown*, Chief Justice Warren was concerned that the opinion be nonaccusatory in nature. It is difficult to envision a contemporary, nonaccusatory opinion holding that gays and lesbians are a suspect class. The three-tiered framework virtually requires gays and lesbians to accuse society of oppressing them and discriminating against them in order to get the courts to apply strict scrutiny. It is one thing to ask

79. B. Schwartz, *History of the Supreme Court*, 293.

the courts to accept that a particular law is discriminatory. It is quite another to ask the courts for a blanket statement that gays and lesbians are an oppressed class.

The concept of oppression lies at the very heart of the political process rationale. Thus, rather than framing their arguments in terms of equality, gays and lesbians must frame their arguments in terms of oppression and difference. This renders gays and lesbians vulnerable to charges that they are seeking special rights rather than equal rights.[80] The three-tiered framework means that, when gays and lesbians, for example, challenge the military's ban on homosexual soldiers, they must argue that, while the military can expel bald people or whomever else, the military cannot expel gays and lesbians because they are a suspect class.

Since suspect classes are treated differently by the courts, it is difficult even for those who support making gays and lesbians a suspect class to avoid using language that makes it seem that gays and lesbians are seeking "special rights." For example, Ellen Chaitin and Roy Lefcourt state that the objective of their article, "Is Gay Suspect," is to "analyze and formulate possible approaches to establishing homosexuality as a 'suspect class,' thereby automatically entitling homosexuals to special protection that the courts have previously extended only to a few groups."[81]

If the class-based approach is so unwieldy, why did the Court eventually decide to turn to it? Why does the Court repeatedly insist that only discrete and insular minorities are entitled to the protection of strict scrutiny? In the next chapter I argue that the Court turned to this approach in the 1970s precisely because it is so cumbersome. Conservative justices developed the three-tiered framework to beat back the then-rapid expansion of the equal protection clause. The primary intention of this effort was not to lock out gays and lesbians from the protection of strict scrutiny—it was to lock out the poor.

80. As will be discussed extensively in chapter 5, proponents of Amendment 2 placed great weight on the argument that gays and lesbians desire "special rights" rather than equal rights.

81. Ellen Chaitin and V. Roy Lefcourt, "Is Gay Suspect?" *Lincoln Law Review* 8 (1973): 24.

The Three-Tiered Framework as a System of Exclusion

Post-*Brown* Developments in Equal Protection Doctrine

By the mid-1960s, the political and racial climate in the United States had changed substantially from the days of *Brown*. By this time both the civil rights movement and the activist Warren Court were in full throttle, and Congress was taking the lead in prohibiting racial discrimination in many areas of public life. The Court was now ready to strike down all varieties of overtly racist laws. In 1964, in *McLaughlin v. Florida*,[1] the Court struck down a law prohibiting unmarried interracial couples from living together. By this time, the Court was ready to hold that laws that classified by race were unconstitutional unless they were necessary to achieve an overriding governmental purpose. By the mid-1960s, the Court was willing to follow a rule against racial classifications to its logical conclusion and venture where it had not previously dared. Three years after *McLaughlin*, in *Loving v. Virginia*,[2] the Court struck down prohibitions against interracial marriage.

By this time it was becoming clear that a two-tiered system was in place for applying the equal protection clause. In the vast majority of cases, the Court still applied the highly deferential "rational basis" standard of review. Indeed, in 1961 the Supreme Court described the rational-basis test in the most deferential terms possible. In *McGowan v. Maryland*, the Court stated that a "statutory discrimination will not be set aside if *any* state of facts reasonably may be conceived to justify it."[3] Meanwhile, in *McLaughlin* and *Loving*, the Court was declaring that racial classifications must be subjected to "the most rigid scrutiny."

1. 379 U.S. 184 (1964).
2. 388 U.S. 1 (1967).
3. 366 U.S. 420, 426 (1961) (emphasis added). This case involved an equal protection challenge to a state law that required stores to be closed on Sundays but included numerous exceptions.

Interestingly, when the Court finally arrived at the point of applying strict scrutiny to all racial classifications, it decided not to rely on the political-process rationale. Instead, the Court described race as sui generis, a special category with a special place under the Fourteenth Amendment. Despite the Court's own hesitancy in *Brown* to hold that all racial classifications are suspect, it argued in *Loving* that the Fourteenth Amendment "has traditionally required of state statutes drawn according to race" a "very heavy burden of justification."[4] The Court brushed aside Virginia's argument that "statements in the 39th Congress indicate that the Framers did not intend the Amendment to make unconstitutional state miscegenation laws." The Court simply responded that the purpose of a constitutional amendment is "broad" and "organic."[5] The two-tiered framework was premised on the "traditionally" special place of race under the Fourteenth Amendment.

This two-tiered approach kept the Court clear of the economic regulation issues that had proved so detrimental to its authority in the 1930s. Meanwhile, the Court had empowered itself to strike down virtually all racial classifications in the law. But the price the Court paid for this bargain was that the two-tiered system proved inflexible. Its simplicity and clarity limited its utility to the Court. When legislation did not involve race or national origin, the Court was required to use the extremely deferential rational-basis test. This proved to be a price the Court was unwilling to pay. Throughout this nation's complex legal history, discriminatory laws have hardly been limited to the subjects of race and national origin. The Court was simply unwilling to sit back and let pass the multiplicity of laws that harshly treated the less powerful in our society.

During the late 1960s and early 1970s the Court rebelled against the limits of the two-tiered framework. The Court expanded its power to strike down laws under the equal protection clause in three ways: (1) it turned to the *Carolene Products* rationale to make "alienage" a suspect classification; (2) it continued developing the list of "fundamental rights" that are also protected by strict scrutiny; and (3) perhaps most significantly, it began to put some real bite into the rational-basis test. Also, the Court hinted that it might expand equal protection doctrine in a way that would have had greater consequences than these three developments combined. By the late 1960s, the Court was strongly hinting that it was considering making the "poor" a suspect class. As will be discussed below, this would have vastly expanded the number of laws subject to strict scrutiny by the courts.

4. *Loving*, 388 U.S. at 9.
5. *Id.*

The Court briefly but dramatically overreached by expanding the scope of equal protection in these ways. The combined result of these three expansions of the two-tiered framework was to turn the equal protection clause into a potentially awesome instrument for judicial power. The possibility of expanding strict scrutiny to wealth classifications would have increased the reach of the equal protection clause even more. As will be discussed below, the three-tiered framework was constructed by the Court at the zenith of the equal protection clause's scope, in order to scale back its expansion. We will see first how the Court expanded the reach of the equal protection clause and then how the Court reined it in.

The Brief Return to *Carolene Products* to Create a New Suspect Class

In 1971, in *Graham v. Richardson*,[6] the Court for the first time applied the *Carolene Products*/political-process rationale to the equal protection clause. In *Graham* the Court struck down an Arizona law that denied welfare payments to aliens unless they had been living in the country for at least fifteen years. The Court held that the Arizona law was subject to strict scrutiny. Without acknowledging that it had never before used the political-process rationale in an equal protection case, the Court held, "Aliens as a class are a prime example of a 'discrete and insular' minority (see *United States v. Carolene Products Co.*) for whom such heightened judicial solicitude is appropriate."[7]

This was to be the last (and only) time that the Court used the *Carolene Products* rationale to expand the list of groups entitled to the "heightened judicial solicitude" of strict scrutiny. As will be discussed below, the next time the Court returned to *Carolene Products*, it was to contract rather than expand the scope of the equal protection clause.

Giving Teeth to the Rational-Basis Test

Graham turned out to be an aberration in the history of the equal protection clause. The Court did not continue to find new groups that qualified for strict scrutiny.[8] Even before *Graham*, however, the Court began to do something with much greater potential significance: it began to put some serious bite into the formerly deferential rational-basis test.

---

6. 403 U.S. 365 (1971).

7. *Graham*, 403 U.S. at 372.

8. The Court did later hold that classifications based on gender or illegitimacy were quasi-suspect and therefore subject to intermediate scrutiny. However, as will be discussed below, these decisions were actually post hoc explanations for why the Court had been striking down these classifications under a quietly strengthened rational-basis test.

In 1968, in *Levy v. Louisiana*,[9] the Court struck down a state law that discriminated against illegitimate children. The Louisiana law prohibited certain illegitimate children from recovering damages for the wrongful death of their mother. It is easy to see why the Warren Court was inclined to strike down a law that piled economic hardship on blameless and unfortunate children who had already suffered the loss of their mother. However, the two-tiered framework created a clear problem for the Court because the Court was unable to apply strict scrutiny (this was three years before *Graham*, and the Court had never used the political-process rationale to expand the scope of strict scrutiny). The Court therefore chose another option to strike down the Louisiana statute: it applied the rational-basis test in a stricter fashion than normal.

The *Levy* Court stated the rational-basis test in the traditionally deferential way, asking "whether the line drawn [by the Louisiana law] is a rational one."[10] Unfortunately, the Louisiana law, while harsh in its impact, was not irrational. The state argued that its refusal to recognize the claims of illegitimate children avoided potentially difficult problems of proof of parentage and discouraged out-of-wedlock births. The Court concluded, however, that the law had "no relation" to the interests articulated by the state of Louisiana. The Court averred that punishing illegitimate children was irrational since they can not help being born out of wedlock. However, this hardly makes the law irrational. While it is obviously hard on the child, there is nothing irrational about trying to discourage parents from having illegitimate children by denying illegitimate children certain benefits. Under a true rational-basis test, the law would have been upheld if it possibly had even a slight effect of discouraging out-of-wedlock births. The Court, therefore, was clearly applying a higher level of scrutiny than the traditional rational-basis test; in fact, many legal scholars interpreted *Levy* to mean that illegitimacy was now a suspect classification.[11]

By the early 1970s, it was becoming clear that the Supreme Court was unwilling to treat certain types of legislation in the deferential manner dic-

9. 391 U.S. 68 (1968).

10. *Levy,* 391 U.S. at 71.

11. John C. Gray Jr. and David Rudovsky, "The Court Acknowledges the Illegitimate," *University of Pennsylvania Law Review* 118 (1969): 1–39; Harry D. Krause, "Legitimate and Illegitimate Off-Spring of *Levy v. Louisiana*—First Decisions on Equal Protection and Paternity," *University of Chicago Law Review* 36 (1969): 338–63; Untitled Note, *Texas Law Review* 47 (1969): 329; all cited in Karen C. Cathey, "Note: Refining the Methods of Middle-Tier Scrutiny: A New Proposal for Equal Protection," *Texas Law Review* 61 (1983): 1507–8 n. 29; "Developments in the Law—Equal Protection," *Harvard Law Review* 82 (1969): 1087.

tated by the rational-basis test. In 1971, in *Reed v. Reed*,[12] the Court unanimously struck down an Idaho law that preferred men over women as probate administrators. This time the Court was clearer that, while it was applying something it called the rational-basis test, it was actually subjecting the Idaho law to a higher level of scrutiny. In *Reed*, the Court did two things that were clear departures from the traditional rational-basis test. First, it rejected Idaho's contention that the purpose of the preference for males was to increase the likelihood that administrators would have some experience in the business world.[13] The Court assumed that the actual purpose of the law was "administrative convenience." Second, the Court held that the rationale of "administrative convenience" was insufficient to justify the preference for males.

As a result of these decisions, by 1972 there was speculation that "truly startling and intriguing developments" were taking place—a new rational-basis standard was being born, one with real bite.[14] In his foreword to the 1972 *Harvard Law Review*, Gerald Gunther argued, "At least one pervasive element of the new mood is clear: a majority of the Justices is prepared to acknowledge substantial equal protection claims on minimum rationality grounds."[15]

The Articulation of "Fundamental Rights" under the Equal Protection Clause

During this period, the Court began expanding the number of "fundamental rights" that are protected under the equal protection clause. Laws that hamper these rights are subject to strict scrutiny regardless of whether they involve suspect classifications. These fundamental rights include the right to vote, the right to engage in interstate travel, and the right to decide whether "to bear or beget a child."[16]

By 1972 the Court appeared ready to break out of the two-tiered framework altogether by merging the less deferential version of the rational-

---

12. 404 U.S. 71 (1971).

13. Karen C. Cathey, "Note: Refining the Methods of Middle-Tier Scrutiny: A New Proposal for Equal Protection," *Texas Law Review* 61 (1983): 1509–10.

14. Gunther, "Foreword," 19.

15. *Ibid*.

16. The first case to hold that the equal protection clause protects certain fundamental rights was *Skinner v. Oklahoma*, 316 U.S. 535 (1942). However, it was not until the mid-1960s that the Court began to seriously expand the number of fundamental rights protected under the equal protection clause. See *Harper v. Virginia Board of Elections*, 383 U.S. 663 (1966) (voting); *Shapiro v. Thompson*, 394 U.S. 618 (1969) (interstate travel); *Eisenstadt v. Baird*, 405 U.S. 438 (1972) (childbearing).

basis test with the fundamental-rights doctrine. In *Weber v. Aetna Casualty & Surety Co.*,[17] the Court strongly suggested that the two-tiered system would be replaced with a sliding-scale test in which the level of scrutiny would be more or less strict depending on the nature of the right at issue. *Weber* involved a Louisiana workman's compensation law that treated unacknowledged illegitimate children of injured workers less favorably than legitimate or acknowledged illegitimate children. Louisiana argued that the statute, unlike the statute in *Levy*, had a rational basis because it was limited to *unacknowledged* illegitimate children. As it can be difficult to establish the true paternity of unacknowledged illegitimate children, subordinating their claims to those of legitimate or acknowledged children had a rational basis.

The *Weber* Court struck down this law. However, in contrast to *Levy*, the Court was willing to acknowledge that it was applying a stricter test than the traditional rational-basis test:

> The tests to determine the validity of the state statutes under the Equal Protection Clause have been variously expressed, but this Court requires, at a minimum, that a statutory classification bear some rational relationship to a legitimate state purpose. Though the latitude given state social and economic legislation is necessarily broad, when state statutory classifications approach sensitive and fundamental personal rights, this Court exercises a stricter scrutiny. The essential inquiry in all the foregoing cases is, however, inevitably a dual one: What legitimate state interest does the classification promote? What fundamental personal rights might the classification endanger?[18]

Thus, by the early 1970s, the equal protection clause had become a powerful and multi-faceted judicial instrument. There seemed to be no clear limit to the reach of the new tougher rational-basis test or to the doctrine of fundamental rights. The Court was applying a tough rational-basis test to classifications based on gender and legitimacy. It was stating that all laws affecting sensitive and fundamental personal rights were going to be subjected to a vaguely defined higher level of scrutiny. If laws disadvantaging the poor, the elderly, and even gays and lesbians were to be subjected to the same tough "rational basis" scrutiny as laws affecting women and illegitimate children, then the Court was poised for a major new era of judicial activity.

Then, in 1973, the Court blinked.

17. 406 U.S. 164 (1972).
18. *Weber*, 406 U.S. at 172–73 (citations omitted).

San Antonio v. Rodriguez: The Court Uses Carolene Products to Pull Back the Scope of Equal Protection

The Court's activist approach to the equal protection clause was not without its critics and dissenters. In contrast to the more cautious *Brown* decision, the opinions expanding the scope of the equal protection clause were not unanimous. Among the most ardent dissenters was Justice William Rehnquist, who had recently joined the Court. Rehnquist wrote a stinging dissent in *Weber*, raising the specter of a return to the *Lochner* era. He reminded the Court of its past expansion of the Fourteenth Amendment and the humiliating defeat that ultimately resulted. He urged the Court to return to a strict two-tiered framework, with judicial deference to all laws except those that classify according to race or national origin.

Rehnquist's invocation of *Lochner* was not without basis. The Court's more expansive interpretation of the equal protection clause, especially adding bite to the rational-basis test, had potentially enormous consequences. After all, *Lochner* and its progeny were also ostensibly striking down laws because they lacked a rational basis. Even beyond this, Rehnquist and other judicial conservatives had another reason to fear that the Court was on the brink of a major expansion of equal protection activism. In addition to strengthening the rational-basis test and finding new fundamental rights under the equal protection clause, the Court was seriously hinting that it might find laws that discriminated on the basis of wealth to be suspect.

For decades, the Court had demonstrated its concern for protecting the constitutional rights of indigent criminal defendants. In 1956 the Court had held that such defendants had a constitutional right to a free trial transcript for purposes of appeal.[19] In 1963 the Court held that indigent defendants had a right to court-appointed counsel at trial and on direct appeal.[20] While these decisions demonstrated its concern for the rights of indigent criminal defendants, the Court did not imply more generally that the poor would be treated as a suspect class. However, in the mid-1960s, the Court began using language that strongly implied that "wealth" might join race and national origin as a suspect classification.

In 1966, in *Harper v. Virginia State Board of Elections*,[21] the Court struck down a state poll tax on equal protection grounds. While the Court emphasized the special nature of the right to vote, it also implied that laws

---

19. *Griffin v. Illinois*, 351 U.S. 12 (1956).
20. *Gideon v. Wainwright*, 372 U.S. 335 (1963); *Douglas v. California*, 372 U.S. 353 (1963), respectively.
21. 383 U.S. 663 (1966).

that classified on the basis of wealth are analogous to racial classifications. Writing for the Court, Justice Douglas stated, "Lines drawn on the basis of wealth or property, like those of race, are traditionally disfavored."[22] In 1969 the Court even more strongly implied that wealth was akin to race for the purposes of the equal protection clause. In *McDonald v. Board of Elections*, the Court stated, "a careful examination on our part is especially warranted where lines are drawn on the basis of wealth or race, two factors which would *independently* render a classification highly suspect and thereby demand a more exacting judicial scrutiny."[23]

If this were not enough to imply that the Court considered wealth and race to be on a similar constitutional footing, the Court followed this statement with citations to *Douglas v. California* and *McLaughlin v. Florida*. *Douglas* held that poor defendants had the right to counsel on appeal. *McLaughlin* was the decision that finally announced the blanket presumption against racial classifications. To cite these two cases side by side to support a statement that wealth and race "independently render a classification highly suspect" brought the Court to the brink of making the poor a suspect class.

By the early 1970s, many lower courts believed that the Supreme Court had indeed made wealth a suspect classification. The issue often arose in the context of school funding cases. Most states had systems of school funding that were based on local property taxes. Under this system, school districts with a small property tax base had much less money to spend per pupil than did wealthier districts. In 1971 and 1972, a number of state and federal courts held that this system of school funding violated the equal protection clause because it discriminated on the basis of wealth.[24] Each of these courts relied on the cases discussed above to hold that wealth was a suspect classification, especially where an important right such as education was involved. These cases also held that education was a fundamental right, citing *Brown v. Board of Education*. There were thus two independent

22. *Harper*, 383 U.S. at 668.

23. *McDonald v. Board of Elections*, 394 U.S. 802, 807 (1969) (citations omitted; emphasis added). Even though the Court stated that wealth classifications are suspect, in this case the Court actually *upheld* the State of Illinois' practice of excluding unsentenced jail inmates from receiving absentee voting ballots. This is because the Court held that disadvantaging unsentenced inmates does not create a wealth classification.

24. *Rodriguez v. San Antonio Independent School District*, 337 F. Supp. 280 (W.D. Tex. 1971), *reversed*, 411 U.S. 1 (1973); *Van Dusartz v. Hatfield*, 334 F. Supp. 870 (D. Minn. 1971); *Serrano v. Priest*, 487 P.2d 1241 (Calif. 1971), *cert. denied*, 432 U.S. 907 (1977); *Milliken v. Green*, 203 N.W.2d 457 (Mich. 1972), *vacated*, 212 N.E.2d 711 (Mich. 1973); *Robinson v. Cahill*, 303 A.2d 273 (N.J.), *cert. denied*, 414 U.S. 976 (1973).

reasons to subject the school financing systems to strict scrutiny: (1) wealth is a suspect classification; and (2) education is a fundamental right.

Realizing that "far-reaching constitutional questions" were at stake, the Supreme Court granted certiorari in one of these cases, *San Antonio Independent School District v. Rodriguez.*[25] The five to four majority (which included two recent Nixon appointees, Justices Lewis Powell and William Rehnquist) reversed. Writing for the majority, Justice Powell emphasized that, if wealth were a suspect classification, virtually all local fiscal arrangements would be subjected to strict scrutiny: "No scheme of taxation, whether the tax is imposed on property, income, or purchases of goods and services, has yet been devised which is free of all discriminatory impact. In such a complex arena in which no perfect alternatives exist, the Court does well not to impose too rigorous a standard of scrutiny lest all local fiscal schemes become subjects of criticism under the Equal Protection Clause."[26]

Rodriguez was therefore a crucial turning point in constitutional history. As the Court stated, to unambiguously hold that wealth was a suspect classification would hurl the Court into the arena of fiscal policy; once again the Court would become the final arbiter of legislative wisdom. The Court was unwilling to step into this role. It held that wealth is not a suspect classification.

The Court could have taken the intermediate route of holding that wealth is suspect only in the context of educational policy because an adequate education is essential to effectively exercise such rights as freedom of speech and the right to vote. The appellees, who were challenging the school funding system, made this argument. The Court balked at this option, holding that this argument has no logical stopping point:

> Furthermore, the logical limitations on appellees' nexus theory are difficult to perceive. How, for instance, is education to be distinguished from the significant personal interests in the basics of decent food and shelter? Empirical examination might well buttress an assumption that the ill-fed, ill-clothed, and ill-housed are among the most ineffective participants in the political process, and that they derive the least enjoyment from the benefits of the First Amendment.[27]

Unwilling to enter this breach, the majority unambiguously declared that the poor are not a suspect class. Yet, on what principle was the major-

25. 411 U.S. 1, 6 (1973).
26. *Rodriguez,* 411 U.S. at 41.
27. *Id.* at 37.

ity to base this decision? The lower courts that had held the school funding systems unconstitutional seemed to have ample Supreme Court precedent for their decisions. In the post-*Brown* era, how could they distinguish between a school system that discriminates on the basis of race and one that discriminates on the basis of wealth? After all, poor school children could no more alter their status than could African American school children.

Ironically, the *Rodriguez* majority turned to the very logic the Court had avoided in the *Brown* decision. They relied on the *Carolene Products* logic and held that the only suspect classes are those that require extraordinary protection from democratic majorities. They also held that the poor are not such a suspect class: "The system of alleged discrimination and the class it defines have none of the traditional indicia of suspectness: the class is not saddled with such disabilities, or subjected to such a history of purposeful unequal treatment, or relegated to such a position of political powerlessness as to command extraordinary protection from the majoritarian political process."[28] The Court noted as well that the class of people living in poorer school districts was "large, diverse and amorphous."[29] By definition such a group is not a discrete and insular minority. Such language obviously did not bode well for a large, amorphous, and diverse group such as gays and lesbians either.

The *Rodriguez* majority also had to deal with the argument that education is a fundamental right. This was not an argument to be dealt with lightly, since the *Brown* Court had said that "education is perhaps the most important function of state and local government."[30] The *Rodriguez* majority responded that the *Brown* decision was "in the context of racial discrimination."[31] Education is not, in and of itself, a fundamental right. The Court held that "the key to discovering whether education is 'fundamental' is not to be found in comparisons of the relative societal significance of education as opposed to subsistence or housing."[32]

Having distinguished *Brown* as a race case, the Court went well beyond the education issue. It held that the only rights protected by the equal protection clause as "fundamental" are rights that are "explicitly or implicitly

28. *Id.* at 28. Interestingly, the Court did not specifically cite *Carolene Products* as authority for this point. In fact, the Court cited no precedent whatsoever. Neither of these facts is surprising since, other than in *Graham*, the Court had never applied *Carolene Products* to the equal protection clause. Nevertheless, the Court's description of which groups are suspect classes is a paraphrase of *Carolene Products'* footnote 4.

29. *Rodriguez*, 411 U.S. at 28.

30. *Brown v. Board of Education*, 347 U.S. 483, 493 (1954).

31. *Rodriguez*, 411 U.S. at 29.

32. *Id.* at 33.

guaranteed by the Constitution."[33] Education, held the Court, is not explicitly or implicitly guaranteed by the Constitution. As a result, the doctrine of fundamental rights was sharply limited.

Thus, the *Rodriguez* Court recast *Brown* as a case primarily concerned with race, not education. As noted above, it also held that race was a special category because certain groups require extraordinary protection from the political process. The end result was that the school finance system was upheld because the poor are not such a minority and because education is not a fundamental right. Ironically, the Court's judicial conservatives had finally recast *Brown* in the way for which *Brown*'s liberal defenders had argued. *Brown* was now seen as a decision that rested not on the unique importance of education, but on African Americans' status as a discrete and insular minority in need of extraordinary judicial protection.

Finally, the *Rodriguez* Court tackled the issue of how stringent the rational-basis test should be. Several lower courts had held that the property-tax method of school finance lacked a rational basis. A system that penalized poorer school children might fail even the rational-basis test, particularly if the test were applied in the stringent manner used by the Court in *Levy* and *Reed*. If laws disadvantaging women and illegitimate children failed the rational-basis test, perhaps laws disadvantaging the poor might as well. In fact, in his dissenting opinion, Justice Byron White argued that the school funding system used by the San Antonio school district could not pass the rational-basis test as enunciated in *Reed*.[34]

Again, the *Rodriguez* Court took the opportunity to rein in the scope of the equal protection clause: "We need not rest our decision, however, solely on the inappropriateness of the strict-scrutiny test. A century of Supreme Court adjudication under the Equal Protection Clause affirmatively supports the application of the traditional standard of review, which requires only that the State's system be shown to bear some rational relationship to legitimate state purposes."[35] Thus, the Court re-embraced the deferential version of the rational-basis test: a law must "bear some rational relationship" to a legitimate state purpose. *Levy* and *Reed* were not cited.

Rodriguez therefore halted the threatened expansion of the equal protection clause. Suspect-class status was limited to discrete and insular minorities, not large, diverse groups like the poor (or gays and lesbians).[36]

33. *Id.* at 33–34.
34. *Rodriguez*, 411 U.S. at 69 (White, J., dissenting).
35. *Rodriguez*, 411 U.S. at 40.
36. As will be discussed in chapter 4, it is far from clear whether even recognized suspect classes such as African Americans can fairly be characterized as discrete and insular minorities.

Fundamental rights were limited to those rights explicitly or implicitly guaranteed by the Constitution. The rational-basis test was, once again, deferential.

The only question left, then, was what to do about the pre-*Rodriguez* cases that had applied the rational-basis test so forcefully. Was *Reed*, for example, simply to be ignored? Was the Court (which had recently decided *Roe v. Wade*[37]) going to overturn *Reed* and uphold various forms of gender discrimination so long as they bore any rational relationship to a legitimate governmental objective? Or was the Court going to allow *Reed* to stand as precedent for a stringent rational-basis test?

The Court chose none of these options. At first it leaned toward the position that gender classifications are subject to strict scrutiny. Less than two months after the *Rodriguez* decision, in a four-justice plurality opinion in *Frontiero v. Richardson,* Justice William Brennan stated, "[C]lassifications based upon sex, like classifications based on race, alienage, or national origin, are inherently suspect, and must therefore be subject to strict judicial scrutiny."[38] The opinion acknowledged that *Reed* had applied a higher standard than traditional rational-basis review. *Reed*, Brennan said, gave "implicit support" for subjecting gender classifications to strict scrutiny.

Yet subjecting all legal gender distinctions to strict scrutiny had its own problems. Was the Court really ready to strike down a male-only draft? Was it ready to strike down gender distinctions in statutory rape laws and threaten teenage girls with prison sentences for engaging in consensual sex with boys their own age?[39]

Justice Brennan did his utmost in *Frontiero* to put together a majority opinion holding that gender is a suspect classification. But the resistance from the more cautious and conservative justices was simply too great. Justice Potter Stewart had already expressed in a 1973 letter to Justice Powell his fear that overuse of strict scrutiny would "return this Court . . . to the heyday of the Nine Old Men [of the *Lochner* era], who felt that the Constitution enabled them to invalidate almost any state laws they thought unwise."[40] Justice Powell also had serious reservations. In a memo to

37. 410 U.S. 113 (1973).

38. 411 U.S. 677, 688 (1973).

39. Subsequently, the Court decided not to do either of these things. See, respectively, *Rostker v. Goldberg*, 453 U.S. 57 (1981), and *Michael M. v. Superior Court of Sonoma County*, 450 U.S. 464 (1981).

40. Stewart to Powell, 8 February 1973, quoted in Bernard Schwartz, *The Ascent of Pragmatism: The Burger Court in Action* (Reading, Mass.: Addison-Wesley Publishing Co., 1990), 220. For a fuller discussion of the letters, memos, and conference discussions cited in this section, see *The Ascent of Pragmatism*, 218–54.

Brennan regarding *Frontiero*, Powell wrote, "If and when it becomes necessary to consider whether sex is a suspect classification, I will find the issue a difficult one. Women certainly have not been treated as fungible with men (thank God!). Yet, the reasons for different treatment have in no way resembled the purposeful and invidious discrimination directed against blacks and aliens. Nor may it be said any longer that, as a class, women are a discrete minority barred from effective participation in the political process."[41]

Brennan was therefore unable to gain a five-justice majority holding that women are a suspect class. The issue came up again in the 1976 case, *Craig v. Boren*.[42] At the *Craig* conference Brennan again argued that the Court should apply strict scrutiny to gender classifications and again he was met with sharp resistance. However, at least three justices, White, Marshall, and John Paul Stevens, were willing to agree that, in Justice Stevens's words: "some level of scrutiny above mere rationality has to be applied."[43]

Having failed to muster a majority in *Frontiero*, Brennan compromised in *Craig*. He drafted an opinion for the Court holding that gender classifications are subject to an intermediate level of scrutiny, midway between strict scrutiny and rational-basis scrutiny. Justices White, Marshall, Stevens, Powell, and Blackmun all joined the opinion, giving Brennan a six-justice majority for the intermediate standard. Ignoring the plurality opinion in *Frontiero* and citing *Reed*, the opinion stated, "To withstand constitutional challenge, previous cases establish that classifications by gender must serve important governmental objectives and must be substantially related to achievement of those objectives."[44]

Thus, the two-tiered framework became a three-tiered framework with strict, intermediate, and rational-basis scrutiny. While Brennan's compromise secured a majority, it is not clear that he realized all of the implications; the creation of the third tier of the three-tiered framework had the effect of *contracting*, not expanding, the scope of the equal protection clause. By holding that gender was a special classification, the Court insured that *Reed*'s tough application of the rational-basis test would be useless as precedent for challenging any laws except laws with gender classifications. At the same time, the intermediate standard meant that, de-

41. Powell to Brennan, 2 March 1973, quoted in B. Schwartz, *Ascent of Pragmatism*, 224.
42. 429 U.S. 190 (1976).
43. B. Schwartz, *Ascent of Pragmatism*, 227.
44. *Craig*, 429 U.S. at 197.

spite the plurality opinion in *Frontiero*, gender classifications would not be subjected to strict scrutiny.

Thus, *Craig* contracted the scope of the equal protection clause in two important ways. The stringent version of the rational-basis test, now acknowledged as an intermediate form of scrutiny, was limited to gender classifications, while strict scrutiny was precluded from being applied to gender classifications.

The Court dealt with *Levy* and the question of illegitimacy classifications in the same manner. As noted earlier, *Levy* had led many legal scholars to believe that the Court had made illegitimacy a suspect classification. However, in its 1977 decision in *Trimble v. Gordon*,[45] the Court held that classifications based on illegitimacy are subject to intermediate scrutiny.

Coming on the heels of *Rodriguez*, the decisions in *Craig* and *Trimble* fenced in the equal protection clause on all sides. *Rodriguez* limited strict scrutiny to those groups that needed "extraordinary protection from the democratic process." This excluded the poor and, as the Court later held, the elderly.[46] As will be discussed in the next chapter, numerous lower courts have held that gays and lesbians also do not meet this definition. Meanwhile, by holding that gender and illegitimacy are special categories, the Court explained away the tough application of the rational-basis test in *Reed* and *Levy*. In his dissent in *Trimble*, Rehnquist lamented that, "although illegitimates are not members of a 'suspect class,' laws that treat them differently from those born in wedlock will receive a more far-reaching scrutiny than will other laws regulating economic and social conditions."[47] Yet he added, "In one sense this language is a source of consolation, since *it suggests that parts of this Court's analysis used in this case will not be carried over to traditional 'rational basis' or 'minimum scrutiny' cases.*"[48]

Finally, by creating a third tier, the Court excluded gender and illegitimacy classifications from strict scrutiny. Thus, *Craig* and *Trimble* are best understood not as cases that extended the equal protection clause to women and illegitimates, but rather as the cases that: (1) rationalized the enhanced protection these groups were already receiving; (2) rendered *Reed* and *Levy* useless as precedent in cases that did not involve gender or illegitimacy; and (3) made sure that protection against discrimination on the basis of gender or legitimacy did not go so far as strict scrutiny.

I do not intend here to be wholly critical of the Court. The further

45. 430 U.S. 762 (1977).
46. *Massachusetts Board of Retirement v. Murgia*, 427 U.S. 307, 313 (1975).
47. *Trimble*, 430 U.S. at 781 (Rehnquist, J., dissenting).
48. *Id.* (emphasis added).

expansion of the equal protection clause could certainly have, as Justice Powell feared, returned the Court to the days of the *Lochner* era, when judicial policy preferences were all too easily translated into constitutional doctrine. Yet there are also costs to what the Court did, costs that have not been fully recognized.

The most significant cost is that the Court has created a closed system while implicitly promising an open one. In *Rodriguez*, the Court held that the poor cannot qualify for strict scrutiny because they do not need extraordinary protection from the majoritarian process. This implies that the Court will give a fair hearing to those who claim that they are so powerless or despised that they do need such protection. However, this has turned out to be an empty promise. The list of "suspect" and "quasi-suspect" classifications has remained in stasis since 1977. No group—not the poor, not the elderly, not gays or lesbians, nor any one else—has been able to convince the Court to expand this list. For all groups that were not already receiving enhanced protection by the 1970s, the judicial hand has held only short straws.

In sum, the three-tiered framework is far better suited to justifying which classifications are *not* entitled to enhanced scrutiny than to justifying those that are. *McDonald v. Board of Elections* is best remembered for its dictum that wealth is a suspect classification. It is easy to forget that the Court actually said this by way of justifying its decision to uphold a state law refusing absentee ballots to unconvicted jail inmates. Since jail inmates are not a class defined by their wealth or lack of it, the Court refused to subject the law to strict scrutiny.

With the single exception of the *Graham* decision (striking down a law denying welfare payments to aliens), the *Carolene Products* rationale has never been used to justify enhanced scrutiny for any class of people who were not already receiving it. Racial minorities, women, and illegitimates were already receiving enhanced judicial protection by the time the third tier of the three-tiered framework was put in place. Since 1971, the political-process rationale has been used exclusively to deny protection to new groups. The Court's indicia of suspect status, rather than being a method to identify groups that need judicial protection, have "been used primarily to explain why certain classes are *not* accorded suspect status."[49]

When equal protection analysis is placed in its historical context, it is not surprising that the Court is unwilling to create new suspect classifications, including sexual orientation. As discussed above, to suddenly de-

---

49. M. J. Moltenbre, "Alternative Models of Equal Protection Analysis: *Plyler v. Doe*," *Boston College Law Review* 24 (1983): 1373.

clare that gays and lesbians are entitled to enhanced judicial protection would have a drastic impact on all areas of law that distinguish between heterosexuals and homosexuals, including military service, marriage, adoption, and inheritance. If sexual orientation were considered to be even a quasi-suspect category, the Court would still be putting itself in the position of having to strike down all of those laws that the state could not demonstrate are "substantially related to an important governmental interest."

History shows that the Court does not work this way—it does not suddenly take a group and make it a protected class. Ten years passed between the Court's decision in *Brown* and its enunciation and enforcement in *McLaughlin* of a blanket presumption against the constitutionality of racial classifications. The Court struggled for years after *Reed* to decide how it wanted to treat gender classifications. As for aliens, the Court has also struggled, and has "in fact been edging away from [*Graham*'s declaration that aliens are a suspect class] without, however, formally renouncing it."[50] Once the Court boxed itself into the three-tiered framework, the inflexibility of the framework locked out all new groups.

Bernard Schwartz's description of the Court's conference discussion of a case involving the rights of the mentally retarded in 1985[51] well illustrates the prevailing view of the justices that the Court should not create any new suspect or quasi-suspect classes:

> White, Rehnquist and O'Connor agreed with Burger [that the mentally retarded are not a suspect class]. Their dominant theme was a refusal to extend the quasi-suspect classification concept. "I wouldn't create another category of heightened [scrutiny]," stated White, "but [would] use rational basis." Rehnquist stated the same view, saying, "I agree with [White] that we ought not create quasi[-suspect classes]. We should rein in on that trend and create no more." O'Connor also affirmed, "I wouldn't create a new class."[52]

Powell was absent from the conference but stated at a later conference on the same case, "I don't want to add another level of heightened scrutiny."[53] Thus, the judicial exercise of ostensibly evaluating whether such

50. Louis Lusky, "Footnote Redux: A *Carolene Products* Reminiscence," *Columbia Law Review* 82 (1982): 1105 n. 72.

51. *City of Cleburne v. Cleburne Living Center*, 473 U.S. 432 (1985). This case is discussed more thoroughly in chapter 6.

52. B. Schwartz, *Ascent of Pragmatism*, 251.

53. *Ibid.*

groups as the poor, the elderly, and gays and lesbians meet the Court's criteria for suspect-class status is actually a charade. The three-tiered framework was set up to keep new groups out, not to let them in, and the Court has shown no inclination to add new suspect or quasi-suspect classes.

This has created an especially difficult situation for gays and lesbians. As described in the next chapter, gays and lesbians have made many efforts to have the courts recognize them as a suspect class and have always been turned away. Chapter 4 analyzes the reasons various courts have given for holding that gays and lesbians are entitled to only the lowest level of constitutional protection.

In addition, as will be discussed in chapter 5, the empty promise of the three-tiered framework has also created political problems for gays and lesbians. The premise of the framework, that certain groups merit special legal protections if they are powerless and have suffered from a history of discrimination, has penetrated the public consciousness. During the public debate over Amendment 2, much was made over the judicial rulings that gays and lesbians are not entitled to the same level of constitutional protection as racial minorities.

PART TWO

The Impact of Class-Based Equal Protection on Gays and Lesbians

Class-Based Analysis and the Courts

In part 1 we saw that the courts' reluctance to apply strict scrutiny to laws that disadvantage gays and lesbians is best understood when placed in the larger context of the history and overall structure of the three-tiered framework. Three arguments elaborating on this point were advanced:

(1) The Supreme Court has used the concept of the suspect class to sharply limit, not expand, the number of groups that could receive heightened judicial protection under the equal protection clause.

(2) The ostensible criteria for what constitutes a suspect class has almost always been used by the courts to explain why certain groups are *not* suspect classes. The first and last time the Supreme Court used these criteria to create a new suspect class was 1971, when it held that aliens are a suspect class (and the Court has subsequently backed away from protecting aliens as a suspect class).

(3) Courts are extremely reluctant to create new suspect classes because declaring a group to be a suspect class throws all laws disadvantaging that group into question, thus affecting important issues far beyond the scope of whatever issue is being litigated in any given case. Also, the political-process rationale requires the courts to take an accusatory tone, condemning society for its "history of discrimination" against a particular group.

In this chapter I argue that the refusal of numerous courts to hold that gays and lesbians are a suspect class should not be seen as a result of the failure of gays and lesbians to meet the specific criteria of what constitutes a suspect class. The courts' response to gays and lesbians must be viewed within the larger context of the courts' overall reluctance to create any new suspect classes at all.

It should be noted that at times gays and lesbians have come tantalizingly close to convincing a handful of courts below the level of the Supreme Court to hold that they are a suspect class. In one case, a federal court held that gays and lesbians are an "identifiable minority." This satisfied a requirement that allowed a gay student to bring a federal tort action against school officials for not protecting him against violence by other students.[1] However, that court specifically stated that it was not addressing the suspect class issue. Other courts have found that gays and lesbians are a suspect class but have had those opinions reversed or vacated on appeal.[2] Most recently, in *Able v. United States*, a federal district court judge held that gays and lesbians meet the criteria for suspect-class status and that the military's "don't ask, don't tell" policy lacked a rational basis, but the decision was reversed by the appellate court.[3]

The appellate courts have consistently rejected the argument that gays and lesbians are a suspect class. Of course, no court has stated that the day for creating suspect classes has passed. Every court that has considered the issue has stated that gays and lesbians simply do not meet the criteria for a suspect class. As the courts explain their own holdings, the issues raised in part 1 are irrelevant to their decisions. The courts explain their decisions as the logical result of applying a set of legal criteria to a specific class of plaintiffs.[4] This chapter examines the specific reasons given by the courts[5] for holding that gays and lesbians are not a suspect class and shows why these reasons are plainly inadequate to explain the courts' decisions.

The organization of this chapter is based on the decision of the Colorado trial court in *Evans v. Romer*,[6] which held that Amendment 2 violates the equal protection clause. In that case, Judge Jeffrey Bayless held a trial to determine whether gays and lesbians are a suspect class. He held that they are not. In his decision, he laid out the criteria for what constitutes a suspect

1. *Nabozny v. Podlesny*, 92 F.3d 446 (7th Cir. 1996).

2. See, e.g., *Equality Foundation of Greater Cincinnati, Inc. v. City of Cincinnati*, 860 F. Supp. 417 (S.D. Ohio 1994), *reversed*, 54 F.3d 261 (6th Cir. 1995), *vacated and remanded*, 116 S. Ct. 2519 (1996); *Jantz v. Mucci*, 759 F. Supp. 1543 (D. Kansas 1991), *vacated*, 976 F.2d 623 (10th Cir. 1992).

3. 968 F. Supp. 850 (E.D.N.Y. 1997), *reversed*, 1998 U.S. App. LEXIS 23359 (2d Cir. Sept. 23, 1998).

4. This sort of rationale is an example of "legal formalism," that is, the "position that a unique answer in a particular case can be 'deduced' from a rule, or that application of a rule to a particular case is 'analytical.'" Margaret J. Radin, "Reconsidering the Rule of Law," *Boston University Law Review* 69 (1989): 793. I do not argue that legal formalism never describes how courts operate. I merely argue that this is not how most courts operate in applying the three-tiered framework of the equal protection clause.

5. I do not wish to imply that the "courts" are a uniform, undifferentiated entity. However, the various courts that have addressed the issue of whether gays and lesbians are a suspect class have set forth similar explanations for their holdings.

6. No. 92 CV 7223 (District Court, City and County of Denver, Colo., December 14, 1993). The trial court's opinion is reproduced as Appendix C to the defendant's petition to the Supreme Court for writ of certiorari, and at this writing the opinion can also be found at *Bayless at ucsub.colorado.edu* (Web site dated 2 February 1996), http://ucsub.colorado.edu/~pluslbgu/bayless.

class and why gays and lesbians do not fully meet these criteria.[7] This chapter lays out these criteria and examines the reasons given by Judge Bayless and other courts for holding that gays and lesbians are not a suspect class.

The Trial Court's Decision and the Three Criteria for Suspect-Class Status

Judge Bayless held that gays and lesbians are neither a suspect class nor a quasi-suspect class and therefore are not protected by strict or intermediate scrutiny. He noted that "[c]ase law has not clearly differentiated between the elements of a 'suspect' class and a 'quasi-suspect' class."[8] Therefore, he applied the same criteria to determine whether gays and lesbians are a quasi-suspect class or a suspect class.

Judge Bayless relied on two precedents for identifying the criteria for suspect-class status. First, he quoted from *San Antonio Independent School District v. Rodriguez:* "The system of alleged discrimination and the class it defines have none of the traditional indicia of suspectness: the class is not saddled with such disabilities, or subjected to such a history of purposeful unequal treatment, or relegated to such a position of political powerlessness as to command extraordinary protection from the majoritarian political process."[9] As discussed in chapter 3, *Rodriguez* was the turning point in the development of equal protection doctrine. It was the case that reversed the expansion of the equal protection clause by limiting strict scrutiny to those groups that could demonstrate that they are *Carolene*-type "discrete and insular" minorities. Based on *Rodriguez,* Bayless concluded that, to qualify as a suspect class, gays and lesbians must demonstrate: (1) that they have suffered a history of discrimination, and (2) that they are politically powerless.

Bayless also cited a federal circuit court case, *High Tech Gays v. Defense Industrial Security Clearance Office,* as authority for a third characteristic of

7. The plaintiffs decided not to appeal the trial court's determination that homosexuals are not a suspect class. As appellate courts have been hostile to the argument that homosexuals are a suspect class, the plaintiffs viewed an appeal on this issue to be a waste of resources. Jean Dubofsky (lead counsel for plaintiffs), interview by author, Boulder, Colo., 9 March 1995. As a result, neither the U.S. Supreme Court nor the Colorado Supreme Court ruled on this issue.

8. *Evans v. Romer* (trial court opinion), at p. C-18 of Colorado's cert. petition.

9. *Id.* at p. C-16 (quoting *San Antonio Independent School District v. Rodriguez,* 411 U.S. 1, 28 (1973)).

members of a suspect class: they must "exhibit obvious, immutable or distinguishing characteristics that define them as a discrete group."[10]

Bayless thus held that gays and lesbians are a suspect class only if they meet the following three criteria: (1) a history of discrimination; (2) an immutable characteristic, and; (3) political powerlessness. The next three sections of this chapter address these criteria, and how the courts have applied them to gays and lesbians.

History of Discrimination

Gays and lesbians have suffered from numerous legal disadvantages in twentieth-century America. During World War II many enlisted personnel serving in the United States military forces received dishonorable discharges on the basis of their homosexuality.[11] However, in keeping with the emerging perception of homosexuality as a medical condition, attempts were made to cure soldiers of their disability. The military's view of homosexuality as an illness was in keeping with the beliefs of the psychiatric profession at that time. From 1952 to 1973 the American Psychiatric Association listed homosexuality as a mental disorder.[12]

Following World War II, in the wake of the emergence of the Cold War, this process of turning homosexuality into a medical condition receded somewhat, and homosexuality's connotations of immorality and perversion were reinvigorated for a time. At the same time Senator Joseph McCarthy was leading the hunt for communists, the United States Congress also became concerned about purging the federal government of so-called sex perverts.[13] In June 1950 the Senate authorized an inquiry into the "Employment of Homosexuals and Other Moral Perverts in Government."[14] The results of the inquiry were unambiguously damning, concluding that a homosexual "tends to have a corrosive influence upon his fellow employees. These perverts will frequently attempt to entice normal

10. *Id.* at p. C-15 (quoting *High Tech Gays v. Defense Industrial Security Clearance Office*, 895 F.2d 563, 573 (9th Cir. 1990)).

11. Before World War II, the military was concerned about homosexual acts rather than homosexuality as a condition. Beginning in the 1940s, the military became more concerned with homosexuality as a condition and attempted to "cure" homosexuals with psychiatric treatment before expelling them. Charles Moskos, "From Citizens' Army to Social Laboratory," *Wilson Quarterly* 17 (1993): 83–94.

12. Ralph Slovenko, "The Homosexual and Society: A Historical Perspective," *University of Dayton Law Review* 10 (1985): 449.

13. For the connection between the purges of communists and homosexuals from the government, see William B. Rubenstein, ed., *Lesbians, Gay Men, and the Law* (New York: New Press, 1996), 313–18.

14. Slovenko, "The Homosexual and Society," 448.

individuals to engage in perverted practices . . . . One homosexual can pollute a government office."[15] As a result of this report, dismissals from government service on the basis of homosexuality increased twelvefold. Indeed, one of Eisenhower's first tasks as president in 1953 was to issue an executive order barring homosexuals from all federal jobs.[16]

The military's assessment during World War II of the negative impact of homosexuality on its ranks was given credence by this purge of homosexuals from government service instigated by the Senate during the 1950s. The exclusion of gays and lesbians from the military remains an existing policy of the federal government. From 1980 through 1990, approximately seventeen thousand service members were discharged on this basis.[17] President Clinton's "don't ask, don't tell, don't pursue" compromise on the military gay ban remains.[18] Ostensibly, under this policy service members can be discharged only if they somehow indicate that they have homosexual desires. However, the number of homosexuality-related discharges remains high; in 1994, for example, nearly six hundred service members were discharged under the new policy. Indeed, the number of gays and lesbians purged from the military has *risen* 67 percent since "don't ask, don't tell" went into effect.[19] Despite the phrase "don't pursue," the military continues to pursue allegations of homosexuality with extraordinary aggressiveness. As described in chapter 1, the military has even gone as far as demanding the identity of a person who placed a profile of himself with America Online describing his marital status as "gay" because it suspected the person might be a service member.

However, the fate of gays and lesbians in the federal civil service has improved since the 1950s. Sexual orientation is no longer a ground for dismissal, and it has been deemed irrelevant to the hiring process. Until very recently, it remained a de facto barrier to positions requiring a high-level security clearance. In 1995, however, President Clinton issued an executive order eliminating the policy against gays and lesbians receiving high-level security clearance.

15. John D'Emilio and Estelle B. Freedman, *Intimate Matters: A History of Sexuality in America* (New York: Harper & Row, 1988), 293.

16. *Ibid.*

17. Franklin D. Jones and Ronald J. Koshes, "Homosexuality and the Military," *American Journal of Psychiatry* 152 (1995): 16.

18. Although President Clinton had promised to simply rescind the ban on homosexual service members, he agreed, under political pressure, to the "don't ask, don't tell" policy, which was enacted into law in 1994. See 10 U.S.C. § 654(b) (1994).

19. Andrew Sullivan, "Undone by Don't Ask, Don't Tell," *New York Times,* 9 April 1998, op-ed page.

Although federal government policy toward gays and lesbians has significant symbolic value, its practical impact is limited. State laws and regulations play a far greater role in constructing the legal and political environment of gays and lesbians. To begin with, the proscription of criminal conduct is largely within the province of the states, and sodomy remains a crime in many of them. While such laws are difficult to enforce, the threat of prosecution hangs over gays and lesbians, and there have been instances of gays and lesbians receiving significant prison sentences for consensual, private sexual activity.[20]

Gays and lesbians face many other legal disadvantages at the state level. In a custody dispute between former spouses, a gay or lesbian parent can be at a distinct disadvantage.[21] For such parents who are denied custody but granted visitation rights, their sexual orientation frequently elicits special conditions. For example, the court may prohibit the child from staying overnight at the gay or lesbian parent's home.[22] Such a condition can effectively foreclose all access to the child if the gay or lesbian parent lives at such a distance from the custodial parent that an overnight stay is inevitable. Further, courts have mandated in some cases that the homosexual parent keep his or her child away from both the parent's partner and the partner's home.[23]

Thus, homosexuality can be a significant disadvantage in custody disputes between parents. Moreover, some courts have granted custody to a third party rather than to the child's biological, but homosexual parent. Grandparents or even aunts and uncles have been awarded custody of the children of gays and lesbians. For example, the Supreme Court of Virginia recently upheld a decision depriving a mother of the custody of her child primarily because she was living with her same-sex lover. In reaching his decision, the trial judge had stated, "I will tell you first that the mother's conduct is illegal. It is a Class 6 felony in the Commonwealth of Virginia. I will tell you that it is the opinion of this court that her conduct is immoral. And it is the opinion of this court that the conduct of Sharon Bottoms renders her an unfit parent."[24] Given the very serious protection that courts

20. For a description of such cases, see Patricia A. Cain, "Litigating for Lesbian and Gay Rights: A Legal History," *University of Virginia Law Review* 79 (1993): 1588 n. 218.

21. "Courts frequently consider the parent's sexual orientation to be relevant to the child's best interests and several courts have used the best interests standard to deny custody to gay and lesbian parents." Editors of the Harvard Law Review, *Sexual Orientation and the Law* (Cambridge: Harvard University Press, 1990), 120–21.

22. For examples of cases where this condition was imposed, see *J. L. P. (H.) v. D. J. P.*, 643 S.W.2d 865, 871(Mo. Ct. App. 1982); *In re Jane B.*, 380 N.Y.S.2d 848, 860 (Sup. Ct. 1976).

23. For example, see *Dailey v. Dailey*, 635 S.W.2d 391, 396 (Tenn. Ct. App. 1981).

24. *Bottoms v. Bottoms*, 457 S.E.2d 102, 109 (Va. 1995) (Keenan, J., quoting the trial court's

have granted to the concept of parental rights,[25] the favoring of a third party over the biological parent offers a telling insight to the way in which homosexuality has been viewed by some courts.

Homosexuality may also deprive a person of full legal protection against criminal assault. Gays and lesbians are frequently the victims of violent physical attack; indeed, a study commissioned by the National Institute for Justice found that gays and lesbians "are probably the most frequent victims of hate crimes."[26] Many courts allow evidence of a victim's homosexuality and the defendant's impulsive response to that status to be admitted as a possible mitigating factor or even full excuse for attacking (or even killing) a gay or lesbian person. The "homosexual panic" defense and, particularly, the "homosexual advance" defense are admitted into evidence with sufficient regularity and effect that defense lawyers are advised to try to use them.[27] There is no equivalent defense when violence is committed against a heterosexual victim.

Not surprisingly, these two avenues of defense have been strongly criticized by academic commentators for the messages they send about the status of gays and lesbians in our society.[28] These defenses put the victim as well as the defendant on trial—in much the same manner as a rape victim's sexual history used to be made an issue before law reform in this area.[29] The courts' recognition of these defenses sends the message that, although attacking or murdering gay people is against our laws, society understands the impulse.

Based on this history, it seems easy to conclude that gays and lesbians have suffered from significant discrimination. However, some might argue that these legal burdens are not "discrimination" at all, but are merely proper societal expressions of moral disapproval of homosexuality. This is not a simple point to rebut. As Laurence Tribe asks, "how are we to distin-

---

decision in his dissent). For other examples, see *Chaffin v. Frye*, 119 Cal. Rptr. 22 (Ct. App. 1975), and *Roberts v. Roberts*, 212 S.E.2d 410 (N.C. Ct. App. 1975).

25. Indeed, the Supreme Court has declared that parental rights are strongly protected under the Constitution and may be terminated only upon a showing of clear and convincing evidence that a parent is unfit. *Santosky v. Kramer*, 455 U.S. 745 (1982).

26. Kendall Thomas, "Beyond the Privacy Principle," *Columbia Law Review* 92 (1992): 1464.

27. For numerous examples of state courts allowing evidence of a homosexual advance as legal provocation in murder cases, see Robert B. Mison, "Homophobia in Manslaughter: The Homosexual Advance as Insufficient Provocation," *California Law Review* 80 (1992): 134 nn. 4 & 5.

28. Gary D. Comstock, "Dismantling the Homosexual Panic Defense," *Law & Sexuality* 2 (1992): 81–102; Mison, "Homophobia in Manslaughter."

29. Comstock, "Homosexual Panic Defense," 97.

guish ... 'prejudice' from principled, if 'wrong' disapproval?"[30] This question, however, has not troubled the courts at all. Courts that have addressed this issue have held that gays and lesbians have suffered a history of discrimination. In *High Tech Gays v. Defense Industrial Security Clearance Office*,[31] the federal Court of Appeals for the Ninth Circuit ruled that gays and lesbians are not a suspect class but stated, "we do agree that homosexuals have suffered a history of discrimination."[32] In *Evans v. Romer*, Judge Bayless addressed the issue of discrimination in a single paragraph, stating that he agreed with the *High Tech Gays* court that gays and lesbians have suffered a history of discrimination.[33] In fact, *no* court has ever denied suspect-class status to gays and lesbians on the ground that they have not suffered a history of discrimination.

The Issue of Immutability

Having held that gays and lesbians have suffered a history of discrimination, Judge Bayless next turned to the issue of immutability. During the trial, Bayless heard extensive and contradictory expert testimony as to whether homosexuality is immutable or is a matter of choice. He decided that the question is not a legal issue. Rather it is a scientific, philosophical, and sociological issue:

> One of the hot debates among witnesses addressed the question of whether homosexuality is inborn, a product of "nature," or a choice based on life experiences, a product of "nurture." Plaintiffs strongly argue that homosexuality is inborn. All the suspect and quasi-suspect classes, race, alienage, national origin, gender and illegitimacy, are inborn. Defendants argue that homosexuality or bisexuality is either a choice, or its origin has multiple aspects or its origin is unknown. The preponderance of credible evidence suggests that there is *a* biological or genetic "component" of sexual orientation, but even Dr. Hamer, the witness who testified that he is 99.5% sure there is *some* genetic influence in forming sexual orientation, admits that sexual orientation is not completely genetic. The ultimate decision on "nature" vs. "nurture" is a decision for another forum, not this court, and the court makes no determination on this issue.[34]

30. Laurence H. Tribe, "The Puzzling Persistence of Process-Based Constitutional Theories," *Yale Law Journal* 89 (1980): 1073.

31. 895 F.2d 563 (9th Cir. 1990).

32. *High Tech Gays*, 895 F.2d at 573.

33. *Evans* (trial court opinion), at pp. C-17 to C-18 of Colorado's cert. petition.

34. *Id.* at p. C-17.

Thus, Judge Bayless decided that the immutability of sexual orientation is not an issue amenable to legal resolution. However, not all courts have agreed with him. In fact, most courts that have held that gays and lesbians are not a suspect class have explained their holdings by stating that homosexuality is not an immutable characteristic.

The reasoning of these courts can be divided into two basic arguments. One argument is that homosexuality is defined by the behavior of homosexual sodomy—a behavior described by the Supreme Court in *Bowers v. Hardwick*[35] as repulsive to Western morality and unprotected under the Constitution. Because the Supreme Court has declared that homosexual sodomy is unprotected, several courts have held that a group defined by this behavior cannot be constitutionally protected.

The other argument used by the courts is that, regardless of the constitutional status of homosexual sodomy, no group that is defined by behavior rather than by an obvious, immutable characteristic such as skin color can be a suspect class. As one federal circuit court stated the argument, "Those persons who fall within the orbit of legislation concerning sexual orientation are so affected not because of their orientation but rather by their conduct which identifies them as homosexual, bisexual or heterosexual."[36] These two arguments are discussed separately.

Bowers v. Hardwick and the Issue of Homosexual Sodomy

Bowers v. Hardwick did not involve the equal protection clause. In *Bowers*, the Supreme Court had to decide whether Georgia's antisodomy law violated the Fourteenth Amendment's due process clause. The Court had previously held that the due process clause protects a somewhat vaguely defined "right of privacy," which is broad enough to encompass such things as the right to have an abortion and the right to use contraceptives.[37] In *Bowers*, the U.S. Court of Appeals for the Eleventh Circuit had held that Georgia's antisodomy law violated the due process clause, reasoning that the "[Supreme] Court's prior cases had construed the Constitution to confer a right of privacy that extends to homosexual sodomy and for all intents and purposes had decided this case."[38] Georgia sought a writ of certiorari from the Supreme Court, which reversed the Court of Appeals' decision.

---

35. 478 U.S. 186 (1986).

36. *Equality Foundation of Greater Cincinnati v. City of Cincinnati*, 54 F.3d 261 (6th Cir. 1995), *vacated and remanded*, 116 S. Ct. 2519 (1996).

37. See, respectively, *Roe v. Wade*, 410 U.S. 113 (1973), and *Griswold v. Connecticut*, 381 U.S. 479 (1965).

38. *Bowers*, 478 U.S. at 190.

Although the Georgia statute outlawed both homosexual and heterosexual sodomy,[39] the Supreme Court addressed only whether homosexual
sodomy is protected under the due process clause. The Court held that
the due process clause does not protect private, consensual homosexual
sodomy. The majority opinion stressed that only two kinds of rights qualify for heightened judicial protection under the due process clause:
(1) those rights "'implicit in the concept of ordered liberty' such that
'neither liberty nor justice would exist if [they] were sacrificed'"[40] and
(2) rights that implicate "liberties that are 'deeply rooted in this nation's
history and tradition.'"[41]

The Court assumed without discussion that homosexual sodomy does
not qualify as a protected right under the first formulation. Regarding the
second formulation, the Court stated that "proscriptions against [homo-
sexual sodomy] have ancient roots."[42] The Court noted that the setting for
such acts—the privacy of the home—did not entitle them to protection;
many "victimless" crimes, such as adultery and incest, are illegal, even
when performed in the home.[43]

The holding of *Bowers* is quite narrow. It merely states that criminal
prosecution of homosexual sodomy does not violate the due process
clause. However, its implications have been enormous. Numerous federal
courts have held that *Bowers* precludes them from treating gays and lesbians as a suspect or quasi-suspect class under the equal protection
clause.[44] In each of these decisions the court has reasoned that, since homosexual sodomy is not constitutionally protected under the due process
clause, those who practice it cannot receive enhanced judicial protection
under the equal protection clause. For example, in *Padula v. Webster*,[45] the
plaintiff had sued the Federal Bureau of Investigation because it allegedly

39. The statute, Ga. Code Ann. § 16-6-2(a) (1984), defined sodomy as follows: "A person
commits the offense of sodomy when he performs or submits to any sexual act involving the
sex organs of one person and the mouth or anus of another. . . ."

40. *Bowers*, 478 U.S. at 191–92 (quoting *Palko v. Connecticut*, 302 U.S. 319, 325–26 (1937)).

41. *Id.* at 192 (quoting *Moore v. City of East Cleveland*, 431 U.S. 494, 503 (1977)).

42. *Bowers*, 478 U.S. at 192. The Court's historical analysis has been sharply criticized.
Richard Posner, *Sex and Reason* (Cambridge: Harvard University Press, 1992).

43. *Bowers*, 478 U.S. at 196.

44. *Equality Foundation of Greater Cincinnati v. City of Cincinnati*, 54 F.3d 261 (6th Cir. 1995),
vacated and remanded, 116 S. Ct. 2519 (1996); *Steffan v. Perry*, 41 F.3d 677 (D.C. Cir. 1994); *High
Tech Gays v. Defense Industrial Security Clearance Office*, 895 F.2d 563 (9th Cir. 1990); *Woodward v.
United States*, 871 F.2d 1068 (D.C. Cir. 1990); *Ben-Shalom v. Marsh*, 881 F.2d 454 (7th Cir. 1989);
Padula v. Webster, 822 F.2d 97 (D.C. Cir. 1987); *Baker v. Wade*, 769 F.2d 289 (5th Cir. 1985) (en
banc).

45. 822 F.2d 97 (D.C. Cir. 1987).

refused to employ her as a special agent because of her homosexuality. She argued that gays and lesbians constitute a suspect or quasi-suspect class, and the Court of Appeals for the District of Columbia rejected her argument, stating:

> It would be quite anomalous, on its face, to declare status defined by conduct that states may constitutionally criminalize as deserving of strict scrutiny under the equal protection clause. . . . If the [Supreme] Court was unwilling to object to state laws that criminalize the behavior that defines the class, it is hardly open to a lower court to conclude that state sponsored discrimination is invidious. After all, there can hardly be more palpable discrimination against a class than making the conduct that defines the class criminal.[46]

Several other federal circuit courts have also relied on this reasoning.[47] *Bowers* thus prevents courts from finding gays and lesbians to be a suspect or quasi-suspect class even if gays and lesbians are able to demonstrate a history of discrimination and substantial current discrimination against them.

As a result, laws involving—to use the *Padula* court's terminology— "state sponsored discrimination" against homosexuals are very likely to survive a challenge under the equal protection clause. The courts must apply only the rational-basis test. This is why the Supreme Court in *Romer* had to conclude that Amendment 2 was motivated by an irrational "bare desire to harm" gays and lesbians in order to strike it down and why the lower federal courts have consistently upheld other laws that disadvantage gays and lesbians. Thus the impact of *Bowers*, a due process case, on the equal protection claims of gays and lesbians has been enormous.

Upon closer examination, the courts' common reliance on *Bowers* is unwarranted, for there are several serious problems with the courts' line of reasoning. First, and most obvious, the Supreme Court itself did not believe that it was addressing any equal protection issues in *Bowers*. To the contrary, the Court explicitly stated that no equal protection issues were before it. After discussing the defendant's contention that the due process clause prohibits public regulation of private "immoral behavior," the majority opinion states, "We do not agree, and are unpersuaded that the sodomy laws of some 25 states should be invalidated *on this basis*."[48] This statement is immediately followed by the following footnote: "[The

46. *Padula*, 822 F.2d at 103.
47. See cases cited in note 44 above.
48. *Bowers*, 478 U.S. at 186 (emphasis added).

defendant] does not defend the judgment below [which struck down Georgia's sodomy statute] based on the Ninth Amendment, the Equal Protection Clause or the Eighth Amendment." It is therefore clear that the Supreme Court did not intend to bind the lower courts with respect to future equal protection claims. However broadly one may interpret *Bowers,* a clear statement that the Court is not addressing equal protection issues cannot be read to mean that the Court has decided the equal protection issues.

Of course, the lower courts could be correct that *Bowers* at least implies that gays and lesbians cannot be a suspect class. If the due process clause does not protect the "behavior that defines the class" of homosexuals, then how can gays and lesbians be protected under the equal protection clause? This logic, however, is not as compelling as it may seem at first. Indeed, it faces several severe analytic problems.

One problem is that these courts have been strangely casual about using the result in a due process case to decide equal protection cases. It is entirely possible that, while homosexual sodomy is not protected under the due process clause, it is protected under the equal protection clause. Courts do not normally assume that, because a behavior is unprotected under one part of the Constitution, it must also be unprotected under all other parts of the Constitution. A prison sentence for burning the flag might not violate the Eighth Amendment's proscription against cruel and unusual punishment, but it does violate the First Amendment.[49] Indeed, Justice Powell, whose concurrence provided the necessary fifth vote in *Bowers,* specifically stated that Georgia's antisodomy law might violate the Eighth Amendment, but that the issue was not before the Court. Thus, Powell was stating that the Court was not foreclosing all avenues of constitutional challenge to antisodomy statutes merely by deciding the due process issue.

Therefore, for the courts to extrapolate from the due process clause to the equal protection clause, they would have to assume that the due process clause and the equal protection clause are so intimately bound together that decisions interpreting one clause can determine the outcome of decisions interpreting the other. Perhaps there is something to this. Both clauses are part of the Fourteenth Amendment, and the Supreme Court has held that the two clauses are related. In *Bolling v. Sharpe,*[50] the Supreme Court had to decide whether the racial segregation of the District of Columbia school system was constitutional. The Court held that the federal

49. *Texas v. Johnson,* 491 U.S. 397 (1989).
50. 347 U.S. 497 (1954).

government was bound by the dictates of the equal protection clause even though that clause, by its terms, applies only to the states. It reached this result by determining that the due process clause found in the Fifth Amendment (which does apply to the federal government) incorporated the dictates of the equal protection clause: "The Fifth Amendment [does] not contain an equal protection clause as does the Fourteenth Amendment which applies only to the states. But the concepts of equal protection and due process, both stemming from our American ideals of fairness, are not mutually exclusive."[51]

So perhaps the two clauses are so closely related that courts can treat them more or less as a single unit. This would perhaps justify extrapolating from *Bowers*'s due process holding to the issue of equal protection. However, there are strong reasons for rejecting this proposition. After discussing how both clauses stem from the American ideal of fairness, the *Bolling* Court immediately added the following caveat: "The 'equal protection of the laws' is *a more explicit safeguard of prohibited unfairness* than 'due process of law,' and therefore, we do not imply that the two are always interchangeable phrases."[52]

In fact, the Supreme Court has not looked to due process decisions to determine what groups are or are not suspect classes. For example, the Court has held that the due process clause protects a woman's right to an abortion.[53] However, just because decisions regarding pregnancy are given special protection under the due process clause, this does not mean that the category of "pregnant persons" is entitled to strict-scrutiny protection under the equal protection clause. In fact, the Supreme Court has explicitly held otherwise: In *Geduldig v. Aiello*,[54] the Court held that excluding pregnancies from a disability program for state workers that covered virtually all other forms of disability did not violate the equal protection clause, because "pregnant persons" are not entitled to heightened protection under the equal protection clause.

Indeed, the whole enterprise of extrapolating from one clause to the other is bound to produce untenable results. Suppose the Court were to deny a due process challenge by Hispanic groups to "English only" laws. Would this mean that Hispanics are no longer a protected class under the equal protection clause, because speaking Spanish is not protected under the due process clause?

51. *Bolling,* 347 U.S. at 499.
52. *Id.* (emphasis added).
53. *Roe v. Wade,* 410 U.S. 113 (1973).
54. 417 U.S. 484 (1974).

Upon examination, there is simply no reason to assume that courts should consider due process cases to be relevant precedents for equal protection cases. Doing so assumes that the two clauses have similar goals and enshrine similar constitutional values. Yet, while the two clauses may both stem from American ideals of fairness, they have evolved in very different ways. As Cass Sunstein has pointed out, the two clauses have been interpreted to have distinct purposes and to embody different values:

> The Supreme Court based its decision in *Bowers v. Hardwick* on the view that the scope of substantive due process should be defined largely by reference to tradition. Thus the Court looked to whether homosexual sodomy was "implicit in the concept of ordered liberty" or "deeply rooted in this Nation's history and tradition." But a holding that the Due Process Clause extends thus far and no farther does not affect the equal protection claim, which is founded on a different set of values. . . . the Equal Protection Clause is a self-conscious repudiation of history and tradition as defining constitutional values.[55]

Sunstein points out that, while the due process clause protects practices deeply rooted in tradition, the equal protection clause does precisely the opposite: "it protects against traditions, however long-standing and deeply rooted."[56] After all, some of our deeply rooted traditions are distinctly inegalitarian. Thus, while racially segregated schools may have been traditional in much of the United States when *Brown v. Board of Education* was decided, segregated schools still violated the equal protection clause.

Because decisions interpreting one part of the Constitution do not generally control how other parts of the Constitution are interpreted, *Bowers* has little to say about whether or not laws prohibiting homosexual (but not heterosexual) sodomy violate the equal protection clause. Yet, even if *Bowers* could be construed to mean that such laws do not deny gays and lesbians equal protection of the laws, there would still be serious problems with the reasoning of the Courts of Appeals.

It is one thing to say that the act of homosexual sodomy is not protected by the equal protection clause. It is another thing entirely to say that homosexuals are not a suspect class. The latter proposition does not logically follow from the former. As noted above, the Courts of Appeals assumed that

55. Cass R. Sunstein, "Sexual Orientation and the Constitution: A Note on the Relationship between Due Process and Equal Protection," *University of Chicago Law Review* 55 (1988): 1168.

56. *Ibid.*, 1174.

homosexual sodomy is "the act which defines the class" of homosexuals. As the D.C. Circuit court stated in *Padula*, "it would be quite anomalous, on its face, to declare status defined by [engaging in homosexual sodomy] as deserving of strict scrutiny under the equal protection clause."[57]

This assumes that the "status" of being homosexual is "defined" by engaging in homosexual sodomy. For the purposes of constitutional analysis, that assumption is simply incorrect. In fact, the only constitutionally justifiable way to define the term "homosexual" would be to use the definition contained in the particular law under review. It is important to remember that homosexuals as a group can never be put on trial—the issue before the courts is the constitutionality of the challenged law. Therefore, the question is whether the classification *created by the law* is constitutional. Yet, the definition used by the courts (homosexuals are those who engage in homosexual sodomy) is quite incongruous with how homosexuals are defined by the laws that are being challenged under the equal protection clause.

Amendment 2, for example, covers homosexual "orientation" as well as homosexual "conduct" and homosexual "acts." Thus, the language of Amendment 2 clearly defines homosexual orientation as something that exists independently of homosexual conduct or acts. Most of the federal cases that have applied *Bowers* to the equal protection question have involved challenges to the military ban on homosexual service members. Quite clearly, the ban does not define homosexuals as only those who commit homosexual sodomy. The phrase "don't ask, don't tell" refers to the act of stating that one is a homosexual, as opposed to actually performing homosexual acts. Under the new policy, a member of the armed services is considered homosexual if the member "has stated that he or she is homosexual or bisexual or words to that effect."[58] In fact, even before the "don't ask, don't tell" policy was put into effect, the military had stopped defining homosexuals as those persons who commit sodomy. The military once did define homosexuals as those who engaged in homosexual acts, during the period from the 1950s through the 1970s.[59] However, this policy changed in 1982 when, "in an effort to bring about a more uniform policy, the Department of Defense issued new guidelines that for all practical purposes made stated sexual orientation, rather than behavior (unless it was overt) the defining quality of homosexuality."[60]

57. *Padula v. Webster*, 822 F.2d 97, 103 (D.C. Cir. 1987).
58. 10 U.S.C. § 654(b)(2) (1994).
59. Moskos, "From Citizens' Army," 92.
60. *Ibid.*

Indeed, in *Steffan v. Perry*,[61] the Naval Academy expelled a cadet because he admitted he was gay, even though he was never accused, much less convicted, of engaging in homosexual acts. Similarly, in *Ben-Shalom v. Marsh*,[62] the court upheld a servicewoman's expulsion even as it conceded, "it is true that actual lesbian conduct has not been admitted by the plaintiff on any particular occasion, and the Army has offered no evidence of such conduct."

The courts should not assume that homosexual sodomy is the act that "defines the class" of homosexuals because the laws at issue do not define homosexuals this way. In the cases discussed above, a more accurate definition of the class of "homosexuals" would be "those persons who declare themselves to have a gay or lesbian sexual orientation." This would better match reality in cases like *Steffan* and *Ben-Shalom*, where no one had been accused or convicted of committing sodomy.

Indeed, this points to perhaps the most troubling aspect of how the courts have handled cases involving gays and lesbians. The courts have been disturbingly willing to *assume* criminal behavior on the basis of statements people have made about their sexual orientation. In *Ben-Shalom*, the Court of Appeals for the Seventh Circuit held that, "although individual exceptions may exist, a lesbian orientation is compelling evidence that the plaintiff has engaged in homosexual conduct and likely will do so again, and consequently a regulation which classifies lesbians does not categorize merely upon status but upon reasonable inferences perceived from probable past and future sexual conduct."[63]

Similarly, the Supreme Court of Washington, in *Gaylord v. Tacoma School District*, upheld the discharge of an openly gay high school teacher, stating that "an admission of homosexuality connotes illegal as well as immoral acts, because 'sexual gratification with a member of one's own sex is implicit in the term "homosexual."'"[64]

These cases assume criminal guilt without any of the normal protections accorded by the criminal justice system. Further, such assumptions may violate the First Amendment rights of gays and lesbians: it is constitutionally impermissible to assume that a person will engage in illegal behavior because of general statements made by that person.[65] In *Hess v.*

---

61. 41 F.3d 677 (3d Cir. 1994).

62. 881 F.2d 454, 464 (7th Cir. 1989).

63. *Ben-Shalom*, 881 F.2d at 463–64.

64. *Gaylord v. Tacoma School District*, 559 P.2d 1340, 1342 (Wash. 1977) (quoting finding of the trial court).

65. *Brandenburg v. Ohio*, 395 U.S. 444 (1969).

Indiana,[66] for example, after police cleared antiwar demonstrators from a street they had been illegally blocking, a demonstrator yelled, "we'll take the fucking street later." He was arrested, but the Supreme Court held that the government could not assume that the demonstrator was going to perform an illegal act in the future on the basis of the this statement. Statements regarding sexual orientation therefore appear to be unique. In no other context have the courts permitted the government to presume that a person is going to engage in illegal behavior based on that person's speech.[67] The point, of course, is not that gays and lesbians are always celibate (although it is entirely possible that a given soldier may choose to remain celibate during his or her time in the armed forces), but rather, that they are entitled to the same presumption of innocence and First Amendment protections as everyone else.

This blurring of the line between criminal guilt and stated sexual orientation is *inherent* in the way courts have applied *Bowers* to noncriminal contexts. Relying on *Bowers* requires courts to assume that the plaintiff class has engaged in the activity that *Bowers* held the state may criminalize. If Amendment 2, the military's policy on homosexuality, and other challenged laws defined homosexuals as "those persons convicted of committing sodomy," this would be a perfectly reasonable assumption. However, this is not the case. The courts are defining homosexuality in a way that is wholly incongruous with how the challenged statutes themselves define homosexuality and that disregards fundamental constitutional principles such as the presumption of innocence and freedom of speech.

Homosexuality and Immutability

For these reasons, the Supreme Court's holding in *Bowers* has little relevance to where homosexuals fit within the three-tiered framework of equal protection jurisprudence. However, various courts have held that, regardless of *Bowers*, gays and lesbians cannot be a suspect class because homosexuality is defined by voluntary behavior, not immutable characteristics.

It is important to be precise here about what the courts have been holding. Perhaps even more importantly, it is important to be clear about what they have *not* been holding. Some courts have allowed extensive testimony at trial about whether sexual orientation is a "characteristic beyond

---

66. 414 U.S. 105 (1973).

67. While statements such as "your money or your life" are actionable, this is because such threats are intended to coerce the hearer. The statement "I am a homosexual" is clearly not analogous to such a threat.

the control of the individual."[68] Therefore, it is easy to assume that, when courts hold that homosexuality is not immutable, they mean that sexual orientation is a matter of choice. However, such an assumption would be incorrect.

No court has held that gays and lesbians should be denied suspect-class status because they could simply choose to have a heterosexual orientation.[69] Although whether homosexuals could choose to be heterosexuals is discussed in a number of cases, no decision has actually turned on this question. Courts that have relied on the immutability issue have held that homosexuality is not immutable because homosexuals, regardless of their orientation, could simply refrain from homosexual behavior. The Ninth Circuit Court of Appeals explained this proposition succinctly in *High Tech Gays:* "Homosexuality is not an immutable characteristic; it is behavioral and hence is fundamentally different from traits such as race, gender and alienage, which define already existing suspect and quasi-suspect classes. The behavior or conduct of such already recognized classes is irrelevant to their identification."[70] Thus, the issue of whether people can choose their sexual orientation has not been a part of the courts' reasoning.

The argument that gays and lesbians share common behavior rather than a common orientation is a powerful one. As discussed in chapter 2, protecting a group as a suspect class is strong medicine, often resulting in the substitution of judicial judgment for democratic decision making in all areas of law affecting the protected group. If the group seeking such protection is defined by voluntary behavior that flouts majoritarian notions of morality, then it seems reasonable to ask that group to simply stop engaging in that behavior. Society singles out all sorts of behavior-based groups for negative treatment—adulterers, bigamists, and people who use prostitutes, among many other groups. Yet no one would argue that such groups are suspect classes. It is their behavior that must conform to societal standards, not vice versa. However, there are also a number of very serious problems with this argument. One is that behavior is not the complete barrier to membership in a suspect or quasi-suspect class that the *High Tech*

68. *Equality Foundation*, 54 F.3d at 267; see also *Evans v. Romer* (trial court opinion), at p. C-17 of Colorado's cert. petition.

69. There has been an enormous amount of debate among scientists concerning the question of immutability. Most of the literature argues that homosexuality is a result of both biological and environmental factors. W. G. Roper, "The Etiology of Male Homosexuality," *Medical Hypotheses* 46 (1996): 85; T. Ferguson, "Alternative Sexualities and Evolution," *Evolutionary Theory* 11 (1995): 55; B. A. Afzelius, "Inheritance of Randomness," *Medical Hypotheses* 47 (1996): 23.

70. *High Tech Gays*, 895 F.2d at 573–74.

court says it is. For example, being an alien is often a matter of choice rather than compulsion. The Supreme Court's decision in *Sugarman v. Dougall*[71] is a good example of the Court's willingness to protect certain people even if their membership in a group is clearly voluntary. In *Sugarman* the Court was reviewing a New York statute that provided that only United States citizens could hold certain civil service positions. The Court applied the *Carolene Products* reasoning:

> In *Graham v. Richardson*, we observed that aliens as a class "are a prime example of a 'discrete and insular minority,'" and that classifications based on alienage are "subject to close judicial scrutiny."[72]

Applying strict scrutiny, the Court struck down the law because it was not tailored to further a compelling governmental interest. However, as Justice Rehnquist emphasized in his dissent, the plaintiffs' status as aliens was far from immutable. The plaintiffs were eligible for citizenship but chose not to apply. Rehnquist noted that the "records . . . contain[ed] no indication that the aliens suffered any disability that precluded them, either as a group or individually, from applying for and being granted the status of naturalized citizens. The appellees . . . took no steps to obtain citizenship or indicate any affirmative desire to become citizens."[73] Rehnquist also noted that one of the plaintiffs was eligible for naturalization but "elected to remain a citizen of the Netherlands . . . and deliberately chose not to file a declaration of intent [to become an American citizen]."[74]

Alienage is not the only example of the Court protecting behavior rather than immutable characteristics. In *Glona v. American Guarantee & Liability Insurance Co.*,[75] the Court applied heightened scrutiny and struck down a law that prevented an unwed mother from suing for the wrongful death of her illegitimate child. Except in instances of nonconsensual sexual intercourse, one becomes an unwed mother by choosing to engage in the behavior of out-of-wedlock sexual intercourse, a behavior that, like homosexual sodomy, has often been condemned and outlawed in the United States.

In *Sugarman* and *Glona*, therefore, the Court has applied heightened scrutiny even where the plaintiffs are not saddled with an immutable characteristic. The point is not to argue that *Sugarman* and *Glona* are right or

71. 413 U.S. 634 (1973).
72. *Sugarman*, 413 U.S. at 642 (citations omitted).
73. *Id.* at 650.
74. *Id.*
75. 391 U.S. 73 (1967).

wrong. Rather, the point is that these holdings are utterly inconsistent with
the argument that gays and lesbians cannot be a suspect or quasi-suspect
class because homosexuality is not an immutable characteristic.

Beyond these inconsistencies, however, there lurks an even more important issue. We know from *Bowers* that the criminalization of homosexual sodomy does not violate the due process clause. Yet most people are
not identified as gay or lesbian as a result of their sexual practices. People
are far more likely to be identified as gay or lesbian because they have been
seen in an affectionate display with a member of their own sex or because
they have chosen to identify themselves as gay or lesbian. The Court of Appeals for the Sixth Circuit, in upholding Amendment 3 to Cincinnati's City
Charter (which is very similar to Colorado's Amendment 2), was quite
clear about what kinds of behavior gays and lesbians engage in that cause
them to be labeled as homosexuals:

> Those persons having a homosexual "orientation" simply do
> not, as such, comprise an identifiable class. Many homosexuals
> successfully conceal their orientation. Because homosexuals gen-
> erally are not identifiable "on sight" unless they elect to be so iden-
> tifiable by conduct *(such as public displays of homosexual affection
> or self-proclamation of homosexual tendencies)*, they cannot constitute
> a suspect class or quasi-suspect class because they "do not [neces-
> sarily] exhibit obvious, immutable or distinguishing characteris-
> tics that define them as a discrete group."[76]

While the government can regulate sodomy, it presumably cannot regulate "public displays of affection." Even more problematic is the Sixth
Circuit's characterization of "self-proclamation of homosexual tendencies"
as "conduct." As noted earlier, the First Amendment requires the government to distinguish between speech and conduct. Yet, especially in the military cases, the homosexual "conduct" at issue is often a simple statement
by a person that he or she is homosexual. In *Steffan,* for example, a federal
court upheld the discharge of a Navy cadet despite the lack of evidence
that he had engaged in homosexual conduct of any sort. The court held
that the military is entitled to infer that a person who states that he or
she is homosexual intends to engage in homosexual activity, even though
a four-month military investigation found no evidence of homosexual
behavior by Steffan.

Indeed, the whole concept of "homosexual self-identification" is prob-

---

76. *Equality Foundation of Greater Cincinnati v. City of Cincinnati,* 354 F.3d 261, 267 (6th Cir.
1995) (quoting *Bowen v. Gilliard,* 483 U.S. 587, 602 (1987)) (citations omitted; emphasis added),
vacated and remanded, 116 S. Ct. 2519 (1996).

lematic. It is not so easy to distinguish between those who are immutably part of a group and those who choose to identify themselves as part of a group. Race seems to be the paradigm example of an immutable characteristic. Yet many "African Americans" have mixed ancestry and have such light skin that they could easily identify themselves as white.[77] Many such persons of mixed racial ancestry "self-identify" as African Americans.[78] In short, they are African Americans because they have declared themselves to be. In her recent book on the experiences of light-skinned African Americans, *Notes of a White Black Woman*, Judy Scales-Trent compares her decision about whether she should identify herself as African American or "pass" as white to the decision of her lesbian colleague about whether to "come out": "It wasn't until years later that I realized that, like me, gay people are faced with the problem of 'coming out' to people. Dianna has to decide when she should come out to someone and how. She has to worry about how that person will respond. And as long as she keeps meeting new people, she will have to keep dealing with those issues of self-identification and exposure. These are issues I deal with also. When do I tell someone that I am black? And how? And how will they respond?"[79]

Indeed, many "persons of color" are perceived as such only because they choose to self-identify that way. Like Scales-Trent and other very light-skinned blacks, many people who have a mixed racial heritage that includes Native American, Latino, or other minority ancestry are thought of as persons of color because of their own behavior—identifying themselves as racial minorities. Some Latinos have "Anglo" fathers and have chosen to adopt the Spanish last name of their mothers. No court has ever suggested that legal discrimination against them should therefore be subjected to anything less than strict scrutiny. Outside of the area of homosexuality, no one appears to dispute that we all have a right to make decisions about how we identify ourselves without forgoing the equal protection of the laws.

For purposes of the equal protection clause, why is Scales-Trent's insistence on identifying herself as black different from a homosexual's "coming out"? One may be tempted to respond that the issue of race is different from the issue of sexuality. However, it is important to avoid circular reasoning. The issue of "immutable versus behavioral" characteristics is supposed to be the means by which we identify suspect classes. The fact

---

77. Judy Scales-Trent, *Notes of a White Black Woman: Race, Color, and Community* (University Park: Pennsylvania State University Press, 1995).

78. *Ibid.*

79. *Ibid.*, 28.

that racial identity, like sexual identity, is often a question of "coming out" undermines both our intuitions and the legal explanation of why racial and sexual identity are treated so differently under the equal protection clause.[80]

In sum, defining homosexuality as a behavioral characteristic does little to distinguish homosexuals from groups that receive the protection of strict scrutiny, such as aliens who decline to apply for citizenship, parents of illegitimate children, or persons of mixed racial or ethnic ancestry. The next section will examine the third element of suspect-class status: political powerlessness.

Homosexuality and Political Powerlessness

The third element used to identify a suspect or quasi-suspect class is "political powerlessness." This element flows logically from the *Carolene Products* rationale for suspect classes: those who lack political power require special protection from the prejudice of the voters.

Judge Bayless held that gays and lesbians have too much political power to be a suspect or quasi-suspect class:

> The court cannot conclude, however, that homosexuals and bisexuals remain vulnerable or politically powerless and in need of "extraordinary protection from the majoritarian political process" in today's society. . . . According to the figures presented to the court, more than 46% of the Coloradans voting voted against Amendment 2. Testimony placed the percentage of homosexuals in our society at not more than 4%. If 4% of the population gathers the support of an additional 42% of the population, that is a demonstration of power, not powerlessness. The President of the United States has taken an active and leading role in support of gays, and an increasing number of states and localities have adopted gay rights protective statutes and ordinances . . . . No adequate showing has been made of the political vulnerability or powerlessness of gays. . . . *Homosexuals fail to meet the ele-*

80. Janet Halley makes a similar point about the immutability of race in "The Politics of the Closet: Towards Equal Protection for Gay, Lesbian, and Bisexual Identity," *UCLA Law Review* 36 (1989): 915–76. She discusses the Supreme Court's struggle over whether Jews and / or Arabs are racial groups within the meaning of the Civil Rights Amendments. The Court conceded that it could not rely on any modern scientific concept of race. Halley argues, "The mere evidence relied on by the Court reveals that race is historically contingent, that its contours have changed radically since the passage of the Civil Rights Amendments. If the boundaries between the races can shift, the racial categorization of individuals can shift—a profound source of mutability." *Ibid.*, 924.

ment of political powerlessness and therefore fail to meet the elements to be found a suspect class.[81]

The Ninth Circuit has also decided that gays and lesbians are too politically powerful to be a suspect class: "Moreover, legislatures have addressed and continue to address the discrimination suffered by homosexuals on account of their sexual orientation through the passage of anti-discrimination legislation. Thus, homosexuals are not without political power; they have the ability to and do 'attract the attention of lawmakers.'"[82]

Thus, along with the perception that homosexuality is a behavioral rather than an immutable characteristic, the perception of substantial gay and lesbian political power has proven to be a major obstacle to gays and lesbians attaining suspect-class status. The criterion of political powerlessness has proven to be even more problematic than the other criteria for suspect-class status. One major problem is that the courts' discussions of political power are based on what can only be described as nonempirical "guess-timates" of group power. The bases of Judge Bayless's claim that homosexuals are politically powerful are difficult to defend. For example, Bayless cites their success in passing local antidiscrimination laws. Yet, in Colorado, whatever political power gays and lesbians have at the local level had been nullified by Amendment 2.

Perhaps Bayless's point is more valid on the state level than the local level. The ability to gather the support of 46 percent of the voters does seem to indicate that gays and lesbians have at least some political influence. Yet Bayless failed to ask what seems like the obvious question about the issue of gay political powerlessness: "powerless compared to whom?" As with the terms "discrimination" and "immutable," the term "powerlessness" is not self-defining. There must be some yardstick of political power to which the power of gays and lesbians can be compared.

The only logical standard of comparison is other suspect or quasi-suspect classes such as racial minorities or women. If these groups are sufficiently powerless to be suspect or quasi-suspect classes, then logically gays and lesbians must be, at a minimum, more politically powerful than these groups if they are in fact too powerful to be a suspect or quasi-suspect class.

Amazingly, not a single court has ever compared the political power of gays and lesbians to that of women or African Americans. Why have the courts failed to engage in so obvious a comparison? One possible explana-

---

81. *Evans* (trial court opinion), at p. C-18 of Colorado's cert. petition (emphasis added).
82. *High Tech Gays*, 895 F.2d at 574.

tion is that the results of such a comparison would deeply undermine the validity of subjecting racial and gender discrimination to strict scrutiny. For example, if the standards for measuring political power used by Judge Bayless were applied to women, courts would be forced to conclude that women are not a suspect class. Judge Bayless points to President Clinton's "outspoken support" for gay rights. But President Clinton is clearly an even more outspoken advocate of women's rights. Judge Bayless also mentions that gays and lesbians have successfully fought for the enactment of civil rights laws by a number of state and local governments. Yet there are many more laws prohibiting gender discrimination than there are civil rights laws protecting gays and lesbians.

Indeed, when called on to evaluate the political power of women, the Supreme Court has relied on indicators of political power quite different from those used to measure the political power of gays and lesbians:

> It is true, of course, that when viewed in the abstract, women do not constitute a small and powerless minority. Nevertheless, in part because of past discrimination, women are vastly under-represented in this Nation's decision making councils. There has never been a female President, nor a female member of this Court. Not a single woman presently sits in the United States Senate and only 14 women hold seats in the House of Representatives. And, as appellants point out, this under-representation is present throughout all levels of our State and Federal government.[83]

Juxtaposing the standards used to measure the political powerlessness of gays and lesbians with the standards used to measure the political powerlessness of women yields a striking result: *the two standards are completely different.* Neither Bayless nor the *High Tech* court looked at how many openly homosexual people are in the House or Senate or on the Supreme Court.[84] There are only two openly homosexual members of the House. There are no openly homosexual Senators or Supreme Court justices.

The double standard in how the political power of homosexuals and women is measured is most apparent in the way courts have looked at civil rights legislation. As discussed above, Bayless regarded the existence

---

83. *Frontiero v. Richardson*, 411 U.S. 677, 686 n. 17 (1972). Since 1972 two women have been appointed to the Supreme Court and the number of female legislators at all levels of government has increased substantially.

84. I focus on the issue of "openly homosexual" legislators for two reasons. First, there is no way to measure how many legislators are secretly homosexual. More importantly, if there are a substantial number of homosexual legislators who feel compelled to hide their homosexuality, this would hardly be an indicator that homosexuals are politically powerful.

of some state and local civil rights protections for gays and lesbians as proof that they are not politically powerless. Yet federal laws such as the Equal Pay Act of 1963 and the Civil Rights Act of 1964 have long prohibited sex discrimination, and this fact was regarded as a reason *for* subjecting gender discrimination to strict scrutiny. The Supreme Court has stated, "Thus, Congress itself has concluded that classifications based upon sex are inherently invidious . . . ."[85]

So it is clear that gay and lesbian political power has been measured by a standard that is completely different from that used to measure women's political power. The point, of course, is not that the courts should tolerate gender discrimination. The point is that the courts are applying a very different standard to gays and lesbians than they have been applying to other groups. No court has been willing to evaluate the political power of women or racial minorities by the same standard that they have applied to gays and lesbians. While the equal protection of the laws does not require the same result for all groups seeking suspect-class status, surely it requires that courts apply the same *standards* to all who seek judicial protection. There is a complete judicial unwillingness to ask whether currently recognized suspect classes are still powerless by the criteria applied to gays and lesbians.

Even more significantly, the discrepancy between judicial treatment of gay and lesbian political power and the political power of women and racial minorities represents just the tip of the iceberg. In the context of affirmative action and in other cases, the courts have applied strict scrutiny to laws that discriminate against *whites* and *males*. This has produced the bizarre result that gays and lesbians are considered too politically powerful to receive the benefit of strict scrutiny, but whites and males are not.

Courts have protected white males as a group by applying various forms of heightened scrutiny to laws that disadvantage them. The Supreme Court has struck down numerous affirmative action programs[86] and has held that males may not be discriminated against in such contexts as jury selection or university admissions.[87]

The argument that gays and lesbians are too powerful to benefit from strict or heightened scrutiny appears to be inconsistent with the argument

---

85. *Frontiero,* 411 U.S. at 687.

86. *Adarand Constructors v. Pena,* 515 U.S. 200 (1995); *City of Richmond v. J. A. Croson Co.,* 488 U.S. 469 (1989); *Wygant v. Jackson Board of Education,* 476 U.S. 267 (1986); *Regents of the University of California v. Bakke,* 438 U.S. 265 (1978).

87. Respectively, *J. E. B. v. Alabama ex rel. T. B.,* 511 U.S. 127 (1994); *Mississippi University for Women v. Hogan,* 458 U.S. 718 (1982).

that programs and laws that burden whites and males should be subjected to heightened scrutiny. How then has the law produced both these results simultaneously? The explanation, I believe, lies with some extremely faulty analysis by the Supreme Court creating inconsistency and confusion that has filtered down to the lower courts. This is discussed in the section below.

The Confusion over "Class" and "Classification"

For some time, the Supreme Court has been juggling two incompatible legal concepts without acknowledging their incompatibility. These two concepts are "suspect class" and "suspect classifications." While these two terms appear similar, this surface resemblance conceals crucial differences.

The concept of "suspect class" has already been discussed at some length. It flows from the *Carolene Products* / political-process theory of equal protection. Some groups (because they suffer from majority prejudice, political powerlessness, etc.) need enhanced judicial protection from discriminatory laws. These groups are suspect classes. These groups and how they are defined are discussed at length in part 1.

The other concept is "suspect classifications." This term refers not to specific groups, but to specific characteristics such as race or gender. For every suspect class, there is a parallel suspect classification. Racial minorities are a suspect class and race is a suspect classification; women are a suspect class and gender is a suspect classification. The key is that suspect classification is a much more inclusive term than is suspect class. Only a certain set of people are considered racial minorities, but everyone has a race. Not everyone is a female, but everyone has a gender.

When the Court strikes down affirmative action programs, it states that race is a suspect classification and that race-based laws are therefore subject to strict scrutiny.[88] Thus, whites receive the benefits of strict scrutiny without having to establish that they meet the various criteria of a suspect class such as political powerlessness and a history of discrimination.

The concepts of suspect classes and suspect classifications are simply incompatible. Analysis based on suspect classes asks the plaintiff class to establish that it suffers from disabilities that require courts to apply strict or heightened scrutiny to laws that target them. Suspect-classification

88. *Wygant*, 476 U.S. at 274 ("[A]ny racial classification must be justified by a compelling governmental interest . . . .") (quoting *Palmore v. Sidoti*, 466 U.S. 429 (1984)); *Adarand Constructors*, 515 U.S. at 220 ("Racial classifications of any sort must be subject to 'strict scrutiny.'") (quoting O'Connor concurrence in *Wygant*, 476 U.S. at 285).

analysis protects the powerless and the powerful at the same time. Since race is a suspect classification, laws that burden whites are just as suspect as those that burden blacks.

The Supreme Court uses the language of suspect classifications to apply strict scrutiny to affirmative action programs, but it uses the language of suspect-class analysis to deny many groups' request for the Court to apply strict scrutiny to discriminatory laws. As discussed in chapter 3, the Court held in *Rodriguez* that laws disadvantaging the poor are not subject to strict scrutiny because the poor are not a group that is "saddled with such disabilities, or subjected to such a history of purposeful unequal treatment, or relegated to such a position of political powerlessness as to command extraordinary protection from the majoritarian process."[89]

Similarly, the Supreme Court has held that the elderly are not entitled to heightened scrutiny of laws that discriminate on the basis of age, because the elderly are not a suspect class. In *Massachusetts Board of Retirement v. Murgia*,[90] a police officer challenged the constitutionality of a state law mandating that police officers retire on their fiftieth birthday. Citing *Carolene Products*, the Court rejected the challenge: "Nor does the class of uniformed state officers over 50 constitute a suspect class for purposes of equal protection. . . . old age does not define a 'discrete and insular' group in need of 'extraordinary protection from the majoritarian process.'"[91]

Since the Court found that the elderly are not a suspect class, it applied the highly deferential rational-basis test. The Court found that the mandatory retirement rule was rationally related to the goal of "assuring physical preparedness of its uniformed police."[92] The Court held that the state was under no obligation to individually test the physical fitness of fifty-year-old officers.

The Supreme Court has not addressed the issue of homosexuality directly, but as discussed above, lower courts have relied on suspect-class language to avoid applying strict scrutiny to laws that disadvantage homosexuals. Yet, when government programs disadvantage whites and men, there is a shift to the language of suspect classifications.

In *Regents of the University of California v. Bakke*,[93] the Court was asked to determine if an affirmative action program being administered by the Medical School of the University of California at Davis was constitutional.

89. *Rodriguez*, 411 U.S. at 28.
90. 427 U.S. 307 (1975).
91. *Murgia*, 427 U.S. at 313 (citation omitted).
92. *Id.* at 314.
93. 438 U.S. 265 (1977).

The program set aside sixteen of one hundred medical seats for members of disadvantaged groups, including racial minorities. Alan Bakke argued that he was disadvantaged because he was white.

Had the Court applied the test to Bakke that it applied in *Rodriguez* and *Murgia*, or that lower courts have applied to gays and lesbians, Bakke would have lost. Whites as a group have obviously not been saddled with such disabilities as to require extraordinary protection from the democratic process. However, the Court did not apply the same test. It did not ask whether whites have suffered from a history of discrimination or are politically powerless. Indeed it did not ask whether whites are a suspect class. The *Bakke* Court specifically disclaimed reliance on *Carolene Products*, stating that, while discreteness and insularity "may be relevant in deciding whether to add new types of classifications to the list of 'suspect' categories," such considerations were irrelevant to claims of discrimination based on race, national origin, or ethnicity.[94] The Court held that laws based on the *classification* of race, not just laws discriminating against the *class* of racial minorities, are suspect. The Court explained its reasoning in a remarkable paragraph:

> There is no principled basis for deciding which groups would merit "heightened judicial solicitude" and which would not. Courts would be asked to evaluate the extent of the prejudice and consequent harm suffered by various minority groups. Those whose societal injury is thought to exceed some arbitrary level of tolerability then would be entitled to preferential classifications at the expense of individuals belonging to other groups. Those classifications would be free from exacting judicial scrutiny. As these preferences began to have their desired effect, and the consequences of past discrimination were undone, new judicial rankings would be necessary. *The kind of variable sociological and political analysis necessary to produce such rankings simply does not lie within judicial competence—even if they otherwise were politically feasible and socially desirable.*[95]

This is a powerful argument, but it is no less powerful with respect to gays, lesbians, the elderly, or the poor than it is with respect to whites. If it is beyond judicial competence to determine the level of societal injury suffered by particular racial or ethnic groups, why is it not beyond judicial competence to make the same determination with regard to gays and lesbians or the elderly? Thus, in *Bakke*, the Supreme Court disclaimed judicial

94. *Bakke*, 438 U.S. at 290.
95. *Id.* at 296–97 (emphasis added).

competence to make exactly the kind of sociological and political evaluations that are the very foundation of the three-tiered framework. Gays and lesbians and other groups are cast in the role of Sisyphus, asked to prove sociological and political facts that the Supreme Court itself has declared courts incompetent to evaluate. If the Court is not competent to evaluate which groups do and do not suffer from a history of discrimination, are or are not lacking in political power, then it is no surprise that the Court has created no new "suspect classes." Whites are not a suspect class, but because race is a "suspect classification" whites receive the judicial protection unattainable by homosexuals.

Nor are whites the only beneficiary of this double standard. The Supreme Court has used the concept of suspect classification to apply heightened scrutiny to laws that disadvantage males even though males could not be considered a suspect class. For example, in *Craig v. Boren*,[96] the Supreme Court invalidated a law forbidding the sale of beer containing 3.2 percent alcohol to males under the age of twenty-one and females under the age of eighteen. This law discriminated against males since women between the ages of eighteen and twenty could buy such beer but men of the same age could not. In support of the law, the state cited statistics showing that men in this age group were more likely than their female counterparts to drink and drive. The Court stuck down the law as sex discrimination, since there is only a loose fit between gender and the tendency to drink and drive.

In his dissent, Rehnquist noted that there "is no suggestion . . . that males in this age group are in any way particularly disadvantaged, subject to systematic discriminatory treatment, or otherwise in need of special solicitude from the courts."[97] In other words, men between the ages of eighteen and twenty are not a suspect class. He also pointed out that the law was not based on any paternalistic or outdated notions that could be construed as discriminatory toward women. Yet the Court struck down the law, which discriminated against men, because "administrative ease and convenience [are not] sufficiently important objectives to justify gender-based classifications."[98]

One can argue that discrimination toward young men is somehow wrong, but this argument has nothing to do with the goal of protecting those who need extraordinary protection from the majoritarian process. If the Court holds that discrimination against young men is unconstitu-

96. 429 U.S. 190 (1976).
97. *Craig*, 429 U.S. at 219 (Rehnquist, J., dissenting).
98. *Craig*, 429 U.S. at 198.

tional, it must state why this is so. Only then can gays and lesbians and other groups have a fair opportunity to argue that they should be protected for the same reason. If the Court believes that young men should be protected from the stereotype that they are irresponsible, then gays and lesbians should have the opportunity to argue that they too should be protected from the same stereotype.

With sufficient imagination, one might construct an argument that this law somehow discriminates against women rather than men. But the Court did not do so and, in any event, the male plaintiff would not have had standing to press this claim. Clearly, the Court was protecting the rights of men, not women. Similarly, one could speculate that striking down affirmative action programs actually protects African Americans from "backlash." But that would be quite a stretch—it is difficult to imagine the Court striking down aid for the inner cities or any other program to avoid white backlash. In any event, such an argument stands the criterion of political powerlessness on its head. It would mean that the Court should actually protect the most powerful members of society, so as to avoid backlash against the least powerful. Further, there is again the problem of standing—why would white plaintiffs have standing to assert injuries by African Americans? And, finally, the courts are quite clear that they are protecting whites, not blacks. In *Bakke,* for instance, it is the white plaintiff whose injuries are recognized and the white plaintiff who benefits from the remedy. To say the *Bakke* Court was actually vindicating the rights of powerless African Americans would truly be to turn black into white.

It is now well settled that whites and men are protected from race and gender discrimination by heightened judicial scrutiny. The number of cases holding that race and gender are, respectively, suspect and quasi-suspect classifications are too numerous to cite. Yet when gays seek similar protection, the judicial language subtly shifts. The courts ask not whether sexual orientation is a suspect classification but whether homosexuals are a suspect class.[99] The legal discourse of suspect classes allows courts to apply criteria to homosexuals that whites and males could never meet and are not asked to meet.

99. *Equality Foundation of Greater Cincinnati v. City of Cincinnati,* 54 F.3d 261 (6th Cir. 1995) ("Since *Bowers,* every circuit court which has addressed the issue has decreed that homosexuals are entitled to no special constitutional protection, either as a suspect or a quasi-suspect class...."), *vacated and remanded,* 116 S. Ct. 2519 (1996); *High Tech Gays v. Defense Industrial Security Clearance Office,* 895 F.2d 563, 574 (9th Cir. 1990) ("Our review compels us to agree with the other circuits that have ruled on this issue that homosexuals do not constitute a suspect or quasi-suspect class."); *Evans v. Romer* (trial court opinion), at p. C-18 of Colorado's cert. petition ("Homosexuals fail to meet the element of political powerlessness and therefore fail to meet the elements to be found a suspect class.").

Thus, it is only by a subtle yet crucial change of terminology that the status quo is maintained. If the courts asked whether men are a suspect class the answer would be obviously no. If the courts asked whether sexual orientation is a suspect class, the question would be nonsensical. It is only by asking whether race and gender are "suspect classifications" and whether homosexuals are a "suspect class" that the status quo can be maintained.

The Court's oscillation between suspect class and suspect classification has escaped analytic attack because, at a surface level, it seems sensible. If the Court decides that African Americans are a suspect class, then it seems natural to say that all racial classifications should be subject to strict scrutiny. But there is nothing natural, or even logical, about this. If African Americans are being protected because they suffer from a history of discrimination and political powerlessness, then the Court should give heightened protection to African Americans but not to whites. Under the suspect-class rationale, there is no need for racial symmetry—Jim Crow laws should be subjected to strict scrutiny, but affirmative action programs should not be. The same is true for men and women. Perhaps it is a mistake to tell groups that they will be protected by strict scrutiny only if they are powerless victims of discrimination. (Indeed, in the last chapter I argue that it *is* a mistake.) But if that is the case, the courts should not ask gays and lesbians (or other groups) to prove that *they* are powerless victims.

This chapter is not intended as an argument that gays and lesbians should receive greater protection against discrimination than do heterosexuals or that *any* group should receive more protection than any other group. Indeed, I will argue in the final chapter that the whole notion of suspect classes, and tying people's rights to such criteria as immutability and political powerlessness, is a mistake and that equal protection law should be reformed. Rather, the principal argument here is that equal protection jurisprudence is so inconsistent, disorganized, and ambiguous that decisions denying equal protection to gays and lesbians cannot be taken at face value. Gays and lesbians attempting to establish that they meet the judicially created criteria for a suspect class find that the criteria are not equal for all comers, but shift and change depending on the identity of the group seeking judicial protection from discrimination. The courts consistently apply the criteria for suspect-class status differently for different classes of plaintiffs.

Nor do I argue that these decisions are the result of "negative attitudes" by judges and justices toward gays and lesbians. The argument is that the courts, especially the Supreme Court, have gotten out of the business of creating new suspect classes.

The chaotic and inconsistent state of equal protection doctrine has important consequences for gays and lesbians. First, it denies gays and lesbians "equal protection of the laws" under any conceivable definition of that term. Gays and lesbians are told that they are too powerful to be a suspect class, while the courts offer enhanced judicial protection to far more powerful groups. Gays and lesbians are told that their status as homosexuals is voluntary and mutable, while the courts protect other groups that are united by voluntary behavior.

While the equal protection clause does not require similar outcomes when different persons challenge discriminatory laws, it surely requires that the courts apply the same legal standards to their claims. To do otherwise represents a devolution to a premodern legal era. As Max Weber has explained, a crucial defining characteristic of the modern Western legal system is the evolution from an array of special laws that applied only to specific groups to general laws that apply uniformly to all citizens. Under premodern systems of special laws, a person's legal rights depended on his or her group status (such as tribe membership in the Frankish Empire, or religious affiliation in some parts of the Near East). To a great extent, the evolution of modern law is the story of the movement away from such group-based special laws to a more general, uniform law pursuant to which the claims of all citizens are subjected to uniform criteria.[100] By, for example, measuring the political power of gays and lesbians by completely different standards than those used to measure the political power of women, or by failing to raise the issue of political power at all with respect to the claims of white men, the courts are operating in a premodern mode that is utterly inimical to the equal protection of the laws.

Furthermore, these flawed legal constructions have become part of the broader public debate over the legal rights claims of gays and lesbians. The judicial message that the world can be divided into groups that deserve special protection and groups that do not has penetrated the public consciousness. Much of the debate in Colorado over Amendment 2 was framed in terms that parallel the judicial debate. This will be taken up in the next chapter.

100. Max Weber, *Law in Economy and Society*, trans. Max Rheinstein (New York: Simon & Schuster, 1967), 140–88.

Class-Based Analysis and the Public Debate over Amendment 2

So far we have seen that the three-tiered framework asks the courts to focus on how closely gays and lesbians resemble recognized suspect classes such as racial minorities. In this chapter we will see that the premises of the three-tiered framework penetrated the public consciousness during the debate over Amendment 2 to Colorado's constitution. As a result, the public debate paralleled the judicial debate in many ways. Whether gays and lesbians are "genuine minorities" who deserve or need "special rights" was central to the campaigns for and against the amendment. While the terminology is somewhat different, the Colorado voters were debating the same basic issue as the courts: are gays and lesbians so politically powerless and discriminated against that they merit special legal protection from discrimination?

Furthermore, the fact that the issues were framed in this way created the same problems for gays and lesbians politically as the three-tiered framework creates for them judicially. The courts are reluctant to declare gays and lesbians to be a suspect class because doing so would affect an extremely wide range of issues ranging from discrimination in public employment to gay and lesbian marriage. Similarly, the debate over Amendment 2 was framed in such a way that voters were led to believe that they were addressing issues well beyond basic antidiscrimination laws for gays and lesbians. *Polls showed that Colorado voters did not want to discriminate against gays and lesbians. Proponents of Amendment 2 were therefore acutely aware that it was advantageous to frame the debate not in terms of discrimination, but as a debate over whether gays and lesbians should enjoy a special legal status.* Many of the voters believed they were debating whether gays and lesbians should benefit from the whole panoply of civil rights that racial minorities receive—especially qualification for affirmative action programs.

Amendment 2's proponents used constitutional doctrine to legitimate their argument that the debate over Amendment 2 was a debate over whether gays and lesbians should be treated as a "protected" or "special" class. Political scientists have not paid attention to the impact of constitutional doctrine on the political debate over the amendment. This is probably because most scholars are skeptical about whether the Supreme Court and constitutional doctrine have much impact on public opinion. While much of the relevant scholarship on the Court and public opinion provides good grounds for this skepticism, this literature also shows how constitutional doctrine can affect the way that people think about gay and lesbian rights and why there is good reason to believe that this happened in the battle over Amendment 2.

The Supreme Court and Public Opinion

The political science literature on the effect of the Supreme Court on public opinion is still somewhat inchoate. As recently as 1991, Gregory Caldeira noted, "Surprisingly, we have little systematic empirical research on the important question of judicial impact on public opinion."[1] While there has been additional research since Caldeira's assessment, the literature in this area is still sparse compared with other areas of public law research.

The literature has been concerned with two major questions: Does the public know what the Court does? And does the public care what the Court does? The latter question is often framed in terms of whether the Court enjoys enough "institutional legitimacy" or "diffuse support" among members of the public for judicial decisions to influence public opinion.[2] My analysis indicates that the legal terminology of the Court's class-based equal protection doctrine played an important part in the political debate over Amendment 2. My analysis is based on thirty semistructured interviews with leading participants in the debate—activists, media editors, public officials, and legislators as well as the lead attorneys for the plaintiffs challenging the amendment's constitutionality, the solicitor general of Colorado at time of the litigation, and Jeffrey Bayless, the judge who initially held that the amendment violates the equal protection clause.[3] I also use data from focus group research commissioned by the anti–

1. Gregory A. Caldeira, "Courts and Public Opinion," in *The American Courts: A Critical Assessment*, ed. John B. Gates and Charles A. Johnson (Washington, D.C.: Congressional Quarterly Press, 1991), 305.

2. Jeffery J. Mondak, "Institutional Legitimacy, Policy Legitimacy, and the Supreme Court," *American Politics Quarterly* 20 (1992): 457–77.

3. For the first quotation from each person interviewed, information about the interview is supplied in a footnote. Unless otherwise noted, any other quotations attributed to the individual later in the text come from the same interview.

Amendment 2 advocacy group EPOC[4] and data from a series of public opinion polls commissioned by the *Denver Post* and conducted by Talmey-Drake Research & Strategy, Inc. Although the number of semistructured interviews is relatively small, there was remarkable agreement on many points among the interviewees, even among those on opposite sides of the debate. The focus-group and polling data are also consistent with these points.

Advocates of Amendment 2 successfully framed the debate in terms of whether gays and lesbians are "real minorities" who need "special rights." These terms are a public echo of the judicial debate over whether gays and lesbians are a "suspect class" who should receive the benefit of "strict scrutiny." Are these similarities a coincidence? To decide, we must answer two questions. First, was the public aware, even if only vaguely, of the Supreme Court's three-tiered framework and the accompanying legal structures of suspect classes and strict scrutiny? Second, if they were, what effect did these legal constructions have on the debate over Amendment 2? These questions are addressed separately in the following two sections.

Public Awareness of Constitutional Doctrine

As Gregory Caldeira has stated, "Until quite recently, the empirical basis of the Court's ability to change public opinion has largely gone unexamined."[5] While the Supreme Court justices themselves seem to believe that they can influence public opinion,[6] the research in this area concludes that the public is generally quite ignorant about what the Court does and says.

Walter Murphy, Joseph Tanenhaus, and Daniel Kastner examined the results of interviews with a national sample of 1,285 voting-age Americans conducted by the Survey Research Center of the University of Michigan in 1966. Based on their study, they argue that constitutional courts might "have quite limited capacities to reach the general public."[7] They found that the general public knows little about even the most well publicized and controversial actions of the Supreme Court: "The Warren Court had handed out a torrent of decisions regarding race relations, church and

---

4. EPOC stands for Equal Protection Ordinance Colorado. It was formed to help pass an antidiscrimination ordinance in Denver; subsequently, it led the opposition to Amendment 2.

5. Caldeira, "Courts and Public Opinion," 304.

6. *Ibid.*

7. Walter F. Murphy, Joseph Tanenhaus, and Daniel L. Kastner, "Public Evaluations of Constitutional Courts: Alternative Explanations," in *American Court Systems: Readings in Judicial Process and Behavior,* ed. Sheldon Goldman and Austin Sarat (San Francisco: W. H. Freeman, 1978), 185.

state, criminal justice and voting rights, and had endured several crises in its relations with Congress. *Yet in the face of these dramatic events, only 46% of the sample in 1966 could recall anything at all that the Court had recently done.*"[8]

Early accounts of the Court assumed that it had "mythic and symbolic prestige in American politics."[9] However, it has more recently become apparent that the public knows little about most of what the Court does: "[M]any (and probably nearly all) Supreme Court decisions pass by virtually unnoticed by most Americans—either because the decision receives little press attention, or because many Americans pay little attention to the Court itself."[10] Since the public generally does not pay attention to what the Court does, this obviously limits the impact the Court can have on public opinion. Surveying the literature in the field, Bradley Canon concluded that "considerable evidence indicates that the Court has at best a very limited impact on public opinion."[11]

Thus, the courts, even the Supreme Court, do not appear to have a significant direct effect on public opinion due to lack of public knowledge of their decisions. However, Murphy, Tanenhaus, and Kastner have suggested that the Court may have a substantial *indirect* effect when the public becomes aware of doctrine through "mediating processes"—an effect that probably cannot be measured by means of survey research:

> Indirectly, of course, a constitutional court may reach much wider audiences through the mediating processes of columnists, news analysts on television, lawyers, high school teachers, college professors, public officials, and informed private citizens. Doctrines inherent in recent decisions could thus have been received and accepted or rejected by many people who did not at all associate these ideals with a court. Thus the judges could have been educating and performing a legitimating function for huge numbers of people and doing so in ways that are almost invulnerable to survey research.[12]

So even if the general public does not follow the decisions of the Court they may be influenced by judicial doctrine that they are exposed to via "mediating" sources. In Colorado one such mediating source was Colorado for

8. *Ibid.* (emphasis added).

9. Thomas R. Marshall, "The Supreme Court as an Opinion Leader: Court Decisions and the Mass Public," *American Politics Quarterly* 15 (1987): 147.

10. Thomas R. Marshall, *Public Opinion and the Supreme Court* (Boston: Unwin Hyman, 1989), 137.

11. Bradley C. Canon, "The Supreme Court as a Cheerleader in Politico-Moral Disputes," *Journal of Politics* 54 (1992): 641.

12. Murphy, Tanenhaus, and Kastner, "Public Evaluations of Constitutional Courts," 185.

Family Values (CFV), the primary interest group supporting Amendment 2. Early in the campaign CFV realized the benefits of using arguments and slogans based on the three-tiered framework in support of Amendment 2. According to Tony Marco, co-chair and director of communications for CFV during the campaign, "the Supreme Court standards were at the center of the campaign."[13]

Before the referendum, CFV distributed 750,000 copies of an eight-page tabloid with the headline: "Equal Rights—Not Special Rights! Stop special class status for homosexuality." Opponents of Amendment 2 were unanimous that the tabloid was extremely effective in building support for the amendment. This was stated most simply by Richard Evans, who was involved in the campaign against Amendment 2 and was the lead plaintiff in *Evans v. Romer:* "This [the tabloid] is what did us in."[14] Another anti–Amendment 2 activist, Sue Anderson, stated that the tabloid "was very effective at reaching the people in the middle."[15]

The tabloid relied explicitly on the Supreme Court and the criteria the Court uses in evaluating whether groups such as gays and lesbians qualify for suspect-class status. In it, CFV made the following argument:

> Amendment 2 upholds common sense civil rights laws and Supreme Court decisions, which say that people who want protected class status have to show they need it in three fair, logical ways:
> 1. A group wanting true minority rights must show that it's discriminated against to the point that its members cannot earn average income, get an adequate education or enjoy a fulfilling cultural life.
> 2. The group must be clearly identifiable by unchangeable physical characteristics like skin color, gender, handicap, etc. (not behavior).
> 3. The group must clearly show that it is politically powerless.

Although the first criterion is slightly different from the criterion of "a history of discrimination," the CFV tabloid is clearly tracking the three-tiered framework. Kevin Tebedo, a major participant in CFV's campaign, describes the three criteria listed in the tabloid as "the system used by the courts to determine if a group should get protected class status."[16] CFV became aware of the three-tiered framework when its attorneys researched whether Amendment 2 could withstand constitutional challenge. Accord-

---

13. Tony Marco, telephone interview by author, 18 April 1995.
14. Richard Evans, interview by author, Denver, 8 March 1995.
15. Sue Anderson, interview by author, Denver, 9 March 1995.
16. Kevin Tebedo, telephone interview by author, 18 April 1995.

ing to Marco, CFV realized that these criteria would be useful terms for the
pro–Amendment 2 campaign because "it is pretty obvious that the Court
is trying to fence out groups which don't meet these standards." CFV
strongly wished to avoid giving the impression that it was trying to per-
secute gays and lesbians. According to Tebedo, when CFV workers discovered the three-tiered framework and the accompanying criteria, they
realized "this could be it. . . . the bottom line was that the homosexual
lobby was claiming strict scrutiny."

Of course there is no reason that statutory civil rights protection must
be limited to constitutionally recognized suspect classes.[17] But the three-
tiered framework allowed CFV to argue that Amendment 2 was merely a
political confirmation of what the Supreme Court had already decided—
that gays and lesbians do not merit the same types of legal protection that
groups such as racial minorities receive. Indeed, a major thrust of CFV's
campaign was that gays and lesbians are not comparable to racial minorities because they have not suffered the same history of discrimination. The
following graph featured prominently in the CFV tabloid:

Equal Rights—Not Special Rights!
Sound like an oppressed minority to you? Judge for yourself—
Take a look at the hardships Black Americans have had to face.
Then see if homosexuals compare. Special rights for homosexuals
just isn't fair—especially to disadvantaged minorities in Colo-
rado. Please vote YES! on Amendment 2.

Historically Accepted Evidences of Discrimination	Black Americans	Homosexuals
Ever denied the right to vote?	Yes	No
Ever faced legal segregation?	Yes	No
Ever denied access by law to public drinking fountains, restrooms?	Yes	No
Ever denied access by law to businesses, restaurants, barber shops, etc.?	Yes	No
Evidence of Systematic Discrimination in housing and jobs in Colorado today?	Yes	No
Verifiable economic hardship as a result of discrimination?	Yes	No

17. Indeed, as Jane Schacter has pointed out, statutory civil rights law protects many
groups, such as the physically handicapped, who are not suspect classes. Jane S. Schacter,
"The Gay Civil Rights Debate in the States: Decoding the Discourse of Equivalents," *Harvard
Civil Rights–Civil Liberties Law Review* 29 (1994): 296–300.

Thus, constitutional doctrine appears to have had a significant impact on the terms of the public debate over Amendment 2. The criteria of the three-tiered framework allowed CFV to move the debate away from why discrimination should be allowed against gays and lesbians and toward whether gays and lesbians are sufficiently similar to African Americans to merit "special rights."

The Influence of the Court on Public Opinion

While it is clear that Supreme Court doctrine had an important impact on the terms of the political debate over Amendment 2, it is harder to evaluate the impact it had on the minds of the voters. It is an inherently difficult task to determine how people respond to Supreme Court doctrine. "Establishing the interpretation of a decision and a population's attitude toward it or toward the original policymaker may be difficult for the researcher since this involves essentially nonbehavioral reactions to the judicial policy."[18]

Political scientists often refer to the level of abstract public support for the Supreme Court as "diffuse" support. There is no consensus among researchers as to how great a level of diffuse support the Court enjoys:

> The Supreme Court does benefit from considerable abstract mass approval, though no consensus exists as to the precise level of diffuse support enjoyed by the Court. Some analysts maintain that the Court maintains a high level of authority but others argue that the public holds only moderate support for this institution. Further, the origin of the Court's approval is unclear, though the strength of the Constitution as a symbol may foster a mythical view of the Court.[19]

Some researchers believe that "the Court has won public deference because of the reverence and tradition that has surrounded it as an institution."[20] Others are not so optimistic about the Court's influence. Indeed, some research has indicated that Court decisions might even push public opinion in the opposite direction from the decision:

> There are indications, on the other hand, that interest groups and perhaps the courts (in recent years) actually have negative effects. That is, when their statements and actions push in one direction

18. Charles A. Johnson, "The Implementation and Impact of Judicial Policies: A Heuristic Model," in *Public Law and Public Policy*, ed. John Gardiner (New York: Praeger, 1977), 113.

19. Jeffery J. Mondak, "Perceived Legitimacy of Supreme Court Decisions: Three Functions of Source Credibility," *Political Behavior* 12 (1990): 363 (citations omitted).

20. Jesse H. Choper, *Judicial Review and the National Political Process: A Functional Reconsideration of the Role of the Supreme Court* (Chicago: University of Chicago Press, 1980), 138.

(e.g., when corporations demand subsidies or a federal court orders school integration through busing) public opinion tends to
move in the opposite direction. We are not certain about the negative effect of courts, however, because of the instability of coeffi-
cients across data sets.[21]

Political scientists believe that strong diffuse support for the Court con-
fers legitimacy on its decisions and facilitates acceptance of its policies.[22]
"However, critics have noted a lack of empirical support for this legitimacy
conferring potential."[23] Attempts to measure the power of the Court to legitimate a particular point of view have taken two basic forms: One set of
experiments compares the reactions of a test group to a viewpoint attributed to the Supreme Court with the reactions of a control group to the same
viewpoint when it is not attributed to the Court. The other line of research
looks at pre- and post-decision polling data to measure the effect of an important Court decision on public opinion. Neither line of research has produced dispositive results.

Larry Bass and Dan Thomas did not find that attributing policies to
the Court increased agreement with those policies.[24] However, Valerie
Hoekstra criticized their work because they failed to attribute policies
given to the control groups to any particular source. She repeated the ex-
periment, attributing policies to one of three sources: the Court, Congress,
or a nonpartisan think tank. She found that attributing policies to the Court
has at least some positive impact: "The results seem to suggest . . . that the
Court can persuade those who hold it in high esteem. Additionally, although the Court does not seem able to persuade those who are not among
its biggest fans, they are at least not reacting against its message. These
findings support the hypothesis that individuals who regard the Court in
high esteem are more likely to be persuaded by its rulings."[25]

Thomas Marshall has studied pre- and post-decision polling data extensively. His research indicates that the Court has some impact on public
opinion when its decisions are in a liberal or activist direction.[26]

21. Benjamin I. Page, Robert Y. Shapiro, and Glenn R. Dempsey, "What Moves Public
Opinion?" *American Political Science Review* 81 (1987): 31–32.
22. Charles A. Johnson and Bradley C. Canon, *Judicial Policies: Implementation and Impact*
(Washington, D.C.: Congressional Quarterly Press, 1984).
23. Mondak, "Institutional Legitimacy," 459.
24. Larry R. Bass and Dan Thomas, "The Supreme Court and Policy Legitimation: Experimental Tests," *American Politics Quarterly* 12 (1984): 335–60.
25. Valerie J. Hoekstra, "The Supreme Court and Opinion Change: An Experimental
Study of the Court's Ability to Change Opinion," *American Politics Quarterly* 23 (1995): 121.
26. Marshall, *Public Opinion*; Marshall, "Supreme Court as an Opinion Leader."

However, the impact of Supreme Court decisions is probably more complicated than mere agreement or disagreement by the public. For example, Charles Franklin and Liane Kosaki found that the abortion decisions of the Court had a polarizing effect. They found that a high-profile decision can direct public attention to a particular policy and thereby increase public debate. They also found that social environment had an effect on opinion: "The nature of the contextual effect also depends upon the homogeneity of opinion within the social environment. If the environment is consensual, the individual is likely to encounter a stream of reinforcements consistently favoring the modal position."[27]

CFV's invocation of suspect classes and other legal terminology in the campaign for Amendment 2 may have been effective because it reinforced already existing widespread public perceptions. The three-tiered framework and the accompanying criteria for suspect-class status are premised on the legal assumption that the strongest form of constitutional protection goes to groups that are powerless, immutable, and oppressed. CFV used this to reinforce the Colorado public's impression that civil rights are a package of "special rights" that goes only to deserving minorities. Indeed, as will be discussed below, leaders of both sides of the debate over Amendment 2 agreed that this perception was more influential in passing Amendment 2 than was animus toward gays and lesbians.[28]

Colorado Voters, Amendment 2, and the Issue of "Special Rights"

At first blush, the passage of Amendment 2 seems somewhat mysterious. Colorado has long had a reputation as a state where people "live and let live," and polling data appear to validate this perception. The *Denver Post* commissioned a series of polls of Colorado voters' attitudes toward gays and lesbians both before and after the vote on Amendment 2.[29] The polling data paint a portrait of a remarkably tolerant population.

The polling data do show that a slight plurality of Coloradans morally

27. Charles H. Franklin and Liane C. Kosaki, "Republican Schoolmaster: The U.S. Supreme Court, Public Opinion, and Abortion," *American Political Science Review* 83 (1989): 763.

28. However, the issues of animus and the public perception of how civil rights work cannot be neatly separated. The impression that gays and lesbians are seeking "special rights" can feed into or generate animus. This will also be discussed in the section below.

29. According to the firm that conducted these polls, Talmey-Drake Research & Strategy, Inc., the margin of error for these questions (with a 95 percent confidence interval) is plus or minus 4 percent. (Because of rounding, the sum of the percentages for two of the poll questions discussed in this chapter exceeds 100.)

disapprove of homosexuality. When asked to respond to the statement "Homosexuality is morally wrong," poll respondents reacted as follows:

Strongly agree	32%
Somewhat agree	14%
Neutral	7%
Somewhat disagree	16%
Strongly disagree	24%
Don't know	7%

However, this moral disapprobation of homosexuality does not appear to translate into intolerant attitudes toward gays and lesbians. For example, Colorado voters are strongly against outlawing homosexual behavior. The response to the statement "Homosexual behavior should be against the law, even if it occurs between consenting adults" was as follows:

Strongly agree	10%
Somewhat agree	6%
Neutral	4%
Somewhat disagree	22%
Strongly disagree	55%
Don't know	3%

The same series of polls shows that Coloradans strongly reject unfounded stereotypes toward gays and lesbians. Large majorities disagree with statements such as "A homosexual is more likely to sexually molest children than a person who is heterosexual," or "Homosexuals should not be allowed to teach in the public schools." Furthermore, 59 percent of Coloradans believe that "Homosexuals should be allowed to serve in the armed forces."

Even more significantly, Coloradans appear to favor by enormous margins the very legal protections that Amendment 2 annulled. When presented with the statement "An employer should have the right to not hire someone because he or she is a homosexual," they responded as follows:

Strongly agree	13%
Somewhat agree	13%
Neutral	2%
Somewhat disagree	19%
Strongly disagree	51%
Don't know	7%

The statement "A landlord should have the right to evict a tenant on the grounds that he or she is a homosexual" produced an even stronger negative response:

Strongly agree	8%
Somewhat agree	5%
Neutral	3%
Somewhat disagree	22%
Strongly disagree	59%
Don't know	4%

Of course, there are reasons to be skeptical of polling data—the results might be skewed by people giving the answers they believe they should give rather than honest answers. However, the margins by which the polls show that Coloradans believe that gays and lesbians should not be denied jobs or housing on account of their sexual orientation are extremely large. Further, the polling data correlate with the conclusions drawn by Miller Research Group, Inc. (MRG), which was hired by EPOC to conduct focus group research on public opinion and Amendment 2. MRG conducted six focus-group discussions in three different geographic areas within Colorado: Grand Junction, Englewood, and Westminster. In each area, one group consisted of men, the other of women. Each group consisted of eight to twelve participants who had not definitely made up their minds about Amendment 2.

Based on the focus-group discussions, MRG concluded that Colorado citizens have little tolerance for discrimination of any kind, including discrimination against gays and lesbians: "Coloradans support the notion that no segment of the population should be subject to discrimination. The assertion in the U.S. Constitution that 'all men are created equal' is well accepted.[30] People recognize that this should protect groups as well as individuals. People should not be subject to discrimination on the basis of age, gender, race, national origin, physical disabilities *or* sexual orientation. In short, discrimination is a dirty word."[31]

Given these highly tolerant attitudes, the natural question is "why did Amendment 2 pass?" Two common but incorrect explanations are that (1) pro–Amendment 2 forces outspent their opposition and (2) the amendment's language was confusing, and some people who voted for it really intended to vote against it. In fact, anti–Amendment 2 forces outspent

30. [The phrase "all men are created equal" actually appears in the Declaration of Independence. The Constitution contains the phrase "equal protection of the laws."—AUTHOR]

31. Miller Research Group, Inc., "Focus Groups regarding Gay Rights Amendments to the Colorado Constitution," report to Equal Protection Ordinance Colorado, April 1992 (hereafter cited as "MRG Report"), 9–10 (emphasis in original, internal footnote added).

32. "Amendment 2's opponents out-spent its supporters by a nearly 2–1 margin." State of Colorado's petition to the Supreme Court of Colorado for writ of certiorari.

pro–Amendment 2 forces.[32] Voter confusion is also an unlikely explanation for Amendment 2's passage. Even if the language of Amendment 2 is somewhat confusing, there is no reason to believe that substantially more people mistakenly voted for it than mistakenly voted against it. Polling data also indicate that voters understood what they were voting for. In a Talmey-Drake poll in December 1992, after there had been widespread coverage and debate over Amendment 2, only 4 percent of respondents indicated that they would change their vote if they had the opportunity.

I argue that the passage of Amendment 2 has more to do with how people think about civil rights than it does about how people feel about gays and lesbians. I reject the notions that Coloradans lied about their beliefs to pollsters and focus-group interviewers, or that people did not understand what they were voting for. Rather, *the most plausible explanation for Amendment 2's success is that people have come to perceive civil rights as a package of rights that certain groups get, rather than a basic set of legal protections for everybody.* The pro–Amendment 2 forces were able to tap into and amplify this perception by the use of the term "special rights" and the selective invocation of legal and constitutional doctrine as campaign slogans. This explanation best fits the polling, focus-group, and interview data, and it accords with the rhetoric of the campaign and the strategy of CFV.

According to anti–Amendment 2 activist Sue Anderson, "'special rights' was a very effective sound bite . . . . special rights is perceived to mean that a group of people will get rights . . . something [others] don't have." Tina Scardina, a member of EPOC and an active opponent of Amendment 2, stated that public conceptions of what civil rights means pushed voters toward Amendment 2. "A lot of the public thinks of civil rights as affirmative action, quota preferences, and special treatment . . . [and believes that] only 'real' minorities should have those protections, not gays and lesbians."[33] Support for Amendment 2 was thus generated by the fear that civil rights laws that protect against discrimination on the basis of sexual orientation would result in special rights for gays and lesbians. According to Scardina, "a prevalent attitude was 'I don't want them to lose their job, but I don't want them to get any special rights.'"

A major source of the power of the special-rights argument is public antipathy toward affirmative action.[34] According to Lesley Dahlkemper,

33. Tina Scardina, interview by author, Denver, 8 March 1995.
34. Affirmative action is, of course, a broad term defined differently by different people. The interviewees consistently used the term to refer to quotas, preferences, set-asides, and other forms of special treatment, rather than such things as casting a broad net in the search process of filling a job vacancy or taking other affirmative steps to avoid an insular recruitment process.

associate news director and public affairs reporter for Colorado Public Radio, "the phrase 'special rights' was largely interpreted to mean affirmative action. Special rights and fear of affirmative action was a very powerful force in the election."[35]

When asked why Amendment 2 passed, Richard Evans did not mention the Christian right or homophobia. Instead, he responded:

> My feeling is that the reason it passed is the last sentence [of the ballot initiative], which talks about quota preferences. If any affirmative action policy were given to the voters in any jurisdiction they would vote it down. I think there is a fundamental belief in this country that affirmative action is wrong. People feel it takes away their competitiveness: "It takes away an opportunity for my family to earn or for me to do better." And I think people are out to repeal affirmative action and I think that's what happened.

It is ironic that the Supreme Court held that the only possible motivation for voting for Amendment 2 was "animus" toward gays and lesbians.[36] Opponents of Amendment 2 all agreed that fear of special rights and affirmative action was at the heart of the vote.[37] Jean Dubofsky, the lead attorney for the parties seeking to overturn Amendment 2, who argued *Evans v. Romer* before the Supreme Court, believes that the vote measured people's attitudes toward affirmative action rather than gay or lesbian civil rights. She stated:

> The "no special rights" slogan was very clever, particularly given a time when at least white males don't like affirmative action. The Amendment 2 people spent a lot of time talking about [how] you don't want gays and lesbians getting in front of you in line for jobs or scholarships or college. Of course that wasn't what Amendment 2 was about overall, but that's the way it was sold. [Question: Was that the key argument?] Oh yeah, I'm sure it was. People

35. Lesley Dahlkemper, interview by author, Denver, 6 March 1995.

36. Justice Kennedy reasoned that Amendment 2's "sheer breadth is so discontinuous with the reasons offered for it that the amendment seems inexplicable by anything but animus toward the class that it affects; it lacks a rational relationship to legitimate state interests." *Romer v. Evans*, 517 U.S. at 620, 632 (1996). This decision is discussed at length in the next chapter.

37. One interviewee who might be a partial exception is Judy Harrington, the director of the anti–Amendment 2 campaign. Harrington stated that she believes that fear of special rights and hostility to affirmative action were significant factors in the vote, but that she could not assess their importance relative to other factors without examining polling data. Judy Harrington, telephone interview by author, 14 November 1996.

I talked with voted for it because they felt gays and lesbians shouldn't get affirmative action.[38]

Evans expressed virtually the identical opinion: "Colorado is very liberal in most regards to personal lifestyle. I would guess that affirmative action played a much greater part in this [than did antigay sentiment]. Maybe sixty-five / thirty-five [percent]." Vince Carol, editorial page editor for the *Rocky Mountain News*, is even more emphatic on this point: "It is safe to say that public resentment over affirmative action policies was indispensable to the amendment's success."[39]

Proponents of Amendment 2 also generally agreed that special rights and affirmative action were the central issues.[40] Mark Paschall, a Colorado state legislator and outspoken supporter of Amendment 2, held this view. When I asked him why public backlash against affirmative action was being directed toward gays and lesbians instead of groups that actually qualify for affirmative action programs, he responded: "Gays are the straw that broke the camel's back. They were in the wrong place at the wrong time."[41]

Despite the Supreme Court's assumption of "animus" on the part of Colorado voters as the only possible explanation for Amendment 2, not a single interviewee, whether for, against, or neutral on the issue of Amendment 2 agreed. According to Scardina, "the vast majority of people who voted yes genuinely felt they don't hate gays and lesbians." Vince Carol believes that "the majority of Coloradans don't want to discriminate against people because of sexual orientation but don't want to see homosexuals recognized as a political minority which will eventually be categorized with other political minorities and racial minorities."[42] Don Bain, chair of the Colorado Republican Party, who described Amendment 2 as "a close call on the merits," believes, "If Amendment 2 were limited to the issue of discrimination instead of quotas and preferences, it would have lost."[43] Fred Brown, political editor for the *Denver Post*, stated that "a vote for Amendment 2 was seen by many people as a vote against affirmative action rather than as a vote against gay rights."[44] Phil Nash, an anti–

38. Jean Dubofsky, interview by author, Boulder, Colo., 9 March 1995.

39. See John F. Niblock, "Anti-Gay Initiatives: A Call for Heightened Judicial Scrutiny," *UCLA Law Review* 41 (1993): 191.

40. This is not to say that fear of special rights or affirmative action for gays and lesbians is what motivated the initial drive to put Amendment 2 on the ballot. However, the special rights argument caused many people to vote for the amendment once it was on the ballot.

41. Mark Paschall, telephone interview by author, 17 February 1995.

42. Vince Carol, interview by author, Denver, 7 March 1995.

43. Don Bain, interview by author, Denver, 8 March 1995.

44. Fred Brown, interview by author, Denver, 6 March 1995.

Amendment 2 fundraiser, sums it up this way: "The vote on Amendment 2 was very complicated. Some people who are friendly to gays voted for it. Some people who hate gays voted against it."[45]

The opponents of Amendment 2 were well aware that widespread opposition to affirmative action posed a major problem for them. This was clearly reported to them in MRG's report on its focus-group discussions:

> Many people disagree that homosexuals should receive special consideration. With regard to hiring practices, the prevailing attitude is that one's homosexuality, if revealed during the interview process, should not enter into the employer's hiring decision. People are quick to add, though, that they do not feel this individual should receive special consideration because of his sexual orientation. This smacks of quotas, leading to reverse discrimination. People note that such a situation exists at present with regard to race. It is not a popular notion, but it can be rationalized to some degree on the basis of severe restrictions which have been placed on blacks in the past. People do not perceive that homosexuals have been victimized to the same extent and therefore, they are much more resistant to the concept of quotas or affirmative action with regard to this group of prospective employees.[46]

Indeed, the focus group research indicated that public fear of affirmative action was so great that anti–Amendment 2 forces should avoid even discussing the issue of hiring gays and lesbians or accepting them as tenants: "The public is wary of anything that hints of "affirmative action." EPOC would be well advised, in discussing discrimination in the workplace or housing, to place emphasis on *retaining* one's job or one's residence after the employer or landlord learns that the person is homosexual. When the subject turns to *hiring* homosexuals or *accepting* them as tenants, the specter of quotas arises in many people's minds."[47]

Opponents of Amendment 2 understood the problem they were facing. However, they were unsure how to respond. According to Anderson, "there is no one good phrase or slogan to counter 'special rights.' It takes fifteen minutes of real discussion to undo the damage that phrase does." Opponents of Amendment 2 were afraid to loudly proclaim that gays and lesbians were not seeking special treatment because they did not want to shift the debate from the issue of discrimination to the issue of affirmative action.

45. Phil Nash, interview by author, Denver, 7 March 1995.
46. MRG Report, 13–14.
47. *Ibid.*, 5 (emphasis in original).

Supporters of Amendment 2, however, had every reason to keep the debate centered on affirmative action, quotas, and preferences. Indeed, the amendment itself was drafted in such a way as to focus voters' attention on these issues. As the MRG report notes:

> The ballot description is cleverly devised to suggest that gays want extra privileges. While the Denver and Boulder ordinances grant *equal* rights to gays, lesbians and bisexual citizens, the proposed amendment implies that gays seek *special* rights. The ballot wording makes explicit reference to "minority status, quota preferences, protected status" as well as discrimination. The word "quota" is especially inflammatory since it suggests that gays wish to be given special consideration when it comes to jobs, housing and public accommodations. This leads many to express concern about reverse discrimination.[48]

The role of public antipathy toward affirmative action in the debate over Amendment 2 is ironic because anti–affirmative action sentiment could just as easily be seen as a reason to *favor* protections against discrimination on the basis of sexual orientation. The arguments for such antidiscrimination laws and the argument against affirmative action (in its most heavy-handed form of quotas and preferences) are essentially the same. Economic opportunities should be available on the basis of merit, not on the basis of characteristics like race, gender, or sexual orientation that are irrelevant to performance.

However, the concept of suspect classes blurs the distinction between affirmative action and antidiscrimination laws because the focus is group-based. The Supreme Court asks whether gays and lesbians are so powerless and victimized that they should receive the same protections as racial minorities, and CFV put the Court's standards for suspect-class status "at the center of the campaign." Since racial minorities receive the benefit of affirmative action as well as antidiscrimination laws, it is not surprising that the public was so sensitive to the issue of gays and lesbians getting affirmative action.[49] Thus, CFV's decision to put the Supreme Court standards

48. *Ibid.*, 9 (emphasis in original).

49. Fear that gays and lesbians might become beneficiaries of affirmative action programs may be a very powerful and underestimated factor in public resistance to gay rights throughout society. In his recent study, Paul Koegal discovered that "the most sharply expressed concern" of police and firefighters about gays and lesbians joining their departments "was the fear that gays and lesbians would achieve—indeed, in some instances had achieved—special class status." Paul Koegal, "Lessons Learned from the Experience of Domestic Police and Fire Departments," in *Out in Force: Sexual Orientation and the Military*, ed. Gregory M. Herek, Jared B. Jobe, and Ralph M. Carney (Chicago: University of Chicago Press,

for suspect class status "at the center of the campaign," along with the wording of the ballot measure, helped move the focus from discrimination to affirmative action. Nor did it hurt CFV's cause that courts have consistently ruled that gays and lesbians are not a suspect class. According to Al Knight, perspectives editor and opinion columnist for the *Denver Post*, "People will do what is easy to do absent some sort of alarm or barrier. People came along and told them essentially that the Constitution of the United States doesn't require us to provide civil rights inclusion for this particular group. We the people of Colorado, the implied message was, don't think this special protected status should be extended. So it was a relatively appealing argument."[50]

The focus group research of the anti–Amendment 2 forces also indicated that people's perceptions of whether gays and lesbians are protected under the Constitution were an important factor in how they would vote:

> The U.S. Constitution is not perceived to protect against discrimination. Voters are quite willing to give strong verbal support to the terms of the Constitution. Some people note that this country has achieved its position of greatness precisely because of adherence to the proposition that "all men are created equal." Some people conclude that this phrase settles this problem of discrimination for posterity. Many more, though, recognize that the Constitution is a blueprint—an ideal—and legislation is required so that barriers to adherence are removed. Thus, while many express dissatisfaction at the number of laws enacted by federal, state and local governments, they recognize that some laws are required to assure that the lofty ideals of the U.S. Constitution are in fact translated into appropriate behavior. That means that they will accept new laws or amendments that, in their view, correct inequalities in pursuit of the precepts of the Constitution.[51]

As a result, MRG advised, "In the present case, [voters] must be shown that enactment of this amendment would in fact *subtract from* the rights guaranteed from the U.S. Constitution."[52] However, since the courts have consistently held that gays and lesbians are not a suspect class, it was difficult

1996), 144. Koegal discovered that police and firefighters spontaneously and frequently brought the subject up during focus groups on attitudes toward gays and lesbians: "Outrage was consistently voiced at the possibility that gays and lesbians might be disproportionately hired, receive special promotional opportunities, be held to a lower standard, or afforded special class protections (such as unique procedural pathways for lodging complaints)." *Ibid.*

50. Al Knight, interview by author, Denver, 7 March 1995.

51. MRG report, 10–11.

52. *Ibid.*, 11 (emphasis in original).

to argue that Amendment 2 would subtract from rights granted by the Constitution. This is another example of the Court's influence on the political debate over the amendment.

As discussed in chapter 4, the Supreme Court is currently juggling two incompatible concepts: suspect classes (which are group-based) and suspect characteristics (which apply to individuals). Since the Colorado public is opposed to discrimination on the basis of sexual orientation, CFV wanted to focus the public's attention on group rights rather than discrimination. Framing the issues the same way that the courts do, in terms of whether gays and lesbians should be entitled to the same protections as African Americans, helped CFV accomplish this goal. The strategy appears to have been quite effective. Not one person interviewed described the debate over Amendment 2 as a debate over what *characteristics* should be considered irrelevant to job and housing opportunities.

CFV was also able to turn the Court's schizophrenic approach to equal protection to its advantage. Whites as a group are of course no more a "traditional minority" than are gays and lesbians. Yet they benefit from strict scrutiny in affirmative action cases. Logically, this should undermine CFV's argument that only traditional minorities get the benefit of enhanced legal protection. However, CFV argued that cases such as *Regents of the University of California v. Bakke* meant that gays and lesbians were seeking *greater* protection from discrimination than whites have. In the tabloid, CFV made the following argument:

> *Example:* Young-Caucasian-males-without-disabilities aren't a protected class. Claims of discrimination are not accepted on the basis of being a Caucasian-male-without-disabilities. But does that mean that someone belonging to this group has no legal recourse? Of course not. Just ask a Caucasian male, Alan Bakke. If he hadn't had legal recourse, there wouldn't be a famous Supreme Court reverse-discrimination case named after him. For Bakke to get that recourse, however, we didn't have to make Caucasian-males a specially protected class, or declare them, as a group, immune from discrimination. That would have destroyed the whole meaning of civil-rights. And so will protected status for homosexuals.

The argument in the tabloid continued:

> Once more for the record: anti-discrimination laws were written to protect specially protected classes—groups who've proven they need help.

On this point CFV is clearly distorting the law. Laws that prohibit discrimination on the basis of sexual orientation do not give gays and lesbians more protection than white men receive. They give both heterosexuals and homosexuals the *same* protections that blacks and whites receive. Yet on this point CFV is no more confused than the courts, which consistently hold that gays and lesbians must show that they are victimized, powerless minorities to benefit from strict scrutiny, even while the courts protect whites and men by applying strict scrutiny to affirmative action programs. Also, CFV's argument that "anti-discrimination laws were written to protect specially protected classes—groups who've proven they need help" is completely in tune with the class-based equal protection rhetoric of the Supreme Court. Thus, it is no surprise that CFV found that constitutional doctrine was quite useful to its campaign.

The CFV campaign, with its emphasis on special rights and protected classes, tapped into a general sentiment among the public that affirmative action and protection against discrimination are part of the same slippery slope—that the former follows from the latter. Leanna Ware is the director of the Civil Rights Bureau for the State of Wisconsin and testified against Amendment 2 at the Colorado trial. Ware states that "people mix up affirmative action and equal opportunity—they don't make the distinction."[53] According to Ware, employers often ask her if civil rights protection on the basis of sexual orientation means that Wisconsin requires affirmative action for gays and lesbians. (It does not.) In fact, even though Wisconsin's laws are clearly written to protect against discrimination on the basis of *characteristics* such as race and sexual orientation, even Ware herself sometimes refers to minorities and gays as "protected groups." When asked why she did this, she responded, "it's a common phrase—a shorthand."

There appears to be a widespread failure to understand that making provision for "protected groups" is *not* synonymous with outlawing discrimination on the basis of certain characteristics. Although the general public obviously does not follow the legal debate closely, the confusion between protecting groups and protecting all individuals from discrimination on the basis of certain characteristics blurs the line between protection from discrimination and affirmative action. Cliff May, associate editor at the *Rocky Mountain News*, says: "the average Joe Sixpack isn't discussing suspect classes or freedom of association but they have an intuitive feel for their resistance to affirmative action—there is a fear that goals, quotas and timetables are on the horizon."[54]

The phrase "special rights" means more than just affirmative action. It taps into a public fear that, if gays and lesbians are considered a protected class, then they will become protected from the vagaries of the economic

---

53. Leanna Ware, interview by author, Madison, Wis., 24 October 1994.
54. Cliff May, interview by author, Denver, 8 March 1995.

marketplace. People fear that employers will lay off heterosexuals instead of gays and lesbians out of fear of being sued by a "protected class." As May puts it, "people worry that we'll start with someone saying 'you can't fire me because I'm gay' but this will turn into: 'you can't fire *me* . . . because I'm gay.'"

Paschall agrees with May. He is adamant that his constituents' fears of gay untouchability at times of layoffs or hiring are realistic: "Corporations are reluctant to fire protected minorities. Also, practically speaking, it's easier for an employer not to hire a white man than a black female. It's not fair to put one group above the other. [Gays and lesbians] don't deserve the same protected status as racial minorities." Although Paschall is a strong supporter of Amendment 2, he says he would like to support laws that simply protect gays and lesbians from being fired on the basis of their sexual orientation. However, he quickly adds, "but I don't trust the government and its lawyers—any law would end up going past that."

People active on both sides of the debate saw the political context as one in which most people now perceive civil rights as a zero-sum commodity—a set of protections that must be carefully parceled out to only the most deserving groups. Anderson puts it this way: "They really play on that economic jealousy factor that people are going to take their jobs away and it plays on their whole idea that civil rights are finite and that there's a pie and that the more people that are in the pie, the more it takes away from another group's civil rights."

Colorado state senator Charles Duke's point of view on the merits of Amendment 2 is the polar opposite from Anderson's—he is an ardent and outspoken supporter of the amendment. But he makes the same point about people's perceptions: "When you take a set of privileges and grant them to some people you must take them away from the overall set, it's an exhaustive set. . . . people are tired of whacking off a slice of the Constitution for a select group of people and giving them special privileges at our expense. When you do that you take rights away from me."[55]

As a result, the public, at least in Colorado, is wary of legal protections for *any* group.[56] Fred Brown believes that Amendment 2 would have passed even if it had been targeted at "blue eyed people." Cliff May uses a similar analogy: "The result would have been the same for left-handed people."

---

55. Charles Duke, interview by author, Denver, 7 March 1995.

56. It is worth noting that this wariness parallels that of the Supreme Court, which during the past twenty years has refused to find that *any* additional group meets the criteria for suspect-class status.

"Special Rights" and the Issue of the "Gay Lifestyle"

As important as concerns over affirmative action and economic issues were in the debate over Amendment 2, they were not the only issues. Most of the interviewees agreed that the public concern over a perceived "gay lifestyle" also played an important role in the debate. According to Lesley Dahlkemper, Amendment 2 "was born out of a fear to some degree of the gay lifestyle and what that's about. You only need look at some of the campaign material that was issued by CFV— "The Gay Agenda" was a video that was used. Even [CFV] acknowledged this only illustrates one segment of the gay population, but certainly looking at that piece, which I think can be very manipulative, you get the sense that the entire gay community is like this and that really plays upon fears."

CFV was especially aggressive about promoting the fear that gay men are predatory toward children. Widely distributed CFV literature included the following statements:

TARGET: CHILDREN

Lately, America has been hearing a lot about the subject of childhood sexual abuse. This terrible epidemic has scarred countless young lives and destroyed thousands of families. But what militant homosexuals don't want you to know is the large role they play in this epidemic. In fact, pedophilia (the sexual molestation of children) is actually an accepted part of the homosexual community!

Under the same banner—"TARGET: CHILDREN"—CFV literature asserted:

Don't let gay militant double-talk hide their true intentions. Sexual molestation of children is a large part of many homosexuals' lifestyle—part of the very lifestyle "gay rights" activists want government to give special class, ethnic status! Say no to sexual perversion with children—vote YES! on Amendment 2!

However, the issue of special rights and the issue of the "gay lifestyle" cannot be neatly separated. In fact, concerns over gays and lesbians having special rights exacerbated concerns about the "gay lifestyle." CFV played up the idea that, if gays and lesbians were a protected class, they could behave any way they wanted to in public and would be legally protected from criticism. Will Perkins, the chairman of the board of CFV, emphasized that the purpose of Amendment 2 was "to prevent sexual orientation from being used as a club to bludgeon their ways onto society."[57]

57. Will Perkins, interview by author, Colorado Springs, 10 March 1995.

CFV literature repeatedly mentioned a proposed "Ethnic Anti-Harassment Bill" that had been introduced in the Colorado legislature. CFV argued that the bill "would have made it a felony hate crime to speak negatively about homosexuality." The boundaries of what does and does not constitute harassment are still developing and are currently somewhat vague.[58] By raising the specter that freedom of speech was threatened by gay and lesbian rights, CFV tapped into the recent spate of publicity and public uncertainty over the meaning of workplace harassment. In other areas, however, CFV made arguments that are clear distortions of the law. As noted, CFV was particularly aggressive about exploiting the public's protective instincts toward children. CFV combined the argument about children with the argument that gays and lesbians were seeking "special" or "minority" status that would make them immune from normal legal accountability. Included in the tabloid was the following argument:

> In Laguna Beach, California, a city with one of the country's largest gay communities and strongest "gay-rights" ordinances, a three year old boy entered a public park restroom. What he saw there traumatized him severely. Three grown gay men were engaging in group sex, right there in the bathroom! When he ran out to his mother, crying and upset, she attempted to file a complaint with the Laguna Beach Police Department. Their reply: with a "gay-rights" ordinance in place, there was nothing they could do. You can stop this from happening in Colorado with your "YES" vote on Amendment 2.

Thus, CFV raised the specter of some very frightening things happening in Colorado if gays and lesbians were protected by civil rights laws. Some of these claims, such as the possibility of workplace harassment suits based on expressions of negative feelings regarding homosexuality, were within the broad realm of possibility given the inchoate state of harassment law in general. Others were obvious exaggerations. However, even if the dangers were remote, most people did not see that there was anything to lose by voting for Amendment 2. There is a widespread perception that it is already illegal to fire a worthy employee just because he or she is gay. According to Anderson, "most people don't realize that a gay person can be fired without recourse just because they are gay." Thus, even if the scenarios raised by CFV seemed unlikely, for many people, as Al Knight puts it, "voting for Amendment 2 was [seen as] a harmless vote."

58. Kingsley Browne, "Title VII as Censorship: Hostile Environment Harassment and the First Amendment," *Ohio State Law Journal* 52 (1991): 481–550; Eugene Volokh, "Freedom of Speech and Workplace Harassment," *UCLA Law Review* 39 (1992): 1791–872.

Thus, CFV combined the special-rights argument with attacks on the "gay lifestyle" to paint a frightening picture of out-of-control child molesters who would be protected from the law by the shield of special rights. Polling data indicate that the special-rights message was more effective than the more volatile, but less credible argument about homosexuals and children. When asked to agree or disagree with the statement "A homosexual is more likely to molest children than a person who is heterosexual," Coloradans responded:

Strongly agree	5%
Somewhat agree	5%
Neutral	4%
Somewhat disagree	18%
Strongly disagree	54%
Don't know	14%

However, Coloradans responded to the statement "When homosexuals talk about gay rights, what they really mean is that they want special treatment" as follows:

Strongly agree	40%
Somewhat agree	19%
Neutral	3%
Somewhat disagree	12%
Strongly disagree	21%
Don't know	5%

The polling data indicate that CFV's special rights argument was far more persuasive to Colorado voters than its provocative rhetoric about the gay lifestyle and child molestation. So while CFV used both special rights and the gay lifestyle as political rhetoric, Coloradans appear to have been more persuaded by the former than the latter.

The vote for Amendment 2 is best understood as the confluence of a variety of concerns. Voters were concerned over the issue of affirmative action for gays and lesbians, that others would be fired before gays and lesbians when layoffs occurred, and that gays and lesbians would become legally protected from public criticism or accountability for their actions. It should be noted that no interviewee was able to give an actual example of gays and lesbians receiving the benefit of affirmative action or being spared the brunt of layoffs (although it is impossible to predict what might happen in the near or distant future). As for the other concerns mentioned, they ranged from the speculative to the virtually impossible. However, what links all of these concerns is the slogan of special rights—the idea that civil rights protection is a package of special rights that give certain groups special protection. Equal protection jurisprudence relies on the same assumption. Thus CFV was able to use constitutional doctrine to buttress and legitimate its argument that gays and lesbians were seeking special rights that should be made available only to traditional minorities.

While it is impossible to know just how powerful an impact constitutional doctrine had on the vote on Amendment 2, two things seem clear. First, class-based equal protection doctrine provided CFV with the rhetorical tools to shift the debate from the issue of discrimination to the issue of how closely gays and lesbians resemble "real minorities" such as African Americans. Second, public skepticism about affirmative action and concern about "special rights" meant that this shift in the terms of the debate worked in favor of the proponents of Amendment 2.

Once the voters passed Amendment 2, the debate moved to the judicial system, where opponents of the amendment argued that it denied gays and lesbians equal protection of the laws. We have seen how the class-based legal formulations of the courts obfuscated the political debate. We shall next see how these formulations obfuscated the legal debate. The next chapter explores how the courts, including the United States Supreme Court, struggled with the issues posed by the passage of Amendment 2.

The Judicial Response to Amendment 2

As we saw in the previous chapter, the public debate over Amendment 2 was an often jumbled mixture of legal and political arguments. Political arguments over affirmative action and civil rights were colored by constitutional arguments about whether gays and lesbians should be considered a protected class.

Once the Colorado voters passed Amendment 2, the battle moved to the Colorado state courts and eventually to the United States Supreme Court. The legal battle over Amendment 2 provides several vital lessons about the state of equal protection doctrine. Although three different courts wrote opinions about the constitutionality of Amendment 2, none gave any clear reason why Amendment 2 does or does not violate the equal protection clause. The litigation revealed how inadequate the three-tiered framework is for navigating the complex political terrain at the turn of the twenty-first century. The litigation was ultimately decided at an emotional level rather than a legal level. The ostensible standards for deciding equal protection cases were largely ignored, and the case ultimately came down to the Supreme Court's intuitions about how the Colorado voters felt about gays and lesbians.

The litigation also demonstrated how thin the line between law and politics is in the area of gay and lesbian rights. Political considerations weighed heavily in the plaintiffs' decisions about legal strategy. Further, the law itself proved to be so ambiguous and confusing that the judges and justices were left with no choice but to fall back on their own intuitions of fairness. This was especially true in the Supreme Court's bitterly divided 6–3 decision striking down Amendment 2.

Since nothing quite like Amendment 2 had ever existed before, the courts seemed as uncertain of how to deal with the amendment as the voters did. The law of equal protection proved to be confusing terrain. We have already seen that the three-tiered framework is an area loaded with vague, often internally inconsistent jargon. The legal challenge to Amendment 2 forced the courts to grapple with all the ambiguities and complexities of equal protection doctrine. The courts had to deal not only with whether gays and lesbians are a suspect class, but also with whether moral disapproval of homosexuality is a "rational basis" for a law. Also, the courts had to decide whether Amendment 2 violated the "fundamental rights" of gays and lesbians. In navigating this terrain, opponents of Amendment 2 had to make many strategic choices, both legally and politically.[1]

Challenging Amendment 2 in the Courts

The lead plaintiff in the legal case was Richard Evans. In 1992 Evans was the director of the Denver Mayor's Office of Citizen Response and served on the Mayor's Gay and Lesbian Advisory Committee. Evans was involved in the fight against Amendment 2 almost from the beginning. He had been watching nervously in February 1992, when CFV began gathering signatures to place Amendment 2 on the ballot. The ballot initiative seemed to strike a chord with at least a part of the citizenry, and CFV easily gathered far more signatures than were needed to place Amendment 2 on the ballot.

In May 1992, members of the mayor's Gay and Lesbian Advisory Committee decided to explore how a legal challenge could be mounted in case Amendment 2 passed. However, according to Evans, EPOC—the leading force in the anti–Amendment 2 campaign—did not want to prepare a legal challenge. EPOC's leaders did not believe such a step would be a wise use of resources because the polls at that time showed that, despite CFV's success at gathering signatures, Amendment 2 would not pass. They also feared that preparing a legal challenge might send a signal to Colorado gays and lesbians that Amendment 2 stood a good chance of passing.

Evans wanted a fallback option in case Amendment 2 did pass. Along with other members of the Gay and Lesbian Advisory Committee, he formed the Colorado Legal Initiatives Project (CLIP) to explore legal strategies in the event Amendment 2 passed. Lacking financial resources,

1. Much of the information in this chapter comes from my interviews with Jeffrey Bayless, the state trial court judge who initially prevented the enforcement of Amendment 2; Jean Dubofsky, lead counsel for the plaintiffs; Richard Evans, the lead plaintiff in the litigation; Matthew Coles, now the director of the ACLU Lesbian & Gay Rights Project, who was an ACLU staff attorney involved in the litigation; Suzanne Goldberg, staff attorney for the Lambda Legal Defense and Education Fund, who was also involved in the litigation; and Tim Tymkovich, the solicitor general of Colorado, who argued the State's case before the U.S. Supreme Court. This chapter is also based on the legal briefs of both sides of the litigation, the transcripts of the various oral arguments, and the written opinions of the various courts that heard this case.

CLIP needed a highly qualified local lawyer who would volunteer substantial amounts of time to devising a legal strategy to challenge Amendment 2. CLIP turned to Jean Dubofsky, a Harvard Law School graduate who had previously served for eight years as a justice on the Colorado Supreme Court. Dubofsky turned out to be an extremely able advocate. She had not only a sharp legal mind, but also a firsthand knowledge of what sort of legal arguments the Colorado Supreme Court might be willing to accept. CLIP was also aided by a formidable team of advocacy-group attorneys, including Matthew Coles of the ACLU and Suzanne Goldberg of the Lambda Legal Defense and Education Fund.

Dubofsky believed that the Colorado Supreme Court was too cautious to accept the argument that gays and lesbians are a suspect class. However, she felt that the court might well be persuaded that Amendment 2 lacked even a rational basis and therefore violated the equal protection clause. (Recall that, under the three-tiered framework, even a law that does not discriminate against a suspect or quasi-suspect class must have a rational basis.) Unlike a decision that gays and lesbians are a suspect class, such a ruling would affect only the relatively narrow issue of Amendment 2. Thus, she felt this would be CLIP's strongest argument in the eyes of the court.

When Amendment 2 passed in November 1992, CLIP felt tremendous pressure to act quickly. Evans, who is gay and is a public employee, agreed to serve as the lead plaintiff. Denver, Boulder, and other local governmental units also joined the suit.

A major question facing CLIP was when to bring the lawsuit. Amendment 2 was to take effect mid-January 1993, still nearly two months off. Normally, to challenge a law like Amendment 2 in court the plaintiffs must show that they have been harmed by the law in some way. Legally, the easiest approach would be to wait until Amendment 2 took effect and someone was refused a job or was discriminated against on the basis of sexual orientation. That person could then show that he or she had been harmed by Amendment 2. However, that would have meant holding off on legal action until CLIP could find a suitable plaintiff.

While it might be legally safer to postpone filing until a specific victim of discrimination could be found, there were important political reasons for bringing a legal challenge to Amendment 2 immediately. According to Evans, "there was a lot of anger [within the gay and lesbian community] and the pressure to do something as soon as possible—to take action—was tremendous." There was also great fear within the gay and lesbian community about what might happen in other states if Amendment 2 were not challenged immediately. According to Suzanne Goldberg of the

Lambda Legal Defense and Education Fund, "There was fear of a snowball effect—there could be a landslide [of Amendment 2–type initiatives] in other states if Amendment 2 went into effect. We wanted to come out fighting."[2] Further, it could be difficult to find a victim of discrimination willing to bring a suit. The ACLU's Matt Coles was worried that Amendment 2 would be "the dog that didn't bark—even if Amendment 2 meant open season on gays and lesbians, most people just walk away from situations of discrimination."[3] If CLIP waited for a suitable plaintiff and one did not come along reasonably quickly, this could undermine, fairly or unfairly, CLIP's argument that Amendment 2 was a severe blow to the rights of gays and lesbians.

As a result, CLIP decided to pursue a risky legal strategy and challenge Amendment 2 "on its face." That meant that it would seek an injunction against the amendment ever being enforced. CLIP would also be asking a state trial court to issue a "preliminary injunction," an order preventing Amendment 2 from being enforced even before the courts had decided whether or not the amendment is constitutional. Dubofsky was nervous about this because it meant that the plaintiffs would have to convince a court that the very existence of Amendment 2 not only harmed gays and lesbians but also violated their "fundamental rights."[4] Fundamental rights are those rights most strongly protected by the U.S. Constitution. They include such rights as freedom of speech and freedom of religion as well as a small number of rights the courts have held are protected by the equal protection clause.

Therefore, CLIP faced a dilemma. Dubofsky felt that the best legal argument against Amendment 2 was that it had no rational relationship to any legitimate state objective. It merely endorsed and gave effect to people's private biases against gays and lesbians. If the courts agreed with this, Amendment 2 would be struck down under the equal protection clause. However, even if the court agreed that Amendment 2 was irrational, that would not necessarily be enough for a preliminary injunction. Without a preliminary injunction, it might be years before the courts struck down Amendment 2, assuming they struck it down at all. As a result, CLIP

2. Suzanne Goldberg, telephone interview by author, 4 September 1997.
3. Matthew Coles, telephone interview by author, 15 August 1997.
4. The plaintiffs' attorneys were not all of one mind on this. The ACLU believed that, if the court could be convinced that Amendment 2 was an irrational act of animus, it would grant a preliminary injunction simply because the amendment was, as the ACLU's Matt Coles put it, "so over the top." Nevertheless, the ACLU felt that devising a fundamental-rights argument was crucial since it is extremely uncommon for courts to hold that a law has no rational basis.

decided to pursue a fundamental-rights argument. To understand this theory, we need to briefly take another look at the law of equal protection.

The Fundamental-Rights Strand of Equal Protection

As we have seen, the equal protection clause has given rise to three different levels of protection: strict scrutiny, intermediate scrutiny, and rational-basis scrutiny. The courts apply strict scrutiny to laws that discriminate against suspect classes such as racial minorities and to laws that are based on suspect classifications such as race. In addition, the courts have held that the equal protection clause protects a small number of fundamental rights that are not specifically mentioned anywhere in the Constitution. These rights include the right to marry, the right to travel from state to state, and the right to vote.[5] If a law violates one of these fundamental rights, the courts will apply the same strict scrutiny to that law that they would apply to racially discriminatory laws. This is often referred to as the "fundamental-rights strand" of equal protection jurisprudence.

CLIP hoped that the courts could be persuaded that the equal protection clause protects a fundamental right to *equally* participate in the political process. Since Amendment 2 excludes gays and lesbians, and only gays and lesbians, from seeking civil rights legislation from state and local legislatures, it deprives them of their right to equal political participation. If the courts agreed, they would prevent Amendment 2 from taking effect since it deprived gays and lesbians of this fundamental right. However, there was one problem with this theory: no court had ever held that such a right exists.

The plaintiffs based their hopes largely on a 1969 Supreme Court case called *Hunter v. Erickson*.[6] In *Hunter* the Supreme Court struck down a charter amendment enacted by the voters of Akron, Ohio. The amendment prohibited the Akron city council from passing any "fair housing laws" unless the Akron electorate specifically allowed it. The Akron city council was free to pass any other type of law, but not fair housing laws. The charter amendment was clearly directed at racial minorities—it made it impossible for them to seek the city's protection against housing discrimination. The Supreme Court struck down the law because it "place[d] special burdens on racial minorities within the governmental process."[7]

Dubofsky and the other attorneys believed that Amendment 2 saddled gays and lesbians with the same burden that the Akron law placed on

5. Cathey, "Refining the Methods," 1501.
6. 393 U.S. 385 (1969).
7. *Hunter,* 393 U.S. at 391.

racial minorities. Indeed, Amendment 2 was designed to prevent gays and lesbians from seeking, among other things, the same type of fair housing legislation that racial minorities were seeking in the *Hunter* case. But the courts have tolerated many legal burdens on gays and lesbians that they would not tolerate in the context of race. Also, the Supreme Court had never applied the rationale in *Hunter* outside of a racial context. Nonetheless, Dubofsky hoped that the Colorado courts could be persuaded that the *Hunter* logic should be applied to Amendment 2.

Dubofsky and CLIP decided to go to court immediately and seek a preliminary injunction. Less than two weeks after the voters passed Amendment 2, the plaintiffs filed a complaint in the state trial court seeking the injunction.

The First Round: Seeking Preliminary Relief

The plaintiffs had little time to present their case. The judge assigned to the case, Jeffrey Bayless, had an extremely tight schedule for the remainder of the calendar year. During oral argument on the preliminary injunction, Dubofsky concentrated on what the plaintiffs' attorneys believed were the two strongest arguments against Amendment 2—the amendment lacked a rational basis, and it violated the fundamental rights of gays and lesbians to equally participate in the political process.

The State of Colorado was represented by Deputy Attorney General John Dailey. Dailey argued that no court had ever ruled that there is a fundamental right to equal participation in the political process. *Hunter* was not applicable because it was a race case. Dubofsky countered that the Supreme Court had never explicitly limited *Hunter* to race cases and that the logic of *Hunter* applied to Amendment 2.

Dailey and Dubofsky also clashed over whether there was a rational basis for Amendment 2. Dubofsky argued that the only purpose of the amendment was to endorse and give effect to private bias against gays and lesbians. Dailey countered that Amendment 2 was rationally related to a number of legitimate governmental purposes such as preserving government resources for combating race and gender discrimination and allowing individuals the choice of not associating with gays and lesbians if they did not want to.

The hearing took place in a highly politicized context. Public and media interest in the hearings and in what Judge Bayless would do was enormous. Judge Bayless knew that his ruling would be interpreted not just as a legal ruling, but as a political statement as well. In an interview with the author, Bayless said, "I was hugely aware that I was making a ruling which was going to make people mad. The media hyped this up. There were cameras in the courtroom and all the local networks canceled their programming to cover [Bayless's announcement of his decision]. So I was talking to everyone who was watching television at that time. I was talking to the legal community but also to all the people who had voted for the Amendment and against it."[8]

Judge Bayless announced his decision from the bench on January 15, 1993, the Friday before the day Amendment 2 was scheduled to take effect. His opening remarks were highly unusual. Bayless made it clear that he understood that his decision had political consequences as well as legal consequences. He acknowledged that "the audience [was] made up of two distinct groups . . . a group of legally trained people . . . [and also] non-legally trained folk, just like the people of Colorado who voted on the Amendment." He stated that he had reached his verdict at 2:30 that morning and had been writing continually since that time with just four hours of sleep. He also said that he had tried to write his opinion for both lawyers and ordinary people without insulting either, but he added, "how well I have succeeded will be determined by someone other than me."

Judge Bayless granted the preliminary injunction, but it turned out that he badly mangled the law in doing so. Judge Bayless was working under enormous time pressure and in his hastily written opinion, he confused Dubofsky's two arguments and merged them together into a single legal theory. Dubofsky had argued that Amendment 2 (1) violated a fundamental right to equal protection in the political process and (2) violated the equal protection clause because it irrationally endorsed and gave effect to private bias. Judge Bayless held, however, "there is a fundamental right here, and it's the right not to have the State endorse and give effect to private biases."[9] This confusion meant that he could grant the preliminary injunction without accepting the novel legal theory that there is a fundamental right to equal political participation. He essentially held that there is a fundamental right not to be subjected to an irrational law. Thus, Bayless granted the preliminary injunction, but he left the legal issues even more confused than before.

The Colorado Supreme Court Finds a Fundamental Right to Equally Participate in the Political Process

Colorado's attorney general, Gale Norton, quickly decided to appeal Bayless's ruling to the Colorado Supreme Court. Both sides understood

8. The Hon. Jeffrey Bayless, telephone interview by author, 20 November 1996.

9. *Evans v. Romer* (unpublished trial court opinion), quoted in Colorado's brief to the United States Supreme Court at p. 4 n. 2.

that they needed to disentangle the two legal arguments that had been mixed together by Judge Bayless. At the same time, the plaintiffs had to try to preserve both the result and the judge's good will—which meant clarifying the issues without appearing unduly critical of Bayless's opinion and without deviating too sharply from his reasoning. As the ACLU's Matt Coles put it, "We didn't want to abandon the decision of the trial judge—after all we'd be going back to the trial judge [to permanently strike down Amendment 2] and we didn't want him to think we'd sold him on bad arguments the first time around."

From the plaintiffs' point of view, the key issue was whether the Colorado Supreme Court would hold that Amendment 2 violated the fundamental right of gays and lesbians to equally participate in the political process. If the Court rejected this theory, it could overturn the preliminary injunction and Colorado could begin enforcing Amendment 2.

The State of Colorado argued that the rationale in *Hunter* could not be applied to gays and lesbians since, unlike the plaintiffs in *Hunter*, gays and lesbians are not a suspect class. Colorado's argument appeared quite strong, especially in light of a U.S. Supreme Court case called *James v. Valtierra*.[10] In *James*, California voters had passed a constitutional measure prohibiting state and local governments from creating any new low-income housing projects without the approval of a majority of the voters. The plaintiffs in that case argued that the measure violated the rights of poor people the same way the law in *Hunter* violated the rights of racial minorities. The *James* Court rejected this argument, stating, "It cannot be said that California's [new law] rests on 'distinctions based on race'. . . . the present case could be affirmed only by extending *Hunter* and this we decline to do."[11] The Court reasoned that extending *Hunter* beyond suspect classes would mean that "a State would not be able to require referendums on any subject unless referendums were required on all, because they would always disadvantage some group."[12]

Since gays and lesbians, like the poor, are not a suspect class, *James* appeared to pose a major problem for the plaintiffs. However, Dubofsky still believed that the political-participation argument was the one most likely to lead to a grant of a preliminary injunction, so the plaintiffs emphasized this argument, both in the legal briefs and during oral argument.

The strategy worked. In July 1993, the Colorado Supreme Court voted 6–1 to uphold the preliminary injunction issued by Judge Bayless.[13] The

10. 402 U.S. 137 (1971).
11. *James*, 402 U.S. at 141.
12. *Id.* at 142.
13. *Evans v. Romer*, 854 P.2d 1270 (Colo. 1993).

majority reasoning closely followed the plaintiffs' argument. It held that Amendment 2 violated the fundamental right of gays and lesbians to participate equally in the political process because they were prevented from pursuing their political interests in state and local legislatures. The court also held that, although *Hunter* involved racial minorities, its principle of equal political participation could apply to any group, including gays and lesbians. State constitutions cannot be amended in such a way that makes it more difficult for any group to pursue its political interests through the normal legislative process. The only limitation was that the group had to be "independently identifiable." This means that the group has to have something in common beyond support for a particular law. So, for example, a state constitutional amendment prohibiting the state from issuing new bonds without voter approval does not violate the principle of equal political participation, because people who support the issuance of new bonds have nothing in common besides their agreement on that particular issue. Gays and lesbians, however, are an independently identifiable group and therefore have a fundamental right to attempt to further their own political interests through the normal political processes.[14] Oddly, the court mentioned the *James* case only in a footnote. It said that *James* was better understood as a case denying suspect-class status to the poor than as a case limiting *Hunter* to racial minorities.[15]

The lone dissenter was Justice William H. Erickson. Erickson pointed out that, under the majority's reasoning, a great many state constitutional provisions would be unconstitutional. For example, many states bar convicted felons from holding public office, even after they have served their time. Erickson argued that, if the court's rationale were taken seriously, these laws would be unconstitutional since convicted felons are an independently identifiable group.[16] Erickson argued that the Colorado Supreme Court had simply created a new "fundamental right" out of the blue. He believed that the U.S. Supreme Court had never recognized a right to equally participate in the political process.[17]

Nevertheless, the ruling ended the first stage of the legal battle. Implementation of Amendment 2 was enjoined until the courts, including, as it turned out, the U.S. Supreme Court, finally determined whether or not Amendment 2 was constitutional.

14. *Id.* at 1281–82.

15. *Id.* at 1282 n. 21.

16. Although Erickson did not mention them, many other state constitutional provisions might be voided under the court's reasoning. For example, many states have constitutional provisions outlawing polygamy, provisions that clearly target Mormons.

17. *Evans,* 854 P.2d at 1300–1302 (Erickson, J., dissenting).

The Colorado Trial

The Colorado Supreme Court's decision did not end the legal debate. Even if Amendment 2 violated a fundamental right, it could still be upheld if it withstood strict scrutiny—if it was "narrowly tailored" to further a "compelling governmental interest." The Colorado Supreme Court sent the case back to Judge Bayless so that he could make this determination.

As is probably inevitable among any group of high-powered litigators, the plaintiffs' attorneys had numerous disagreements over legal strategy. At this stage of the litigation, the disagreements became far more serious. Some of the attorneys, including the ACLU's Coles and Lambda's Goldberg, wanted to avoid any sort of a trial. They felt that, with the favorable ruling from the Colorado Supreme Court, the plaintiffs were in a position to seek "summary judgment"—a ruling striking down Amendment 2 permanently without any fact-finding by Bayless beyond what was contained in the legal documents. Indeed, Colorado Solicitor General Timothy Tymkovich admitted, "We expected that the plaintiffs would move for summary judgment, and given the State Supreme Court's ruling, had a very good chance of winning."[18] Dubofsky saw things quite differently. She wanted Bayless to conduct a full-scale trial that could serve as an opportunity "to put on evidence dispelling myths about sexual orientation." She wanted to create a record that "would educate courts about sexual orientation."

Judge Bayless went along with Dubofsky's request and decided to conduct a full-scale trial. He heard evidence about what governmental purposes were served by the amendment. However, the trial turned out to be far more freewheeling than expected. Even though the Colorado Supreme Court had already ruled on the fundamental-rights issue, Judge Bayless decided to allow the plaintiffs full latitude to advance a variety of legal theories. In his interview with the author, Bayless said, "I wanted to give everyone a chance to say what they had to say—I wanted a huge record for the appellate courts."

With the preliminary injunction safely in place, Dubofsky also decided to advance the more ambitious argument that gays and lesbians are a suspect class. If the courts were to accept this argument, the results would be dramatic. All laws burdening gays and lesbians, not just Amendment 2, would be subjected to strict scrutiny by the courts.

Judge Bayless allowed both sides broad latitude in presenting evidence for their arguments. Bayless listened to what he described as "testimony from dueling Classics professors about Greek views [toward homosexual-

18. Timothy Tymkovich, telephone interview by author, 13 September 1996.

ity]."[19] The experts for the State argued that "tolema," Plato's adjective for homosexuality, is properly translated as "abomination." The plaintiffs' experts insisted that the term was properly translated to mean "deed of daring." Judge Bayless heard testimony on issues such as whether "being gay is a lifestyle which leads to happiness."[20] Bayless also heard testimony about whether Amendment 2 furthered any compelling state interests. The State argued that Amendment 2 served the purpose of "preserv[ing] the integrity of the State's political functions."[21] Representatives from CFV testified about the "homosexual agenda" and their alleged push for "protected status." CFV Chair Will Perkins stated that Amendment 2 was necessary to fend off "militant gay aggression." According to Judge Bayless, Perkins used that term half a dozen times during his direct testimony alone.

Kevin Tebedo, also of CFV, was less antagonistic in his testimony. He argued that Amendment 2 was needed to prevent gays and lesbians from receiving "protected-class status" and to prevent them from eventually receiving the benefits of affirmative action. As we saw in the previous chapter, this is the argument that may have been most influential in persuading Coloradans to vote for Amendment 2.

Judge Bayless rejected these arguments, stating, "the evidence does not persuade the court that absent Amendment 2, homosexuals and bisexuals are going to be found to be a suspect or quasi-suspect class and afforded protections based on those classifications."[22] This ruling placed Judge Bayless in a somewhat awkward position, as the plaintiffs were indeed urging him to hold that gays and lesbians are a suspect or quasi-suspect class. As we saw in chapter 4, Judge Bayless ended up ruling that gays and lesbians are too politically powerful to be considered a suspect or quasi-suspect class. The severe problems with this reasoning are discussed in chapter 4. Yet, having just held that "homosexuals and bisexuals are [not] going to be found to be a suspect or quasi-suspect class," it would have been difficult for him to turn around and declare that these groups are just such a class.

The State also argued that Amendment 2 served the purpose of preserving state resources to combat discrimination against recognized suspect classes such as racial minorities. The State presented witnesses who testified that adding gays and lesbians to civil rights statutes would lessen

19. Judge Bayless, interview.
20. Jeffrey Rosen, "Sodom and Demurrer," *New Republic,* 29 November 1993, 17.
21. Colorado's cert. petition at p. C-6.
22. *Evans* (trial court opinion), at p. C-8 of Colorado's cert. petition.

the public's respect for traditional civil rights categories. Bayless rejected this argument as well because it was merely speculation "in the form of opinion and theory as to what *would* occur if a [gay rights ordinance] were adopted as a state statute."[23] Such speculation, he reasoned, cannot amount to a compelling state interest.

The State also argued that Amendment 2 preserved the right of religious institutions to refuse to associate with gays and lesbians if they believed that homosexuality violated their religious principles. The State argued that the City of Boulder's discrimination law did not have an exemption for religious institutions such as churches or religious schools. While Bayless agreed that religious freedom is a compelling state purpose, he found that Amendment 2 was not narrowly tailored to meet those goals. He ruled that "the narrowly focused way of addressing the Boulder ordinance is to add to it a religious exemption such as is found in [other] ordinances, not to deny gays and bisexuals their fundamental right of participation in the political process."[24]

Finally, the State argued that Amendment 2 promoted "the physical and psychological well-being of children." Bayless rejected the argument, noting that the evidence suggests that pedophiles are more likely to be heterosexual than homosexual.[25]

Thus, Judge Bayless ruled that the State had failed to meet its burden of proving that Amendment 2 was narrowly tailored to further a compelling governmental interest. He therefore held that Amendment 2 violated the equal protection clause and would never go into effect.

Moral Judgment and the Colorado Supreme Court

When the State appealed Bayless's final ruling to the Colorado Supreme Court, it added a new argument: Amendment 2 promoted the compelling interest in preserving public morality.[26] The State argued that Amendment 2 promotes public morality by sending the societal message that homosexuality is immoral. The Colorado Supreme Court accepted the argument that the State has a "substantial" interest in promoting morality. However, it held that Amendment 2 could not be sustained on this basis, because even a "substantial" state interest falls short of the "compelling" interest

23. *Id.* at p. C-9.
24. *Id.* at pp. C-11 to C-12.
25. *Evans* (trial court opinion), at p. C-13 of Colorado's cert. petition.
26. The State claimed that this was not a new argument because it mentioned the issue of morality in an introductory paragraph in its brief to the trial court. *Evans v. Romer*, 882 P.2d 1335, 1346 n. 11 (Colo. 1994).

required by strict scrutiny. Also, the court was unconvinced that Amendment 2 furthered the public interest in promoting public morality. In response to the State's argument that antidiscrimination laws might send the message that the government considered homosexuality to be morally acceptable, the court stated, "In short, prohibitions on discrimination against gay men, lesbians, and bisexuals do not imply an endorsement of any particular sexual orientation or practice."[27]

The Colorado Supreme Court thus affirmed the ruling that Amendment 2 was not necessary to serve any compelling state interest. As far as the Colorado courts were concerned, the legal battle had ended. Amendment 2 was permanently enjoined. Then, to many people's surprise, the United State Supreme Court agreed to hear the case, and the stakes were dramatically raised.

Amendment 2 and the Supreme Court

It was far from certain that the Supreme Court would agree to hear the case. The Court has virtually complete discretion over its own docket. Each year the Court is asked to review thousands of cases but it actually hears argument in fewer than one hundred of these.[28] Judge Bayless was "frankly astounded" that the Court agreed to hear the case.

The state-court battle over Amendment 2 had been commanding national attention. Once the Supreme Court agreed to decide the case, *Romer v. Evans* became perhaps the most important constitutional case in the nation that year. The Court had not agreed to review a gay rights case since the homosexual sodomy case, *Bowers v. Hardwick*, in 1986.[29] *Bowers* had been hostile in both tone and substance to arguments for gay rights. As we have seen, gays and lesbians have consistently been granted the lowest possible level of protection under the equal protection clause. Many federal courts had interpreted *Bowers* as placing the Supreme Court's imprimatur on this lack of judicial protection. The plaintiffs in *Romer* hoped that the Court was ready to change course and grant gays and lesbians greater protection under the equal protection clause. The case also had national implications far beyond the issue of gay and lesbian rights. Due to the reasoning of the Colorado courts, *Romer* now raised important issues about

27. *Id.* at 1347.

28. David W. Neubauer, *Judicial Process: Law, Courts, and Politics in the United States,* 2d ed. (Fort Worth, Tex.: Harcourt Brace College Publishers, 1997), 441–47.

29. 478 U.S. 186 (1986). The Court had heard another case involving gay and lesbian plaintiffs, *Hurley v. Irish-American Gay, Lesbian and Bisexual Group of Boston,* 515 U.S. 557 (1995), before *Romer,* but *Hurley* is more fairly characterized as a First Amendment case than a gay rights case.

whether voters could limit the ability of *any* group to lobby for civil rights or affirmative action laws.

Although much was at stake, no one knew what the Court would do. The plaintiffs' "equal political participation" argument was sufficiently novel outside of a racial context that it was impossible to tell how the Court would react to it. During oral argument, Justice Scalia aggressively grilled Dubofsky on that issue and appeared to back her into a logical corner. Scalia asked if the citizens of Colorado could use the state referendum process to repeal a particular city's gay rights ordinance. Dubofsky had to concede that they could. Scalia then pointed out it would produce a bizarre "ping pong game" if the Colorado voters could repeal local laws but could not prohibit a city from simply passing the same law again. The city could keep passing the law over and over again and the Colorado voters would have to keep repealing it over and over again. In the flurry of questioning, Dubofsky was never really able to focus on or respond to Scalia's point.

Ultimately the Court neither rejected nor accepted the "equal political participation" argument. The six-justice majority (which did not include Justice Scalia) simply stated that it was upholding the permanent injunction, "but on a rationale different from that adopted by the State Supreme Court."[30] The Court held that there was no rational basis for Amendment 2 and therefore struck it down. While the decision was cause for enthusiastic celebration by gays, lesbians, and their supporters, no one knows what the long-term consequence of the Court's decision will be. Indeed, few understand exactly how the Court ended up deciding that there is no rational basis for Amendment 2 in the first place. Since both of the Colorado courts had applied strict scrutiny, they had not even considered whether a rational basis existed for Amendment 2. Thus, rather than reviewing the conclusions of the Colorado courts, the Supreme Court, sitting in Washington, D.C., four years after the vote on Amendment 2, took it upon itself to make both the initial and the final determination of whether the Colorado voters had a rational reason for voting for Amendment 2.

To understand how the Court reached the conclusion that the voters had no rational reason for voting for Amendment 2, we must step back and take another look at the rational-basis test and the three-tiered framework. We saw in the previous chapters that the Court has not been able to apply the criteria for who qualifies as a suspect class in a fair or objective manner. For example, we have seen that the courts have applied the "political powerlessness" test to gays and lesbians in a far more exacting manner than they have to women or other protected groups. What we will see now is

30. *Romer,* 517 U.S. at 626.

that the Supreme Court has applied the rational-basis test just as inconsistently as it has applied strict scrutiny.

The Supreme Court and "Second Order" Rational Basis

Up until now, we have looked at the rational-basis test as though it were a single test. The courts will uphold a law under this deferential test so long as there is any possible rational basis for the law. This is the way the test is always stated by the Supreme Court. *In reality, however, the rational-basis test has an unacknowledged sibling, referred to by Justice Thurgood Marshall as "second order" rational-basis review.*[31] This test is far less deferential than the usual rational-basis test and seems to be similar to intermediate or even strict scrutiny. But the Supreme Court has never explicitly acknowledged the existence of this test and has therefore never spelled out exactly what the standard is. However, the Court sometimes applies this stricter test even as it claims to be applying the far tamer version of the rational-basis test.

Perhaps the development of this unacknowledged yet powerful form of judicial scrutiny was inevitable. As we have seen, the three-tiered framework is extremely inflexible. A class either is or is not a beneficiary of enhanced judicial scrutiny. A right either is or is not "fundamental." If a law discriminates on the basis of a classification that is not suspect or quasi-suspect, and it does not violate a fundamental right, the Court must apply the rational-basis test. No matter how harsh the law is, the Court must uphold it so long as it has any rational basis. But the Court has found it difficult to abide such results. Thus, the three-tiered framework's formal inflexibility in theory has led to judicial unpredictability in fact. The three-tiered framework requires the courts to permit discrimination against any group that does not constitute a suspect or quasi-suspect class (assuming that no fundamental right has been violated) so long as the government can articulate *any* rational basis for the discrimination or exclusion. However, when such laws violate the justices' sense of fairness, they have been unable to resist the temptation to silently raise the level of scrutiny they apply to certain laws.

The case of *City of Cleburne v. Cleburne Living Center*[32] is a good example of application of the "second order" rational-basis test. In *Cleburne*, the Supreme Court invalidated a city zoning ordinance that prevented the plaintiffs from building a group home for the mentally retarded. Since

31. *City of Cleburne v. Cleburne Living Center*, 473 U.S. 432, 459–60 (1985) (Marshall, J., concurring).
32. 473 U.S. 432 (1985).

the mentally retarded are not a suspect class, and living in a group home is not a fundamental right, the Court could apply only the rational-basis test to the ordinance. The Court found that there was no rational basis for denying a permit for the group home.

Yet, the law was surely not "irrational," despite its harsh effect on the mentally retarded. As Justice Marshall pointed out in his concurring opinion, the majority ignored the city's "legitimate concerns for fire hazards [and] the serenity of the neighborhood."[33] Indeed, in a case called *Village of Belle Terre v. Boraas*,[34] similar considerations had led the Court to uphold a municipal zoning ordinance restricting land use to single-family dwellings. (The apparent purpose of the law was to keep out, among other groups, college fraternities.) Whatever else may have been wrong with the ordinance in *Cleburne*, it was not irrational.

The *Cleburne* Court stated that it was inappropriate to single out the mentally retarded because other types of group houses might also disrupt the serenity of the neighborhood. However, as Justice Marshall pointed out, courts ordinarily make this type of argument only when they are applying heightened scrutiny. Under the normal rational-basis test, the government can deal with problems "one step at a time," meaning that the government can deal with problems that are perceived to be pressing at the moment, even if it is ignoring other similar problems. For example, a town could ban jet skis to avoid noise problems even if it did not ban other noisy recreational vehicles. The rational-basis test is designed to be deferential to this sort of legislative judgment even if a law arbitrarily deals with only one aspect of a problem.

Looking at *Belle Terre* and *Cleburne* together, we see that the Court has chosen to protect the mentally retarded much more than it protects college fraternities. Towns can zone out fraternities because they fear disruptions, but they cannot zone out group homes for the mentally retarded for the same reasons. A number of scholars have observed that, in *Cleburne* (and in a variety of other cases), the Court applied a stricter level of scrutiny than it described.[35]

Of course there may be good reasons to grant extra protection to the mentally retarded. They are politically vulnerable, and many people have

---

33. *Cleburne*, 473 U.S. at 458 (Marshall, J., concurring). Marshall concurred in the majority opinion with regard to striking down the application of the ordinance in the case before the Court, but argued that the ordinance was unconstitutional on its face.

34. 416 U.S. 1 (1974).

35. Harry N. Hirsch, *A Theory of Liberty: The Constitution and Minorities* (New York: Routledge, 1992), 229; Laurence H. Tribe, *American Constitutional Law*, 2d ed. (Mineola, N.Y.: Foundation Press, 1988), 1444.

irrational negative reactions to them. Yet, as discussed in chapter 3, the Court has long since stopped creating new protected classes. Thus, the Court has adopted the expedient approach of formally adhering to the deferential rational-basis test while applying a stricter test: the "second order" rational basis test.

The Supreme Court has silently applied this test on other occasions as well. In *USDA v. Moreno*,[36] the Court considered a law limiting food-stamp eligibility to "families," which were defined as households in which all the individuals are related to one another. Ostensibly applying the rational-basis test, the Court struck down the law. The Court found that "the legislative history . . . indicates that that [law] was intended to prevent so-called 'hippies' and 'hippie communes' from participating in the food stamp program." In language that would later prove vital in the *Romer* case, the Court stated: "If . . . 'equal protection of the laws' means anything, it must at the very least mean that a bare congressional desire to harm a politically unpopular group cannot constitute a *legitimate* governmental interest."[37]

This language is more emotive than analytical. Is a determination that families should be prioritized over "hippie communes" in distributing antipoverty resources the same thing as "a bare desire to harm" hippies? Social Security will pay survivor benefits to the surviving member of a married couple but not to the surviving member of an unmarried couple, regardless of actual financial dependence. Does this demonstrate a bare desire to harm unmarried couples? Further, the government had defended the law by arguing that households of unrelated individuals have less stable membership than households of people who are related to one another. With more people coming and going it would be harder to detect fraudulent use of the food stamp program. This argument certainly appears strong enough to justify the law under the deferential version of the rational-basis test, but the Court nevertheless invalidated the law.

One can see how stringent the Court's actual level of review was in *Cleburne* and *Moreno* by comparing those cases to a case in which the Court applied the rational-basis test in the more traditional manner. In *Heller v. Doe*,[38] the Court upheld a Kentucky law that granted the mentally retarded less protection against involuntary commitment than it granted to the mentally ill. The *Heller* Court began its analysis by stating that the legislature "need 'not actually articulate at any time the purpose or rationale sup-

36. 413 U.S. 528 (1973).
37. *Moreno*, 413 U.S. at 534 (emphasis in original).
38. 509 U.S. 312 (1993).

porting its classification.'"[39] The Court continued, "Instead, a classification 'must be upheld against equal protection challenge if there is *any reasonably conceivable set of facts* that could provide a rational basis for the classification.'"[40] Further, "A State, moreover, *has no obligation to produce evidence to sustain the rationality of a statutory classification.*"[41] The Court added that "a legislative choice . . . *may be based on rational speculation unsupported by evidence or empirical data.*"[42] Furthermore, "the burden is on the one attacking the legislative arrangement to negate *every conceivable basis* which might support it."[43] Finally, and this language, while less dramatic, is perhaps the most crucial: "courts are compelled under rational basis review to accept a legislature's generalizations even when there is an imperfect fit between means and ends."[44]

Under this highly deferential test, the Kentucky law was of course upheld by the Court. It is extremely difficult to understand how the laws at issue in *Cleburne* and *Moreno* could have been struck down if the Court were genuinely applying such a deferential standard. In *Cleburne* the city argued that a group home for the retarded threatened public serenity and safety. Under the rational-basis test, the legislature need not empirically prove this. If the legislature believes that the mentally retarded are more likely than others to be loud or disruptive in any way, these are not determinations to be second-guessed by the courts. Nor need they be the original reasons the law was passed. As long as any conceivable set of facts can rationally justify any conceivable (and legitimate) purpose for the law, then the law passes the rational-basis test. Similarly, the standard articulated by the *Heller* Court should have forbidden the Court from disputing Congress's assertion in *Moreno* that it is more difficult to detect welfare fraud in households of unrelated individuals because such households have a higher turnover rate than households of related individuals.

Perhaps most importantly, the test articulated in *Heller* says the Court cannot strike down a law merely because the law's means are not tightly related to its ends. It is not enough to challenge a law by saying that other people besides the mentally retarded can be disruptive or that it might be

39. *Heller*, 509 U.S. at 320 (quoting *Nordlinger v. Hahn*, 505 U.S. 1, 15 (1992)).

40. *Id.* at 320 (quoting *FCC v. Beach Communications*, 508 U.S. 307, 313 (1993)) (emphasis added).

41. *Heller*, 509 U.S. at 320 (emphasis added).

42. *Id.* (quoting *Beach Communications*, 508 U.S. at 315) (emphasis added).

43. *Id.* (quoting *Lehnhausen v. Lake Shore Auto Parts*, 410 U.S. 356, 364 (1973)) (emphasis added).

44. *Heller*, 509 U.S. at 320.

difficult to detect fraud in households other than those with unrelated individuals living in them.

Quite clearly, the Supreme Court is cheating. It is applying two very different tests while claiming to apply only one. This type of cheating has serious consequences. The effect of *Cleburne* is to grant the mentally retarded a substantive right to live in a group home in a neighborhood or city that opposes their presence. Yet by striking down the law as "irrational," the Court sets out no legal standards by which other groups can assert a similar claim. Thus, if a city were to apply *Belle Terre*–type zoning ordinances in a way that excluded gay and lesbian couples, the lower courts would have no guidance as to which standard of rationality to apply. Since the rational-basis test has two versions, one strong and one weak, gays and lesbians are left to the sympathy of the judiciary if they challenge such exclusions. If the courts apply the rational-basis test with *Cleburne*-like rigor, gays and lesbians are likely to win. If the courts apply the rational-basis test in its more deferential form, gays and lesbians will lose. Yet, by refusing to acknowledge that *Cleburne* veered from the articulated rational-basis test, the Court has given the lower courts no guidance as to when they should do the same. Thus, gays and lesbians are forced to appeal to the sympathy of judges rather than to any legal principle.

The Majority Opinion in *Romer v. Evans*

It appears that the Court used the rigorous version of the rational-basis test in *Romer*. In fact, in its majority opinion the Court repeatedly flirted with the idea of explicitly applying some form of heightened scrutiny to Amendment 2, but it never quite did so. The majority stated that Amendment 2 "is unprecedented in our jurisprudence"[45] and hinted that the Amendment 2's very novelty might justify a heightened level of scrutiny: "The absence of precedent for Amendment 2 is itself instructive; '[d]iscriminations of an unusual character especially suggest careful consideration to determine whether they are obnoxious to the constitutional provision.'"[46]

The majority also stated, "It is not within our constitutional tradition to enact laws of this sort. Central both to the idea of the rule of law and to our own Constitution's guarantee of equal protection is the principle that government and each of its parts remain open on impartial terms to all who seek its assistance. . . . A law declaring that in general it shall be more

45. *Romer v. Evans,* 517 U.S. at 633.
46. *Id.*

difficult for one group of citizens than for all others to seek aid from the government is itself a denial of equal protection of the laws in the most literal sense."[47] Thus, it appeared that the Court was going to follow the lead of the Colorado courts and subject Amendment 2 to heightened scrutiny because it denied gays and lesbians equal political opportunity to fight for laws that protect them from discrimination.

But it turned out that this language merely set a mood rather than any actual legal standard. The Court held that the appropriate standard for reviewing Amendment 2 is the rational-basis test and it took pains to state the test in the usual deferential manner:

> The Fourteenth Amendment's promise that no person shall be denied the equal protection of the laws must coexist with the practical necessity that most legislation classifies for one purpose or another, with resulting disadvantage to various groups or persons. We have attempted to reconcile the principle with the reality by stating that, if a law neither burdens a fundamental right nor targets a suspect class, we will uphold the legislative classification so long as it bears a rational relation to some legitimate end.[48]

This deferential language turned out to be quite misleading. As it did in *Cleburne* and *Moreno*, the Court set out one standard and proceeded to apply a far stricter one. The Court held that Amendment 2's "sheer breadth is so discontinuous with the reasons offered for it that the amendment seems inexplicable by anything but animus toward the class it affects; it [therefore] lacks a rational relationship to legitimate state interests."[49]

The Court repeatedly emphasized the theme that Amendment 2 could be understood only as an irrational act of hostility to gays and lesbians. Quoting *Moreno*, it repeated the warning that "a bare . . . desire to harm a politically unpopular group cannot constitute a *legitimate* governmental interest."[50] But the majority gave virtually no support for its conclusion that Amendment 2 could be understood only as an act of animus. As discussed in chapter 5, people voted for Amendment 2 for a number of reasons, the most important of which may have been the fear that gays and lesbians were receiving "special rights" unavailable to others. Both sides of the debate over Amendment 2 agreed that the "special rights" argument and concern that gays and lesbians might eventually benefit from affirmative action were at least as important to the voters as was "animus."

47. *Id.*
48. *Id.* at 631 (citations omitted).
49. *Id.* at 632.
50. *Id.* at 634 (quoting *Moreno*, 413 U.S. at 534) (emphasis in original).

Nonetheless, the Court held that Amendment 2 was irrational because it "singled out" a specific group for "disfavored legal status." Yet, many laws do exactly that. Laws that discriminate against illegitimate children single them out for disfavored legal status. While the Supreme Court initially held that discrimination against illegitimate persons fails the rational-basis test, it later conceded that it was applying a stricter test. It is now widely acknowledged that laws disadvantaging illegitimates are subject to the intermediate level of scrutiny, not rational-basis scrutiny.[51]

Perhaps the most striking aspect of the opinion in *Romer* is how little attention the Supreme Court paid to the arguments Colorado gave for Amendment 2's rationality. As noted, the Colorado courts had applied strict scrutiny to Amendment 2. Therefore, the Colorado courts had never ruled on whether there was a rational basis for the amendment. However, the Colorado courts had acknowledged that there were several significant purposes served by Amendment 2. The courts ruled that these purposes were not enough to pass strict scrutiny because either the purposes were not "compelling" or Amendment 2 was not "narrowly tailored" to serve those purposes that could be considered compelling. However, the Supreme Court was applying only the rational-basis test. It should have upheld Amendment 2 if the amendment was only loosely related to any legitimate state purpose.

But the Supreme Court declined to even *mention* many of the legitimate purposes of Amendment 2 that had been acknowledged by the Colorado courts. Colorado argued that gay rights laws could force religious individuals and institutions to accept gay and lesbian tenants and employees and that not all of the gay rights laws in Colorado have religious exemptions. The Colorado Supreme Court correctly held that Amendment 2 was not narrowly tailored to achieve this goal. Religious liberty could be preserved through a narrower constitutional amendment requiring religious-conscience exemptions for all gay rights laws.[52] This is a sensible argument when a court is applying strict scrutiny. However, the rational-basis test does not require that the law be narrowly tailored to achieve its purpose. It requires only that the law be rationally related to that purpose.

Colorado also argued that protecting homosexuality the same way the law protects race and gender might eventually dilute or undermine public support for traditional civil rights. At trial, Colorado presented several witnesses to support this point, including former members of the Col-

---

51. The Court's treatment of laws that disadvantage illegitimate children is discussed in chapter 3.

52. *Evans*, 882 P.2d at 1342–43.

orado Civil Rights Division and the Colorado Civil Rights Commission. The trial court ruled that, because this concern was based on speculation rather than hard evidence, it could not pass strict scrutiny.[53] Yet it is far from clear why this concern cannot be considered a rational basis for Amendment 2. The fact that a concern is speculative does not make it irrational. The Supreme Court failed to even mention this argument or discuss why the Court was rejecting it as irrational.

Colorado also argued that Amendment 2 served the purpose of assuring that the state did not send the message that it was endorsing homosexuality. The Colorado Supreme Court held that legally protecting gays and lesbians did not necessarily amount to an endorsement of homosexuality.[54] This is no doubt correct. Yet there is a world of difference between saying that protection of certain characteristics does not *necessarily* amount to endorsement of those characteristics and saying that it is *irrational* to believe that protection might be construed as endorsement. It would not be irrational for voters to reject, for example, a law protecting the medical use of marijuana because they feared it *might* be construed as endorsing marijuana use more generally. Again, the Supreme Court declined to even mention or discuss this argument, even though the Court was supposedly applying only the rational-basis test to Amendment 2.

Obviously, the Supreme Court was actually applying a test far stricter than rational-basis scrutiny. Although the Colorado courts were applying strict scrutiny and the Supreme Court was ostensibly applying the rational-basis test, the Supreme Court was no more deferential to the judgment of the Colorado voters than were the Colorado courts. There is no indication of why the Court chose to apply this stricter form of rational-basis scrutiny. In fact, a major point of this chapter is that there are no standards at all to restrict the Court's discretion. Therefore, it seems reasonable to assume that Amendment 2 simply struck the Court as unfair to gays and lesbians, much as the City of Cleburne's zoning ordinance struck the Court as being unfair to the mentally retarded.

One reaction to this might be to shrug one's shoulders and simply say "so what?" If the result is "right," why worry about whether the reasoning is defensible or whether the Court is actually applying the deferential legal standard it claims to be applying? After all, many scholars, particularly in political science, believe that the Supreme Court's decisions are influenced primarily by the justices' "attitudes" rather than by legal precedent.[55]

But there are important reasons to be concerned about the Court's

53. *Evans* (trial court opinion), at p. C-9 of Colorado's cert. petition.
54. *Evans*, 882 P.2d at 1347.
55. Segal and Spaeth, *Attitudinal Model.*

sloppy reasoning in *Romer*. While the Supreme Court's decision was widely viewed as a victory for gay and lesbian rights, it is a victory that is narrow and perhaps Pyrrhic. While *Romer* is something of a breakthrough for gays and lesbians, the case really represents a change of sentiment rather than a change in law. Gays and lesbians are still at the bottom of the equal protection hierarchy. The big change from *Bowers* is that the Court spoke of gays and lesbians as a "politically unpopular group,"[56] rather than as a collection of individuals like drug users or prostitutes who happen to engage in certain "immoral" practices. This is a substantial advance for gays and lesbians.

Yet, by formally adhering to rational-basis scrutiny, the Court left gays and lesbians at the mercy of judges' sentiments about fairness and morality. *Romer* sends the signal to lower-court judges that they may have a freer hand to strike down antigay laws that happen to seem unfair to them by silently raising the level of scrutiny applied to those laws. This is not constitutional protection—it leaves gays and lesbians at the whim of the judiciary. When gays and lesbians are denied custody of their own children, denied security clearance, banned from military service, prohibited from serving as foster or adoptive parents or from operating day care centers, or banned from working at the FBI simply because they are homosexual,[57] they can only hope that the particular judges who hear their cases happen to consider that treatment unfair. Most often, they have not.

When a law discriminates against racial minorities, women, illegitimate children, or even white men, these groups are *entitled* to a substantial degree of constitutional protection. Gays and lesbians are still entitled to nothing.[58]

By silently increasing the level of scrutiny in *Romer* the Court failed in its most important role, that of chief interpreter of the Constitution. In his concurrence in *Cleburne*, Justice Marshall eloquently explained why the quiet application of heightened scrutiny in certain cases undermines the rule of law:

> The refusal to acknowledge that something more than minimum rationality review is at work here is, in my view, unfortunate in at least two respects. The suggestion that the traditional rational-

56. The Court was quoting *USDA v. Moreno*, 413 U.S. 528, 534 (1973).

57. See, e.g., *Bottoms v. Bottoms*, 457 S.E.2d 102, 109 (Va. 1995) (child custody); *High Tech Gays v. Defense Industrial Security Clearance Office*, 895 F.2d 563 (9th Cir. 1990) (security clearance); *Opinion of the Justices*, 530 A.2d 21 (N.H. 1987) (foster parents, adoptive parents, day care centers); *Padula v. Webster*, 822 F.2d 97 (D.C. Cir. 1987) (FBI).

58. Indeed, just as this book was going to press, the Supreme Court demonstrated just how narrow *Romer's* holding actually is. In *Equality Foundation of Greater Cincinnati v. Cincinnati*, No. 97-1795 (Oct. 13, 1998), the Court let stand an amendment to Cincinnati's city charter that is virtually identical to Colorado's Amendment 2 but operates on a city-wide level rather than a state-wide level.

basis test allows this sort of searching inquiry creates precedent
for this Court and lower courts to subject economic and commercial classifications to similar and searching "ordinary" rational-
basis review—a small and regrettable step backward to the days
of *Lochner v. New York. Moreover, by failing to articulate the factors that
justify today's "second-order" rational basis review, the Court provides
no principled foundation for determining when more searching inquiry
is to be invoked. Lower courts are thus left in the dark on this important question, and this Court remains unaccountable for its decisions
employing, or refusing to employ, a particularly searching judicial
scrutiny.*[59]

Thus, in many ways the Court's decision in *Romer* is a defeat for both
sides of the gay rights debate. The decision confirms that laws disadvantaging gays and lesbians are still subject to mere rational-basis review.
Therefore, when gays and lesbians challenge discriminatory laws they
have no legal principle to invoke on their own behalf. They must hope that
their case seems sympathetic enough to the judges hearing the case that
they choose to apply the *Cleburne / Moreno / Romer* version of the rational-
basis test. Meanwhile, those who seek to pass laws that condemn or discourage homosexuality are also in a difficult position. They are left to hope
that whatever laws they seek to pass are not struck down under the "second order" rational-basis test.

Thus, after years of litigation and no less than five written judicial opinions
plus dissents, the *Romer* case has left the law of equal protection even
murkier than before. It is still unknown whether there is such a thing as a
fundamental right to equal political participation. Further, the Court still
uses "second order" rational-basis scrutiny without acknowledging its existence.

Any nonsuspect group seeking equal protection of the laws is con-
fronted with highly indeterminate legal terrain:

(1) Although the formal law states that groups with certain characteristics such as a history of discrimination and political vulnerability will be
considered suspect classes, the unacknowledged fact is that no new suspect classes will be created for the foreseeable future.

(2) Although the formal law states that there is one rational-basis test,
there are in fact two completely different tests. As this situation is unacknowledged, there are no legal standards whatsoever to determine or

59. *City of Cleburne v. Cleburne Living Center*, 473 U.S. 432, 459–60 (1985) (Marshall, J., concurring) (emphasis added).

even guide the courts as to which standard to apply in what situation. Therefore it is impossible for any group to make a legal or constitutional argument that it has a right to be protected under the stricter standard. It must simply hope that those with power, that is, members of the judiciary, look upon its situation with sufficient sympathy that they choose to apply the higher standard.

(3) Although the equal protection clause protects something called "fundamental rights," the Supreme Court has never explained how these rights are derived. The Supreme Court declined to even comment on the Colorado Supreme Court's determination that there is a right to equal political participation.

This is not equal protection of the laws. It is the very opposite of equal protection. It is a loose conglomeration of stated legal principles that are, in fact, ignored, and unstated de facto rules that allow courts to apply different standards to different groups at different times based on judicial sentiment rather than judicial reason. The courts can do better than this. They can create legal rules that treat people equally and allow for a modicum of judicial rationality and accountability. The last chapter of this book asks how the law of equal protection might be so reformed.

PART THREE

Moving Forward: A New Direction for Equal Protection

Moving Away from Class-Based Analysis

This chapter suggests some possible directions for reform of equal protection jurisprudence. It looks at approaches that have been suggested by various scholars and jurists and then outlines an alternative approach, which builds on some of these earlier reform proposals. But it should be emphasized that the purpose here is to stimulate and expand the discussion, not to try to settle the law. The goal is not to create a full-blown scheme, which would be impossible to do in any single book, much less in the final chapter of a book. Rather, it is to give the reader a sense of the debate so far and to encourage the future debate to take seriously the idea that there are possible alternatives to class-based, or even classification-based, equal protection.

All of the proposals discussed here reject the class-based three-tiered framework. This is because the framework is a failure on many levels. We have seen that the class-based approach has not been applied in a fair or even coherent way and has contributed to a political discourse in which various groups are pitted against one other in what is perceived as a zero-sum battle for "special rights." These problems cannot be fixed by tinkering with the tiers.

Searching for an Alternative

The serious problems with the three-tiered framework have led many people to search for an alternative approach to equal protection. Justice Stevens suggested one such alternative in his concurring opinion in *Cleburne*. He argued that all legislation should be reviewed under a slightly less deferential version of the rational-basis test:

> "I am inclined to believe that what has become known as the [tiered] analysis of equal protection claims does not describe a completely logical method of deciding cases, but rather is a method the Court has employed to explain decisions that actually apply a single standard in a reasonably consistent fashion." . . . In my own approach to these cases, I have always asked myself

whether I could find a "rational basis" for the classification at issue. The term "rational," of course, includes a requirement that an
impartial lawmaker could logically believe that the classification would serve a legitimate public purpose that transcends
the harm to the members of the disadvantaged class. Thus the
word "rational"—for me at least—includes elements of legitimacy and neutrality that must always characterize the performance of the sovereign's duty to govern impartially.[1]

While this approach has the advantages of simplicity and clarity, it is
probably unworkable for several reasons. Most significantly, it is not a suitable test for a pluralist society such as the United States. In a pluralist society, laws are the result of group competition in the legislative sphere. The
resulting law need not be rational or neutral. Indeed, the law need not have
a particular purpose at all beyond being a satisfactory compromise among
various competing interest groups: "Public choice theory challenges the
assumption that a statute even has a purpose to be identified and analyzed.
Legislatures are viewed as places where special interests trade among
themselves in pursuit of their own agendas. With the legislative process
characterized by agenda manipulation, strategic voting and logrolling, the
end product is simply a result embodying no single purpose or motivating
force."[2]

Searching for a rational basis for a particular piece of legislation is often
a fruitless exercise. Suppose Congress decides to grant a subsidy to wheat
farmers but not to rice farmers. Suppose further that it is well known that
this subsidy was procured not through rational argument but through
generous campaign donations to key senators. While there may be no
rational reason for the subsidy and while the subsidy may cause great
hardship to unsubsidized rice farmers, such a law is clearly not unconstitutional. As will be discussed below, without some substantive principle to
distinguish between issues such as farm subsidies and issues such as employment discrimination, a judicial insistence on rationality would make
the Court busy indeed.

Stevens's approach is flawed for other reasons. He argues:

The Court must be especially vigilant in evaluating the rationality
of any classification involving a group that has been subjected to
a "tradition of disfavor [because] a traditional classification is

---

1. *Cleburne,* 473 U.S. at 452 (Stevens, J., concurring) (quoting *Craig v. Boren,* 429 U.S. 190,
212 (1976) (Stevens, J., concurring)).
2. Don Welch, "Legitimate Government Purposes and State Enforcement of Morality,"
University of Illinois Law Review 1993: 81 (citations omitted).

more likely to be used without pausing to consider its justification than is a newly created classification. Habit, rather than analysis, makes it seem acceptable and natural to distinguish between male and female, alien and citizen, legitimate and illegitimate; for too much of our history there was the same inertia in distinguishing between black and white. But that sort of stereotyped reaction may have no rational relationship—other than pure prejudicial discrimination—to the stated purpose for which the classification is being made."[3]

It is comforting to think that race and gender discrimination is invariably based entirely on "old habits" and is therefore irrational. Unfortunately, one of the very reasons such discrimination can be so hard to eradicate is that discrimination can have a rational basis. It may be, for example, that the customers of a particular business prefer dealing with women rather than men, or vice versa.

As Cass Sunstein has pointed out, "the claim of irrationality disguises the necessary moral argument" as to why society should tolerate certain generalizations but not others.[4] Society bans gender discrimination because it has made the moral choice that it is wrong to limit people's professional opportunities based on their gender. The standard of rationality, in and of itself, has no substance. Peter Westen argues that the rational-basis test is nothing more than a presumption that "like cases be treated alike" unless there are "rational reasons for treating people differently."[5] He avers that such a principle is no principle at all: "As soon as any weight is put on this principle it seems to collapse into the shattering triviality that cases are alike, morally or in any other respect, unless they are different."[6] The rational-basis test has no way to deal with the fact that it is often perfectly rational to *generalize*. Even the vilest forms of discrimination can have at least some rational basis. If some groups, as a whole, commit greater amounts of violent crime than others, then it may be rational for a town to try to exclude members of that group if crime control is the town's highest priority. There is a difference between that which is morally wrong and that which is irrational. Failure to treat people as individuals may be morally wrong, but it is not necessarily irrational. A central challenge of

3. *Cleburne*, 473 U.S. at 453 n. 6 (Stevens, J., concurring) (quoting *Mathews v. Lucas*, 427 U.S. 495, 520–21 (1976) (Stevens, J., dissenting)).

4. Cass R. Sunstein, "Homosexuality and the Constitution," *Indiana Law Journal* 70 (1994): 5.

5. Peter Westen, "The Empty Idea of Equality," *Harvard Law Review* 95 (1982): 547.

6. *Ibid.*, 547 n. 30, quoting Don Locke, "The Trivializability of Universality," *Philosophy Review* 77 (1968): 25.

equal protection doctrine is to demarcate when it is permissible for the government to act on generalizations. To use an example from the previous chapter, why may a city act on the generalization that college fraternities will often disturb public tranquility but not act on the very same generalization with regard to a home for the mentally retarded? Since the rational-basis test gives no standards for distinguishing between permissible and impermissible generalizations, even the most scrupulous judge has nothing to fall back on but his or her own sympathies for the plaintiffs or sense of moral judgement.

So the standard of rationality is superficially tempting but ultimately useless. Other commentators have suggested that the Constitution forbids legal distinctions that are "arbitrary." During oral argument in *Romer v. Evans*, Justice Sandra Day O'Connor suggested that Amendment 2 would authorize libraries to bar gays and lesbians from using their facilities. Hadley Arkes, in the *Weekly Standard*, took O'Connor to task for this suggestion on the ground that such an action by the library would be arbitrary:

> It was jarring, to say the least, to find Justice O'Connor utterly obtuse on this matter during the argument before the Court. She raised the prospect of a public library refusing to allow homosexuals to borrow books, and it appeared to her that Amendment 2 would allow "no relief from that" . . . [O'Connor is wrong because,] in the case of libraries and other public facilities, there may be a provision that bars discrimination on grounds that bear no connection to the service at hand.[7]

Unfortunately, excluding homosexuals from a library might not be arbitrary at all. For example, in *Sex, Art, and American Culture*, Camille Paglia states that the Yale library is (or least has been at times) a "hot spot" for gay sexual encounters.[8] Library administrators at public universities might respond to this by denying guest privileges to individuals whom they know to be gay. Would such an action be arbitrary? It would be hard to say. An administrator is presumably entitled to try to prevent sexual activity in the library, and an exclusionary policy bears a rational relationship to that goal.

This type of preventive action is only "arbitrary" in the sense that it does not treat people as individuals—it excludes an entire group of people on the basis of the rumored actions of a few. Yet the government is entitled to do exactly that, even when it causes great hardship to innocent people.

---

7. Hadley Arkes, "Gay Marriage and the Courts: *Roe v. Wade II?*" *Weekly Standard*, 20 November 1995, 38–39.

8. Camille Paglia, *Sex, Art, and American Culture: Essays* (New York: Vintage Books, 1992), 24.

For example, in *Weinberger v. Salfi*,[9] the Court allowed the government to deny social security benefits to a widow and her children by a previous marriage because she had been married to the deceased for less than nine months. The Social Security Administration had a blanket rule denying such benefits when the death occurred within nine months of the marriage. The purpose of the policy was to avoid sham marriages.

Of course such a policy can cause terrible hardship to innocent people. The government did not need to present evidence that the marriage was actually a sham. Nor did the government have to prove that sham marriages for the purpose of receiving social security benefits were a widespread problem. The situation in *Weinberger* is just as arbitrary as would be denying access to certain public facilities to gays and lesbians. In both cases the government is denying an important government benefit to broad groups of people based on speculation and generalizations, without any evidence that a particular individual has done anything wrong or that the benefits of the policy outweigh the harms. Yet, as *Weinberger* tells us, the government is allowed to act on broad-brush generalizations. This is seen in countless other Supreme Court cases, including *Massachusetts Board of Retirement v. Murgia*,[10] discussed in chapter 4, which held that a fifty-year-old police officer can be forced into retirement even if he or she is just as healthy and fit as younger officers.

Weinberger and *Murgia* uphold the right of the government to rely on arbitrary standards. (Thus, O'Connor may not be so "obtuse" after all.) The standard of arbitrariness is just as useless as the standard of irrationality because it provides no dividing line between permissible and impermissible generalizations. Further, one need not be convinced by the above arguments in order to reject standards such as "irrationality" and "arbitrariness" as the principal methods of evaluating equal protection claims. Even if such terms are not ultimately meaningless, they are, at a minimum, highly subjective. Applying these standards to all laws—welfare reform, the tax code, civil rights laws—would either hopelessly dilute equal protection jurisprudence or place almost unlimited discretion in the hands of judges. Are tax breaks for the wealthy "irrational"? Is the drinking age of twenty-one "arbitrary"?

Justice Brennan has suggested that the equal protection clause prohibits classifications that "reflect deep-seated prejudice rather than legislative rationality in pursuit of some legitimate objective."[11] Yet the term

---

9. 422 U.S. 749 (1975).
10. 427 U.S. 307 (1975).
11. *Plyler v. Doe*, 457 U.S. 202, 216 n. 14 (1982).

"prejudice" is no more helpful than terms such as "rational" or "arbitrary." *High Tech Gays v. Defense Industrial Security Clearance Office*[12] illustrates the uselessness of the term "prejudice." In this case a group called "High Tech Gays" challenged Department of Defense ("DOD") rules that instructed companies not to submit the names of gays and lesbians for Top Secret Security Clearance. The rule prevented gays and lesbians from holding jobs that required such clearance.

The DOD argued that even openly gay people might be subject to blackmail, since someone might threaten to "out" their former lovers. High Tech Gays countered that DOD could not point to a single known instance where this had happened, nor could the DOD present any evidence that homosexuals pose a greater security risk than heterosexuals. Nonetheless, the *High Tech* court held that the DOD's policy was rationally related to its objective of protecting classified material because gays are societal outcasts and might therefore be more willing to betray their country. The court noted that, in one espionage case, the person who committed espionage "was a homosexual and this fact interested the KGB handlers since the homosexual frequently is shunted by society and made to feel like a social outcast. Such a personality may seek to retaliate against a society that has placed him in this unenviable position. [He] was such a person and one of his first assignments on behalf of Soviet Intelligence was to spot other homosexuals in the American Community."[13]

The DOD did not have to demonstrate that gays and lesbians posed a greater security risk than others. It had to show only that it could rationally believe that homosexuals *might* be a greater security risk. Yet many groups might be an equally great security risk according to the DOD's theory. Many Chinese Americans, for example, have been victims of discrimination and stigma, but if the DOD automatically labeled all Chinese Americans as security risks this would be seen as prejudice. Why is it "prejudice" to assume that Chinese Americans might be resentful outcasts,

---

12. 895 F.2d 563 (9th Cir. 1990).

13. *High Tech Gays*, 895 F.2d at 575. Thus, the DOD argued that societal discrimination against homosexuals makes them more likely to "retaliate against society." As discussed in chapter 2, courts usually consider a history of discrimination against a group to be a factor *against* allowing further legal disadvantage to that group. The *High Tech* court, however, authorized a feedback loop of discrimination in which the possible resentment caused by discrimination against gays and lesbians makes it rational to doubt their good citizenship and therefore to further discriminate against them. While this "outcast" theory is at least as applicable to many racial, religious, and ethnic minorities as it is to gays and lesbians, there is no indication that the DOD automatically deemed individuals in any of these groups to be security risks. Since these groups are all suspect classes, the courts would have subjected any attempt to do so to strict scrutiny.

but "rational" to assume the very same thing about gays and lesbians? As Sunstein points out, referring to a policy as prejudiced merely hides the underlying moral argument. "We should think of the category of 'prejudice' as a placeholder for a complex moral argument: the term is usually a conclusion masquerading as an analytic device."[14]

Thus, each of the alternatives to the three-tiered framework discussed so far—the constitutional prohibition of laws that are (1) "irrational," (2) "arbitrary," or (3) "prejudiced"—demonstrate little or no utility. None of these terms provide an answer to a basic question of equal protection law—when may the government base its actions on generalizations? Each of these tests amounts to little more than an invitation for courts to superimpose their own sense of morality, sympathy, or good policy on the judgments of the other branches.

Another approach to equal protection was suggested by the constitutional law scholar Gerald Gunther in his famous 1972 foreword to the *Harvard Law Review*. Gunther suggests that the courts scrutinize the "goodness of fit" between legislative classifications and the purpose served by those classifications: "Stated most simply, [this proposal] would have the Court take seriously a constitutional requirement that has never been formally abandoned: that legislative means must substantially further legislative ends. The equal protection requirement that legislative classifications must have a substantial relationship to legislative purposes is, after all, essentially a more specific formulation of that general principle."[15] According to Gunther, his approach "would concern itself solely with means, not with ends."[16] The courts would no longer evaluate whether a governmental purpose is legitimate or compelling or important. "The yardstick for the acceptability of the means would be the purposes chosen by the legislatures, not the 'constitutional' interests drawn from the value perceptions of the Justices."[17]

Unfortunately, this approach is even less helpful than the others discussed so far. If taken seriously it would mean that all legislation would always be upheld since "every means is related to *some* end."[18] If equal protection is to mean anything, the courts must be willing to say that certain ends are illegitimate state goals. For example, antimiscegenation laws advance the goal of keeping the white race "pure." As Laurence Tribe ar-

14. Sunstein, "Homosexuality and the Constitution," 4.
15. Gunther, "Foreword," 20.
16. *Ibid.*, 21.
17. *Ibid.*
18. Welch, "Legitimate Government Purposes," 85.

gues, without judicial review of the legitimacy of legislative ends, "it would seem useless to demand and discover even the most perfect congruence between means and ends, for each law would provide its own indisputable fit: if the means chosen burdens one group and benefits another, then the means perfectly fit the ends of burdening just those whom the law disadvantages and benefitting just those whom it assists."[19] So for the equal protection clause to have any meaning, courts must assume that certain legislative goals, for example "a bare . . . desire to harm a politically unpopular group,"[20] are constitutionally illegitimate. Without such an assumption, all legislation, no matter how discriminatory, would pass constitutional muster.

Even branding certain legislative ends as illegitimate would not really strengthen Gunther's means-ends test. Even the most reprehensible forms of discrimination can substantially further legitimate state ends. For example, racially segregating schools serves the end of preventing interracial violence in the schools. Such an end is surely legitimate and segregation is an effective means of accomplishing it. In fact, given the seemingly intractable nature of racial violence, it might be the only way to completely avoid racial hate crimes in the public schools. The common-sense response to this argument is that racially segregated schools are unfair to African American children. They diminish their opportunity for an equal education by stigmatizing them, and, in all likelihood, saddling them with less-than-equal facilities. Segregated schools also diminish African American students' economic opportunities by socially isolating them from potential future business partners, employers, investors, and clients. Yet this common-sense response would require the courts to explicitly acknowledge that they are in the business of protecting certain substantive rights that they have heretofore been unwilling to recognize. For example, it would be easy to justify *Brown* if we said that the courts should acknowledge and protect a substantive right to equal educational opportunity. As discussed in chapter 2, the Warren Court actually based its decision in *Brown* on the importance of educational opportunity. It was the Burger Court that later reinterpreted *Brown* as a case protecting discrete and insular minorities.

So far, the Court has been willing to protect only a limited number of narrowly defined "fundamental" rights,[21] which do not include any right to equal educational opportunity. Justice Thurgood Marshall repeatedly

19. Tribe, *American Constitutional Law*, 955, quoted in Welch, "Legitimate Government Purposes," 86.

20. *Moreno*, 413 U.S. at 534.

21. See chapter 6 for a discussion of the concept of fundamental rights.

criticized the Court's narrow approach to protecting substantive rights under the equal protection clause. He often suggested that the Court should aggressively define and protect a broader array of rights. Before laying out my own reform proposals, I discuss Marshall's suggestions to provide background and comparison.

Justice Marshall and the Protection of Substantive Rights

Justice Thurgood Marshall long advocated a balancing approach to equal protection law. He first argued for such an approach in *Dandridge v. Williams*,[22] a case involving a family cap on payments under the federal Aid to Families with Dependent Children ("AFDC") program. The plaintiffs argued that the cap violated the equal protection clause because larger families received smaller payments per child than did smaller families. The Supreme Court held that there was no "fundamental right" to welfare payments and therefore applied the rational-basis test and upheld the law.

Marshall dissented. He argued that the dichotomy between a small number of fundamental rights (protected by strict scrutiny) and all other rights or interests (protected only by the rational-basis test) was too stark and simplistic. People have many interests, including the interest in a decent level of welfare support. The Court should move away from the "fundamental"/"not fundamental" dichotomy and in each case should balance the importance of the plaintiff's interest, be it in welfare benefits or in anything else, against the government's interest in the law at issue. So in *Dandridge*, for example, the Court should have balanced the government's interest in placing an overall family cap on AFDC against the interest a family has in receiving additional support for each new child regardless of the number of children. According to Marshall, "In determining whether or not a state law violates the Equal Protection Clause, we must consider the facts and circumstances behind the law, the interests which the State claims to be protecting, and the interests of those who are disadvantaged by the classification."[23] Marshall averred that such an approach would clarify rather than fundamentally change equal protection law: "This [balancing approach] is essentially what the Court has done in applying equal protection concepts in numerous cases, though the various aspects of the approach appear with a greater or lesser degree of clarity in particular cases."[24]

22. 397 U.S. 471 (1969).
23. *Dandridge*, 397 U.S. at 521 (Marshall, J., dissenting) (quoting *Williams v. Rhodes*, 393 U.S. 23, 30 (1968)).
24. *Dandridge*, 397 U.S. at 521 n. 15.

Marshall believed that equal protection law had to be made more flexible. The Court should examine laws and the groups they affect on a case-by-case basis and grant more protection to less powerful groups. For example, Marshall argued that the Court should give poor families more protection than it gives the business community because most businesses "have more than enough power to protect themselves in the legislative halls."[25]

While Marshall's ideas represented something of a break from the three-tiered framework, they bore many similarities to it. Marshall relied on the same political-process logic that underlies the class-based three-tiered framework. He argued that groups that are not powerful enough to protect themselves "in the legislative halls" should receive greater judicial protections than more politically powerful groups. Therefore, Marshall believed that under his system traditional suspect classes would still receive the greatest protection:

> Some classifications are so invidious that they should be struck down automatically absent the most compelling state interest, and by suggesting the limitations of strict-scrutiny analysis I do not mean to imply otherwise. The analysis should be accomplished, however, not by stratified notions of "suspect" classes and "fundamental" rights, but by individualized assessments of the particular classes and rights involved in each case. *Of course, the traditional suspect classes and fundamental rights would still rank at the top of the list of protected categories.*[26]

Marshall's approach is intriguing but it also has significant drawbacks. One problem is its continued reliance on "political powerlessness" as a trigger for more aggressive judicial review of a statute, although powerlessness would be measured on a sliding scale rather than as a dichotomous variable. As discussed in chapter 4, the Court is in a poor position to measure the political power of various socioeconomic, racial, religious, and other groups and, in fact, it specifically disclaimed the expertise to do so in *Regents of the University of California v. Bakke.*[27] Indeed, some have argued that measuring a group's political power is more of a normative question than an empirical one: "The category of political powerlessness looks like an inquiry into political science, but it really depends on some

25. *Id.* at 520.
26. *Massachusetts Board of Retirement v. Murgia*, 427 U.S. 307, 319 n. 1 (1975) (Marshall, J., dissenting) (emphasis added).
27. 438 U.S. 265 (1978). *Bakke* is discussed in chapter 4.

normative judgments about the legitimacy of the usual grounds for government action."[28]

Further, even if the Court could measure various groups' political power, the results might be quite different from what Marshall expected. Marshall assumed that under his approach African Americans and other traditional suspect classes would still be protected by the highest level of scrutiny. But racial minorities are hardly the most powerless groups in America.[29] In many contexts, African Americans are well able "to protect themselves in legislative halls." In many cities African Americans constitute a majority of the voting-age population. It hardly seems plausible to argue that they are unable to protect their own interests in the city halls of Detroit or Atlanta. On the national level, as of mid-1996 there were thirty-eight African American members of the House of Representatives, and African Americans head several cabinet departments. If Marshall's approach were adopted, African Americans might lose much of the protection against discrimination that they now have under the three-tiered framework.

Neither Justice Marshall nor other thinkers who continue to rely on the political-process rationale have come to grips with the fundamental problems of linking equal protection rights to membership in a "powerless" group. For example, John Hart Ely struggles with how to address legislation that discriminates against women. Women, of course, constitute the majority of the voting-age population. Accordingly, Ely is forced to conclude that legislation passed after the ratification of Nineteenth Amendment is perfectly constitutional no matter how blatantly the law discriminates against women: "[I]f women don't protect themselves from sex discrimination in the future, it won't be because they can't. It will rather be because for one reason or another—substantive disagreement or more likely the assignment of a low priority to the issue—they don't choose to. Many of us may condemn such a choice as benighted on the merits, but that is not a constitutional argument."[30] So if a state were to resuscitate laws such as those barring women from the practice of law or from working as bartenders,[31] in Ely's view this would not violate equal protection of the laws.

This example highlights the fundamental flaw with the political-process logic. *It loses sight of any notion of the equal protection clause as protect-*

---

28. Sunstein, "Homosexuality and the Constitution," 9.

29. Ackerman, "Beyond *Carolene Products*," 718–37.

30. Ely, *Democracy and Distrust*, 169–70.

31. See, respectively, *Bradwell v. Illinois*, 83 U.S. (16 Wall.) 130 (1873), and *Goesaert v. Cleary*, 335 U.S. 464 (1948), upholding the constitutionality of such restrictions.

ing individual rights. Ely is arguing that, since women are not powerless, discrimination against women who want to practice law is constitutional if their fellow women are willing to tolerate it. But why should a woman's right to practice law depend on what other women think? Virtually by definition, an individual's constitutional rights do not turn on the approval of the country as a whole, so why should they depend on the approval of one's "class," be that class women, African Americans, white males, or anybody else?

Thus, Marshall's reliance on political powerlessness presents a problem with his balancing test. A second problem with his test is related to the first—his test would be extremely intrusive on the democratic process. The poor are an exceptionally vulnerable class of people. This is why Marshall believed that the family cap on AFDC payments should be subjected to greater judicial scrutiny than laws that regulate more powerful business interests. Thus Marshall suggested that the Court subject laws affecting this class to a rigorous test balancing "the asserted state interest" furthered by the law against the "relative importance of the benefit" being denied to the poor.

Such an approach would make the Court the legislature of last resort on many, if not all, social welfare issues. In the contemporary debate, many advocates of the family cap argue that it will reduce poverty by breaking a cycle of welfare dependence. How is the Court supposed to factor this presumed benefit to society and to the poor into the analysis? Any balancing would require the Court to evaluate the probability of the program's success—a determination far outside the realm of judicial expertise.

In sum, while Marshall's balancing test is in some ways clearer and more coherent than the three-tiered framework, his approach suffers from two problems: (1) he relies on the same untenable "political-process" rationale that underlies the three-tiered framework, and (2) his approach would plunge the Court into areas of social policy beyond its expertise.

A Rights-Based System of Equal Protection

Any system of equal protection must deal with how the Court should vary its level of scrutiny from case to case. The Court cannot possibly apply the same level of scrutiny to all laws. If it applied strict or intermediate scrutiny to all laws it would virtually replace the legislature as the primary body that balances the burdens and benefits of various laws. If the Court applied rational-basis review to all laws, there would be very little protection against laws that deprive targeted groups of basic rights. Therefore, any system of equal protection cannot be monochromatic—it must allow the Court to vary the level of scrutiny from case to case.

If the Court is to move away from the class-based system while still varying the level of judicial review, the only alternative seems to be varying the level of review according to the type of *right* (as opposed to the type of class) affected by the law at issue. For example, the Court could subject laws that affect a person's right to an equal education to greater scrutiny than laws that affect a person's right to receive the vanity license plate of his or her choice.

How would a rights-based system work? There are many different ways such a system could be constructed. One possible approach was suggested in 1975 by J. Harvie Wilkinson in "The Supreme Court, the Equal Protection Clause, and the Three Faces of Constitutional Equality."[32] Wilkinson argues that the central question should be not *who* has been denied equality but rather *what kind* of equality has been denied. He argues that there are three basic categories of inequality that the Court has attempted to address: inequality of participation within the political process, inequality of competitive opportunity, and economic and material inequality.

While conceding that there is "some intermingling and overlap" among these categories, Wilkinson believes that they provide the best basis for varying the level of judicial review: the Court should apply the strictest level of scrutiny to issues of political equality, an intermediate balancing test to issues of equality of competitive opportunity, and minimal review to issues of economic and material inequality. I believe that Wilkinson's approach could provide the basis for a new system of equal protection that is not based on class. The remainder of this chapter sets out this approach, along with my own thoughts and suggested revisions.

Again, the following is intended as no more than a rough outline of what a reformed equal protection jurisprudence might look like. Constitutional doctrine evolves slowly and incrementally—it is the product of countless legal briefs, scholarly arguments, and ultimately, judicial decisions over long periods of time. So the purpose here is not to lay out a full-blown scheme. The purpose is merely to persuade readers that it would be fruitful to begin a discussion about how a rights-based equal protection jurisprudence might work and whether it would be a viable alternative to the current, deeply flawed, class-based system.

Political Equality

The Court already protects political equality to some degree under the rubric of fundamental rights. The Court has tried to ensure that the right to

32. *Virginia Law Review* 61 (1975): 945–1018.

vote is broadly available, striking down restrictions based on such things as military status and length of residency.[33] In *Baker v. Carr*,[34] the Court constitutionalized the principle of "one person, one vote." The Court has also protected the rights of candidates to appear on ballots, subject to reasonable regulations.[35]

Wilkinson would define the right to political equality more broadly than the Court has. For example, he disagrees with the Court's holding in *Gordon v. Lance*.[36] That case involved a state constitutional amendment providing that political subdivisions "may not incur bonded indebtedness or increase tax rates beyond those established by the [state] Constitution without the approval of 60% of the voters in a referendum election."[37] Wilkinson argues that this law violates political equality. It means that those who favor increased indebtedness or taxes are now at a permanent political disadvantage compared to those who oppose them.[38]

Wilkinson argues that the courts should grant the greatest protection to political equality because "courts have few greater duties in a democracy than to ensure an equal chance to influence government to those whose lives government so intimately affects."[39] For the same reason, I argue that the courts should also give maximum protection to access to the legal system. This would cover such things as right to counsel and right to a fair trial. A natural response to this argument might be, "But doesn't the Constitution already protect access to the legal system and the right to a fair trial?" The answer is in some ways yes and in some ways no. In fact, the class-based system of equal protection can deeply *undermine* a person's right to a fair trial. A discussion of the law of peremptory challenges illustrates the difference between the class-based system and the proposed rights-based system.

In a criminal trial both the state and the defendant have the right to exclude potential jurors "for cause" if there is any articulable reason to believe that the potential juror is biased. For example, if a potential juror is a relative of the defendant or admits to a personal dislike of or affection to-

33. Respectively, *Carrington v. Rash*, 380 U.S. 89 (1965); *Dunn v. Blumstein*, 405 U.S. 330 (1972).

34. 369 U.S. 186 (1962).

35. *Anderson v. Celebrezze*, 460 U.S. 780 (1983); *Williams v. Rhodes*, 393 U.S. 23 (1968).

36. 403 U.S. 1 (1971).

37. *Gordon*, 403 U.S. at 2.

38. Note that this argument would have no connection with the debate over Colorado's Amendment 2, since the amendment had no supermajority requirement—those in favor of gay rights legislation would have needed only the usual bare majority to rescind Amendment 2.

39. Wilkinson, "Three Faces of Constitutional Equality," 976.

ward the defendant, the defendant or the state can ask that the potential juror be excluded from the jury "for cause." Both the state and the defendant may make as many "for cause" challenges as they wish, so long as they can convince the judge that there is an objective reason to believe a potential juror may be biased against or in favor of the defendant. However, an experienced trial attorney may have a strong intuition that a particular potential juror is biased but the attorney might not be able to prove it. Therefore both the state and the defendant are entitled to a certain number of "peremptory challenges" that allow them to disqualify a potential juror without stating any reason for the exclusion. (Similar rules also apply to civil trials.)

In 1986 the Supreme Court held that the equal protection clause prohibits prosecutors from using racial factors in exercising their peremptory challenges.[40] Six years later, in *Georgia v. McCollum*,[41] the Court held that criminal defendants are also barred from using race as a factor in exercising peremptory challenges. These decisions are relatively straightforward applications of the three-tiered framework and the fact that race is a suspect classification.[42] Racial classifications are subject to strict scrutiny. Therefore a juror cannot be excluded on account of his or her race unless there is a "compelling state interest" in doing so.

Yet these decisions do not necessarily protect racial minorities from racial animus. Indeed, they may actually prevent minority defendants from protecting themselves from racial discrimination. For example, take a situation where a black man is accused of raping a white woman in a predominantly white county. The defendant might have good reason to fear an all-white jury.[43] If the jury selection process is race-neutral, there is a good chance he will have to face an all-white jury since the jury pool is predominantly white. The only way he can avoid this is to use many of his

40. *Batson v. Kentucky,* 476 U.S. 79 (1986).

41. 505 U.S. 42 (1992).

42. The dissent in *McCollum* argued that the defendant's attorney is not a state actor and is therefore not subject to the Constitution. The majority rejected this argument because the defendant is excluding people from the jury on account of their race and is exercising state power in doing so. The argument that the defendant's attorney is not a state actor is particularly difficult to make when the attorney is a public defender. It would be difficult to argue that the public defender's office could, for example, constitutionally exclude black and female attorneys on the ground that it is not a public actor. See *Branti v. Finkel,* 445 U.S. 507 (1980) (holding that the public defender is subject to the Constitution in making personnel decisions).

43. See A. Harris, "Race and Essentialism," *Stanford Law Review* 42 (1990): 600–601, for a discussion of rape law and the legal system as a tool for white oppression of African Americans.

peremptory challenges against white potential jurors. If he has twenty peremptory challenges,[44] by excluding white jurors he will have a substantial chance of avoiding an all-white jury even if only a small percentage of the county is nonwhite. Yet the Supreme Court has ruled that this is exactly what he may not do. Thus, we have a system of "equal protection" that cannot distinguish between a black defendant trying to avoid an all-white jury and the State of Mississippi forcing blacks to drink from segregated water fountains. According to the Supreme Court, there is no constitutional difference between the two situations.

We find ourselves in this situation because the three-tiered framework focuses solely on the issue of class or classification instead of looking at the substantive rights at issue. The right to sit on any particular jury is trivial compared to the right to a fair trial, especially when the defendant is accused of a serious crime. Yet the three-tiered framework does not analyze the severity of the injury—all race-based generalizations are equally unconstitutional unless they are narrowly tailored to further a compelling governmental purpose.

A rights-based approach would be most concerned with protecting the defendant's right to a fair trial. The three-tiered approach is too inflexible in its treatment of race and can therefore damage a person's right to a fair trial, whether that person is black or white. In his concurrence in *McCollum*, Justice Clarence Thomas reluctantly admits that the majority decision is dictated by precedent. However, he laments: "In effect, we have exalted the right of citizens to sit on juries over the rights of the criminal defendant, even though it is the defendant, not the jurors, who faces imprisonment or even death. At a minimum, I think that this inversion of priorities should give us pause."[45] Yet this "inversion of priorities" is inherent in the three-tiered framework, which focuses on classes and classifications rather than the nature of the right involved.

The Court next visited the issue of peremptory challenges in *J. E. B. v. Alabama ex rel. T. B.*[46] In that case, the Court held that gender is also an impermissible basis for exercising a peremptory challenge. In *J. E. B.* the Court spent very little time discussing the right to a fair trial. It held: "We have recognized that whether the trial is criminal or civil, potential jurors, as well as litigants, have an equal protection right to jury selection procedures that are free from state-sponsored group stereotypes rooted in, and reflective of, historical prejudice."[47]

---

44. This was the number allowed in *Georgia v. McCollum*.
45. *McCollum*, 505 U.S. at 62 (Thomas, J., concurring).
46. 511 U.S. 127 (1994).
47. *J. E. B.*, 511 U.S. at 128.

One thing the Court does not explain is why this principle is limited to race and gender. Is it fairer to exclude older jurors in an age discrimination case than it is to exclude female jurors in a gender discrimination case? Issues such as immutability and political powerlessness are irrelevant to whether the defendant's right to a fair trial is being jeopardized. If gay jurors are being excluded from a jury in an indecency case against a gay defendant, what difference does it make if gays as a group have political power or if homosexuality is immutable? The issue is whether such exclusions jeopardize the right to a fair trial. The defendant's right to a fair trial is the same, regardless of whether the defendant is black, gay, female, or elderly. A rights-based approach could shift the Court's focus to the crucial issue of assuring a fair trial and an unbiased jury.

Note that the rights-based approach does not dictate any particular result. No approach in the complex field of constitutional law can function like a computer program that spits out the constitutionally required result when it is fed the relevant facts. What is significant is that the rights-based approach focuses the Court on the issue of assuring a fair trial and frees the Court from the clumsy constitutional boxes and categories that have undermined this right.

Under the rights-based approach, the Court could seek to ensure an equal right to a fair trial in many different ways. It could eliminate peremptory challenges altogether, as Justice Marshall once suggested.[48] It could so limit the number of peremptory challenges that racial gerrymandering of juries becomes impractical. It could prohibit racially motivated peremptory challenges under circumstances where the case had strong undertones of racial animosity, and similarly protect gay jurors when that would help preserve the defendant's right to a fair trial.[49] The rights-based approach could move the Court past the three-tiered framework's boxes of classes and classifications.

The Right to Equal Competitive Opportunity

Wilkinson also argues for a right to "equality of opportunity," perhaps better described as a right to equal competitive opportunity. This right should be protected by a balancing test (to be described below) that would provide an intermediate level of protection—less than for political equality

48. *Batson*, 476 U.S. at 107 (Marshall, J., concurring).
49. Further, with the three-tiered framework eliminated, the Court would not have to treat race or gender as having talismanic significance in all cases. In cases involving, for example, a dispute between a Jew or Muslim and a Christian in a predominantly Christian county, the courts could disallow only those peremptory challenges that are based on religious affiliation.

but more than for economic equality. This right would include the equal right to pursue a lawful occupation and the right to an equal education.

The suggestion that the Court should protect the right to pursue a lawful occupation is bound to be greeted with skepticism. All students of constitutional law quickly learn of the infamous *Lochner* era, during which the Court struck down minimum-wage laws, maximum-hour laws, and other laws intended to protect the health and well-being of workers. The Court held that the due process clause protected workers' "liberty" to work for as small a wage and as long a day as the employer could impose. The right to pursue an occupation got lost in the constitutional shuffle during the Court's retreat from the excesses of *Lochner* era. "One may speculate whether the Court's overreaction to the *Lochner* era did not bring about a significant shortchanging of the old right to pursue a lawful calling."[50]

Indeed, there are many good reasons for the Court to recognize a limited right to pursue the occupation of one's choice. First, this right is solidly grounded in the intentions of the Fourteenth Amendment's framers. In his classic work, "The Original Understanding and the Segregation Decision," Alexander Bickel demonstrates that this right has far better grounding in the framers' intentions than do such rights as the right to enter into an interracial marriage or to attend integrated schools: "Thus it is clear that the Moderates wished also to protect rights of free movement, and *a right to engage in the occupations of one's choice.* They doubtless considered that their enumeration somehow accomplished this purpose. . . . The obvious conclusion to which the evidence, thus summarized, easily leads is that section 1 of the fourteenth amendment . . . carried out the relatively narrow objectives of the Moderates . . . ."[51] As Bickel points out later in his article, just because a right, such as the right to attend an integrated public school, was not intended by the framers, this does not mean the Court was wrong to expand constitutional protection in this way. However, there is no reason for the Court to give short shrift to a right so basic as the right to pursue an occupation—a right that is arguably within the original intentions of the framers of the Fourteenth Amendment.

Moreover, as Justice Marshall has argued, there is ample judicial precedent for explicitly recognizing the right to pursue an occupation:

> Whether "fundamental" or not, "the right of the individual . . . to engage in the common occupations of life" has been repeatedly recognized by this Court as falling within the concept of liberty guaranteed by the Fourteenth Amendment. *Board of Regents v.*

---

50. Wilkinson, "Three Faces of Constitutional Equality," 995 n. 249.

51. Alexander M. Bickel, "The Original Understanding and the Segregation Decision," *Harvard Law Review* 69 (1955): 56–58 (emphasis added).

Roth, 408 U.S. 564, 572 (1972), quoting *Meyer v. Nebraska*, 262 U.S. 390, 399 (1923). As long ago as *Butcher's Union Co. v. Crescent City Co.*, 111 U.S. 746 (1884), Mr. Justice Bradley wrote that this right "is an inalienable right; it is formulated as such under the phrase 'pursuit of happiness' in the Declaration of Independence . . . This right is a large ingredient in the civil liberty of the citizen."[52]

Such a right would be a classic negative right, not a positive right. Just as the First Amendment protects our right to criticize the government but does not require the government to finance our speech, the government would not be required to supply anyone with the means to pursue an occupation. However, the government would have to justify whatever barriers it puts in people's way. Through use of a balancing test, protection of this right could be achieved without officious meddling into the regulatory powers of the executive and legislative branches. Wilkinson suggests a three-pronged test: "The constitutional inquiry to test governmental denials of equal opportunity ought to weigh and to balance carefully the following elements[:] (1) the importance of the opportunity being unequally burdened or denied; (2) the strength of the state interest served in denying it; and (3) the character of the groups whose opportunities are denied."[53] For the reasons discussed so far, I would jettison the third criterion—the "character of the group." The equal protection clause must protect all groups equally or it does not truly offer *equal* protection. I would replace this prong with a different standard: the *degree* of the injury to a person's equal competitive opportunity, and I would make "degree of injury" the starting point of the inquiry.

Wilkinson emphasizes that "[s]tate occupational licensing, whether of lawyers or candlestick makers, would normally be valid, where the licensing or examining procedure aided in ensuring honest and competent service to the public." However, he also emphasizes that "occupational licensing is not invariably above reproach."[54] He illustrates this point by reference to a 1947 case, *Kotch v. Board of River Port Pilot Commissioners*.[55] In *Kotch* the State of Louisiana certified river pilots through an apprentice system so that one essentially had to be a friend or relative of a current pilot to become certified, and the Court upheld the certification procedure because it promoted "esprit de corps" among the pilots.

Wilkinson sees this decision as an example of how a balancing test that

---

52. *Massachusetts Board of Retirement v. Murgia*, 427 U.S. 307, 322 (1975) (Marshall, J., dissenting).

53. Wilkinson, "Three Faces of Constitutional Equality," 991.

54. *Ibid.*, 995.

55. 330 U.S. 552 (1947).

recognizes the right to equal competitive opportunity would be superior to the status quo. The modern three-tiered framework would uphold the Louisiana system since no suspect class or fundamental right was at stake. Yet the result is intolerable if we believe that meritorious individuals should not be legally disqualified from competing for a job just because they have no friends or relatives who are river pilots. This case also demonstrates why the "character of the group" being discriminated against should be irrelevant to the constitutional inquiry. Under the three-tiered framework, a woman could probably win an equal protection–based lawsuit against Louisiana if she could show that there is an "old boy" network among river pilots who refuse to take on women as apprentices. Racial minorities, aliens, illegitimate children, and white men could all successfully make this argument if they could show that river pilots were refusing to take on members of their group as apprentices. But if river pilots refused to employ gays, lesbians, members of a lower (or higher) economic class, people with northern accents, and so forth as apprentices, these people would be without recourse. Again, it is hard to see how this is *equal* protection. A rights-based approach would have the great advantage of offering the same degree of protection to everyone.

An advantage of using a rights-based balancing approach in equal competitive opportunity cases is that *it would make explicit what the Court often actually does in practice*. While the Court has never acknowledged a right to an opportunity to pursue an occupation, it actually protects just such a right for whites and males in some cases challenging affirmative action programs. Further, it does so in exactly the fashion suggested in this chapter: it balances the state interest in the unequal treatment against the plaintiffs' right to pursue an occupation.[56]

For example, in *Wygant v. Jackson Board of Education*,[57] the Supreme Court had to decide whether a policy of laying off white teachers ahead of less-senior minority teachers violated the equal protection clause. Following the three-tiered framework, the Court began by dutifully noting that it must apply the same "strict scrutiny" to the plan that it would to any other governmental action that applied a racial classification. Thus, the plan had to "be justified by a compelling governmental interest" and be "narrowly

---

56. Herman Schwartz has argued that the "weight, necessity, and fairness" of the burden imposed on whites by affirmative action programs "seem to be the most important factors in determining which plans are acceptable under the analysis developed by Justice Powell (and apparently adopted, at least in part, by Justices White and O'Connor)." Herman Schwartz, "The 1986 and 1987 Affirmative Action Cases: It's All Over but the Shouting," *University of Michigan Law Review* 86 (1987): 552.

57. 476 U.S. 267 (1986).

tailored to meet that goal." The Court had previously given its imprimatur to race-based hiring plans.[58] Yet the Court struck down the layoff plan because, "while hiring goals impose a diffuse burden, often foreclosing only one of several opportunities, layoffs impose the entire burden of achieving racial equality on particular individuals, often resulting in serious disruption of their lives."[59]

This argument makes sense only if the Court is balancing the burden imposed on the white teachers being laid off against the interest advanced by the program. However, the burden imposed by race-based layoffs has nothing whatsoever to do with whether the layoff plan "is narrowly tailored to serve a compelling governmental interest." In fact, the interest advanced by the layoff plan is exactly the same as the interest advanced by the school board's constitutionally permissible race-based hiring plan—increasing minority representation among the faculty. If the board had used the usual "last hired, first fired" approach to layoffs, it would have laid off most of the minorities who were recruited under the hiring program. Therefore, the layoff plan was narrowly tailored to achieve the same interest as the hiring program. In fact, the layoff plan was more narrowly tailored to the end of achieving faculty diversity than was the hiring program. The board could have tried to recruit minority faculty through means other than race-based hiring, but there was no possible means to save minority faculty from layoffs other than through preferential treatment for racial minorities when it came to layoffs.[60]

There is no getting around the fact that the *Wygant* Court used a balancing approach. The state's interest in faculty diversity was balanced against the burdens on white teachers. However, by balancing *implicitly* rather than *explicitly*, courts do not hold themselves accountable for giving each group of plaintiffs the same fair hearing on whether the burden imposed by the classification outweighs the benefits. If the *Wygant* Court had been more honest about what it was doing, the plaintiffs in *High Tech Gays* could have argued that the bare speculation that disgruntled homosexuals might betray their country was outweighed by the stigma and job loss caused by the blanket denial of security clearance. Since the *Wygant* Court formally relied on the three-tiered framework, gay and lesbian plaintiffs instead had to prostrate themselves before the federal courts in *High Tech*

58. *United Steel Workers of America v. Weber*, 443 U.S. 193 (1979).

59. *Wygant*, 476 U.S. at 283.

60. Herman Schwartz has also noted that the *Wygant* Court's concern for the weight of the burden on white plaintiffs in affirmative action cases is out of sync with the formal law in this area. Schwartz, "Affirmative Action Cases," 551–53.

Gays as victims of societal discrimination, victims of their own political powerlessness, and victims of their own immutable genetic destiny—that is, as a suspect class.

Another advantage of using a balancing approach in equal competitive opportunity cases is that it would allow the Court to respond to the issue of affirmative action more flexibly and rationally than it does now. Under the three-tiered framework, many (perhaps all) affirmative action laws are subject to strict scrutiny. In *City of Richmond v. J. A. Croson Co.*,[61] for example, the Court struck down a municipal law requiring "prime contractors to whom the City awarded construction contracts to subcontract at least 30% of the dollar amount of the contract to minority-owned business enterprises."[62] The Court held that the affirmative action program was subject to strict scrutiny because "the standard of review under the equal protection clause is not dependent on the race of those benefited or burdened by a particular classification."[63] In *Adarand Constructors, Inc. v. Pena*,[64] the Court held that affirmative action programs in federal contracting are also subject to strict scrutiny; federal racial classifications, like those of a state, must serve a compelling governmental interest and must be narrowly tailored to further that interest.[65] Under this standard, few affirmative action programs are likely to survive, at least in the context of government contracting.

It could be argued that the Court simply misapplied the three-tiered framework in *Adarand*. Perhaps affirmative action can be upheld under the three-tiered framework if the highest level of judicial protection is reserved solely for the protection of African Americans. Justice Rehnquist, for example, has argued, "Since the [Fourteenth] Amendment grew out of the Civil War and the freeing of the slaves, the core prohibition was early held to be aimed at the protection of blacks."[66] Yet this approach would drastically scale back judicial protection against discrimination on the basis of characteristics such as gender and national origin. A purely historical approach would mean that discrimination against Latinas and Latinos, Native Americans, Asian Americans, and women would be beyond the protective reach of the equal protection clause. The only way out of this conundrum would be to somehow distinguish between the whites who are

61. 488 U.S. 469 (1989).
62. *Richmond,* 488 U.S. at 477.
63. *Id.* at 494.
64. 515 U.S. 200 (1995).
65. *Adarand Constructors,* 515 U.S. at 227.
66. *Trimble v. Gordon,* 430 U.S. 762, 780 (1977) (Rehnquist, J., dissenting).

disadvantaged by affirmative action and all these other groups. This would mean a renewed commitment to the logic of "discrete and insular minorities" with the multiplicity of problems discussed throughout this book.

A rights-based balancing approach offers a far more coherent way of evaluating the constitutionality of various affirmative action programs. The first inquiry under this analysis is to ask to what degree the law at issue deprives the plaintiffs of equality of competitive opportunity. In *Adarand* the plaintiff suffered a diminished opportunity to compete for a federal subcontract. While this is a serious injury, it is not as severe as the educational or job-related injury blacks have sustained under Jim Crow laws or under discriminatory governmental policies regarding contracting or employment. This is because Jim Crow–type segregation and discrimination are tremendously stigmatizing to blacks.

The class-based approach to equal protection has no way of taking into account the subtleties of an issue like affirmative action. A balancing approach, however, allows the courts to acknowledge that affirmative action programs can harm whites and men while also acknowledging that affirmative action programs are less harmful than Jim Crow laws. Without balancing, equal protection becomes an all-or-nothing issue. Whites are or are not a protected class.

Justice Powell has tried to make the case that many affirmative action programs place only a very small burden on groups that are excluded from them. In his concurring opinion in *Fullilove v. Klutznick*,[67] Powell argued that a federal set-aside program for minority contractors was constitutional because of the extremely small burden it placed on nonminority contractors:

> In this case, the petitioners contend with some force that they have been asked to bear the burden of the set-aside even though they are innocent of wrongdoing. *I do not believe, however, that their burden is so great that the set-aside must be disapproved.* As noted above, Congress knew that minority contractors were receiving only 1% of federal contracts at the time the set-aside was enacted. . . . The Court of Appeals calculated that the set-aside would reserve about 0.25% of all the funds expended yearly on construction work in the United States for approximately 4% of the Nation's contractors who are members of a minority group. The set-aside would have no effect on the ability of the remaining 96% of contractors to compete for 99.75% of construction funds. In my view,

67. 448 U.S. 448 (1980).

the effect of the set-aside is limited and so widely dispersed that its use is consistent with fundamental fairness.[68]

Thus Powell articulates a basis to distinguish between the set-asides at issue in *Fullilove* and much more substantial set-asides in other programs. The problem with Powell's approach, and the reason it has never been formally adopted in a majority opinion, is its incompatibility with the three-tiered framework's reliance on suspect classes and classifications. Powell's approach is clearly a balancing approach. He even uses the language of balancing: "Any marginal unfairness to innocent nonminority contractors is not sufficiently significant—or sufficiently identifiable to *outweigh* the government's interest served by [the set-aside program]."[69]

By explicitly adopting a balancing test in cases involving equality of competitive opportunity, the Court could move away from the all-or-nothing approach to affirmative action. Affirmative action programs could be allowed up to the point where they pose a significant obstacle to the professional advancement of nonbeneficiaries. While there would no doubt be significant and sometimes complex litigation over what this point is, such a determination would be no more complex than other issues that courts are called on to decide, such as defining the relevant market in antitrust cases. Indeed, any thoughtful approach to evaluating the constitutionality of affirmative action *should* sometimes result in complex litigation. Affirmative action is a complex issue, and simplistic line-drawing only serves to polarize both the legal and political debate. The perceived judicial economy of the current approach is a false economy.

This approach would have several important advantages. One advantage is that it offers the same protection to everybody. As discussed in chapter 5, a major concern of those who voted for Amendment 2 was that gays and lesbians would be added to groups that benefit from affirmative action, meaning that another group would "move to the head of the line" for job opportunities, federal contracts, and so forth. The balancing approach would assure that the Court would not allow any person's professional opportunities to be significantly diminished by affirmative action programs, no matter how many groups are included in these programs. If it assured a uniform and significant bottom line of equal protection for all persons, the equal protection clause could help negate the zero-sum mentality currently dominant in the debate over affirmative action and civil rights in general.

68. *Fullilove,* 448 U.S. at 514–15 (Powell, J., concurring) (emphasis added).
69. *Id.* at 515 (emphasis added).

The balancing approach is advantageous in another respect; because it is explicit, it would be fairer to groups that have been locked out by the three-tiered framework. Suspect-class status would lose its talismanic significance under a balancing approach. Gays, lesbians, and the elderly would have the same protection as whites. If the government requires workers to retire at age fifty, as in *Murgia,* or automatically denies high-level security clearance to gays and lesbians, as in *High Tech Gays,* their claims would have to be taken as seriously as the claims of whites who feel they have been harmed by affirmative action programs. Of course, the governmental interests in these policies are different from the state interest in affirmative action policies. Under a balancing approach, the government would have the opportunity to show that the policies are necessary. But the injuries suffered by these groups could no longer be ignored on the basis that they are a less favored class of plaintiffs than are whites.

Equal access to the occupation of one's choice would not be the only right protected by this balancing approach. Wilkinson also advocates intermediate protection for educational opportunity. He argues that "[o]pportunity in America has historically meant education."[70] Further, educational equality is closely and directly linked to political opportunity. Marshall made this point in his dissent in *San Antonio Independent School District v. Rodriguez:*

> I believe that the close nexus between education and our established constitutional values with respect to freedom of speech and participation in the political process makes this a different case from our prior decisions concerning discrimination affecting public welfare or housing. . . . Whatever the severity of the impact of insufficient food or inadequate housing on a person's life, they have never been considered to bear *the same direct and immediate relationship to constitutional concerns for free speech and for our political processes as education has long been recognized to bear* . . . . Education, in terms of constitutional values, is much more analogous, in my judgment, to the right to vote in state elections than to public welfare or public housing.[71]

On numerous occasions the Supreme Court has flirted with the idea of making education a fundamental right. As discussed in chapter 2, the *Brown* Court justified its desegregation mandate by stating that education is fundamental to the rights and privileges of citizenship. Twenty-seven years later, the Court again came very close to declaring education to be a

---

70. Wilkinson, "Three Faces of Constitutional Equality," 977.
71. *Rodriguez,* 411 U.S. at 115 n. 74 (Marshall, J., dissenting) (emphasis added).

fundamental right in *Plyler v. Doe*.[72] The issue in *Plyler* was a Texas law authorizing school districts to deny enrollment in public schools to children who were not legally admitted to the United States. A five-justice majority held that the law violated the equal protection clause. The Brennan-drafted opinion is a masterpiece of strategic vagueness. Four justices were apparently ready to hold that education is a fundamental right for equal protection purposes.[73] But Justice Powell would not add the fifth vote to an opinion creating a new fundamental right. Thus, Brennan's opinion dutifully notes, "Public education is not a 'right' granted to individuals by the Constitution." But Brennan follows this with an extraordinary verbal dance that finds as many different ways to call education a fundamental right as are possible without actually using those exact words:

> But neither is [education] merely some governmental "benefit" indistinguishable from other forms of social welfare legislation. Both the importance of education in maintaining our basic institutions, and the lasting impact of its deprivation on the life of the child, mark the distinction. The "American people have always regarded education and the acquisition of knowledge as matters of supreme importance." *Meyer v. Nebraska*, 262 U.S. 390, 400 (1923). We have recognized "the public schools as a most vital civic institution for the preservation of a democratic system of government." *Abington School District v. Schempp*, 374 U.S. 203, 230 (1963) (Brennan, J., concurring), and as the primary vehicle for transmitting "the values on which our society rests." *Ambach v. Norwalk*, 441 U.S. 68, 76 (1979). . . . In addition, education provides the basic tools by which individuals might lead economically productive lives to the benefit of us all. In sum, education has a fundamental role in maintaining the fabric of our society.[74]

Similarly, in 1986 in *Papasan v. Allain*,[75] the Court refused to dismiss a complaint alleging that unequal division of state resources among school districts violates the equal protection clause. The Court somewhat cryptically stated that, while *Rodriguez* was the law of the land, that case "did not purport to validate all funding variations that might result from a State's public school funding decisions."[76]

The right to an education has existed in a nether state long enough. After some forty years of toying with the idea of making education a funda-

---

72. 457 U.S. 202 (1982).
73. Klarman, "Interpretive History," 288.
74. *Plyler*, 457 U.S. at 221.
75. 478 U.S. 265 (1986).
76. *Papasan*, 478 U.S. at 287.

mental right, the Court needs to make a decision. Wilkinson, Brennan, Marshall, and Warren have all persuasively articulated many reasons for constitutionalizing the right to an education. Protecting the right to an equal education under an intermediate balancing test would not *necessarily* mean overruling *Rodriguez*. The Court would still have to balance poorer students' interest in equal educational opportunity against the state interest in avoiding severe disruption of state educational systems. Many state supreme courts have attempted to equalize school district funding within states, with decidedly mixed results.[77]

The advantage of a balancing approach would not be that it would assure the "right" result, but that it would focus the Court on issues that are more relevant than whether the plaintiffs are part of a protected class. As noted in chapter 1, if a school district segregated gay students in a paranoid reaction to AIDS, under the three-tiered analysis such a law would receive the same low level of scrutiny as a run-of-the-mill administrative regulation. Under a balancing test, however, the Court would be in a position to give substantial weight to the gay students' interest in equal educational opportunity.

Nor would the Court have to be blind to the special context of race. Racial segregation is no doubt especially injurious to the affected students due to the tremendous stigma on African Americans that has always been part and parcel of racial segregation. So in a balancing test, the state would have to articulate a very strong set of interests to justify racial segregation. It would be the functional equivalent of strict scrutiny in that particular case. But under the balancing test the interests of other groups of students—poor, gay, or otherwise—to equal educational opportunity would be given more weight by the courts than under the current system.

One possible objection to a balancing approach is that it might place too much discretion in the hands of judges. There is no getting around the fact that balancing inevitably involves some subjective judgments, and judges' values will undoubtedly affect how they weigh competing concerns. This is a legitimate concern. Indeed, fear of overreaching judicial activism in the form of balancing tests is what gave momentum to the current equal protection jurisprudence in the first place. Recall that the term "discrete and insular minorities" was coined by Justice Stone in 1938. At that time the

---

77. Michael Minstrom, "Why Efforts to Equalize School Funding Have Failed: Towards a Positive Theory," *Political Research Quarterly* 46 (1993): 847; G. Alan Tarr and Russell S. Harrison, "School Finance and Inequality in New Jersey," in *Constitutional Politics in the States: Contemporary Controversies and Historical Patterns*, ed. G. Alan Tarr (Westport, Conn.: Greenwood Press, 1996).

Supreme Court was in full retreat from its decisions during the *Lochner* era of judicial activism.[78] This period of judicial activism was marked by judicial balancing tests.[79] The tiered approach to equal protection ostensibly keeps the Court clear of *Lochner*-type judicial activism. It allows the Court to maintain a formal deference to the majoritarian will except in cases involving politically vulnerable minorities. As Kathleen Sullivan puts it, the tiered approach is "penitence" for the sins of the *Lochner* era: "In equal protection and substantive due process law, for example, the two-tier system was meant to enshrine penitence for the sins of the *Lochner* era by making deferential rationality review the norm and strict scrutiny the emergency exception where 'fundamental rights' or 'suspect classes' were threatened."[80]

However, as discussed in earlier chapters, in practice the three-tiered rubric has not been particularly deferential to the democratic process. Rather, the courts have oscillated between strictly adhering to the three-tiered framework in cases like *Murgia, Rodriguez,* and *High Tech Gays* and silently resorting to a much stricter test in cases like *Romer, Moreno,* and *Cleburne.* Thus, the current situation represents the worst of all possible worlds. When the justices' sense of fair play is offended, they apply a strict test. Yet, because they formally adhere to the three-tiered framework, they do not hold themselves accountable to place the same weight on similar injuries caused by laws that burden groups such as the poor, the elderly, and gays and lesbians.

Another potential objection to using balancing tests in cases involving equal competitive opportunity is the possibility that any balancing test would be too deferential to state interests and would end up weakening important constitutional protections.[81] The debate over whether constitutional rights are better protected by a balancing or by a category-based approach has been particularly vigorous in the area of free speech. According to John Hart Ely, the Warren Court was especially cautious about balancing in the area of government regulation of speech because it believed that a category approach was "more likely to protect expression in crisis times. . . . where messages are proscribed because they are dangerous, balancing tests inevitably become intertwined with the ideological

78. This history is set out more fully in chapter 2.

79. Richard Fielding, "Fundamental Personal Rights: Another Approach to Equal Protection," *University of Chicago Law Review* 40 (1973): 816.

80. Kathleen M. Sullivan, "Categorization, Balancing, and Governmental Interests," in *Public Values in Constitutional Law,* ed. Stephen E. Gottlieb (Ann Arbor: University of Michigan Press, 1993), 242.

81. *Ibid.*

predispositions of those doing the balancing."[82] Thus the Court has tended to avoid First Amendment balancing tests.

Yet a balancing test can be even more protective of constitutional rights than a category-based test. This is especially true in terms of the equal protection clause. In First Amendment jurisprudence, the Court defers to majoritarian sentiment only when the speech at issue falls within narrow categories of "unprotected speech."[83] Otherwise the Court protects the constitutional rights of the speaker unless there is a compelling reason to silence him or her. By contrast, in applying the equal protection clause, the Court *defers* to majoritarian sentiment unless the law falls within certain narrow categories such as race or gender discrimination. Thus, while the category-based approach in First Amendment jurisprudence is a shield against unfettered majoritarianism, the category-based approach to equal protection doctrine is meant to generally defer to the popular will. Yet, as just discussed, this approach also does a poor job of restraining the courts from interfering with the popular will.

Further, even in First Amendment jurisprudence a balancing test can be more protective of constitutional rights than a category-based approach. Gerald Gunther has written about how Justice John Harlan's commitment to a balancing approach often resulted in his protecting freedom of speech in cases where justices who purported to be champions of free speech were willing to allow government censorship. For example, in *Cohen v. California*,[84] a young man was arrested for walking through a courthouse corridor while wearing a jacket that had the words "fuck the draft" on the back. Justice Harlan wrote the majority opinion overturning Cohen's conviction for disturbing the peace. Justice Black, "the most consistent and articulate critic claiming that Justice Harlan's balancing weakened First Amendment protections," joined the dissent.[85] The dissent argued that Cohen's words either were not speech at all—just "absurd and immature" conduct—or fell under the "fighting words" category of unprotected speech.[86] Harlan's opinion, by contrast, balanced the harm done by Cohen against the consti-

82. John Hart Ely, "Flag Desecration: A Case Study in the Roles of Categorization and Balancing in First Amendment Analysis," *Harvard Law Review* 88 (1975): 1500–1501.

83. Such unprotected categories include obscenity and, to a lesser degree, libel and "fighting words." Steven H. Shiffrin and Jesse H. Choper, *The First Amendment: Cases—Comments—Questions* (St. Paul, Minn.: West, 1991).

84. 403 U.S. 15 (1971).

85. Gerald Gunther, "In Search of Judicial Quality on a Changing Court: The Case of Justice Powell," *Stanford Law Review* 24 (1972): 1007.

86. "Fighting words" are words that would cause a person to come to blows or that by their very utterance inflict injury. *Chaplinsky v. New Hampshire*, 315 U.S. 568 (1942).

tutional harm caused by government censorship of Cohen's expression. Regarding the harm caused by censoring even such immature speech as Cohen's, Harlan wrote,

> [M]uch linguistic expression serves a dual communicative function: it conveys not only ideas capable of relatively precise, detached explication, but otherwise inexpressible emotions as well. In fact, words are often chosen as much for their emotive as their cognitive force. We cannot sanction the view that the Constitution, while solicitous of the cognitive content of individual speech, has little or no regard for the emotive function which, practically speaking, may often be the most important element of the overall message communicated.[87]

Harlan also acknowledged that the government has an interest in maintaining "a suitable level of discourse within the body politic" but that this was outweighed by the First Amendment values at stake.[88]

Similarly, in *Street v. New York*,[89] three justices generally regarded as strong protectors of free speech—Black, Warren, and Abe Fortas—dissented from Justice Harlan's majority opinion overturning a conviction for flag burning. Harlan argued that the state had not demonstrated any interest strong enough to outweigh the First Amendment concerns involved in the case. The dissenters argued that flag burning belongs in the category of "conduct" rather than speech. Ironically, Justice Black, even while voting to allow the conviction for flag burning, chastised Harlan for insufficiently protecting freedom of speech. Black wrote, "[Had the conviction been based on words rather than conduct,] I would firmly and automatically agree that the law is unconstitutional. I would not feel constrained . . . to search my imagination to see if I could think of interests the State may have in suppressing this freedom of speech. *I would not balance away the First Amendment mandate that speech not be abridged in any fashion whatsoever.*"[90]

The problems of Black's rigid fidelity to the category-based approach to the First Amendment parallel the difficulties of the categorical, three-tiered approach to equal protection. Once the Court decides that gays and lesbians are not "suspect classes," it upholds laws that disadvantage them regardless of how great a burden the law places on them or how diminutive the government's interest in the classification is. Similarly, once Justice Black de-

---

87. *Cohen*, 403 U.S. at 26.
88. *Id.* at 23.
89. 394 U.S. 576 (1969). This example is also discussed at length in Gunther, "In Search of Judicial Quality," 1008–11.
90. *Street*, 394 U.S. at 609–10 (Black, J., dissenting) (emphasis added).

cides that burning the flag is conduct, he does not require the government to demonstrate that any actual harm is being caused by such expression.

As these examples demonstrate, a category-based approach is not intrinsically more protective of constitutional rights than is a balancing approach. It seems reasonable to believe that a clear and coherent balancing test would be more protective of people's rights than a murky category-based test, since murky categories are easily distorted and manipulated. This book's central argument is that the current categories are beyond murky—they are virtually incoherent. Thus, I believe a balancing test would be superior to the current system of equal protection.

Another possible objection to advocating a balancing approach in competitive economic opportunity cases is that the proposal does not realistically take into account negative public opinion regarding gays and lesbians and the courts' reluctance to venture very far beyond public opinion in protecting the rights of unpopular groups. While scholars are divided over whether the courts are directly influenced by public opinion or are simply affected by the same forces of socialization that shape general public opinion, many have noted that there is usually at least some degree of congruence between judicial and public opinion.[91]

Even if it is true that public opinion has a substantial direct or indirect impact on judicial willingness to protect the rights of various groups, I believe that a rights-based, balancing approach would make it *more* likely that courts would vigorously protect the rights of gays and lesbians. This is because public attitudes toward gay and lesbian rights are actually quite complex and nuanced—indeed, far more nuanced than the current, clumsy jurisprudence of suspect classes.

It is apparently true that the public is still quite hostile to gays and lesbians. "Homosexuals may well be the single most systematically disliked group in the United States."[92] Indeed, Alan Wolfe recently found that, while Americans "are extremely reluctant to judge the behavior of anyone else," homosexuality is the great exception to this tolerant attitude.[93] It

---

91. For a summary and treatment of the discussion and debate in the literature, see Baum, *Puzzle of Judicial Behavior*.

92. Kenneth Sherrill and Steven Yang, "Public Opinion toward Lesbian and Gay Rights," in *The Encyclopedia of Homosexuality*, ed. George Haggerty (Haworth Press, in press). Sherrill and Yang rely on a variety of data sources, including the National Elections Studies conducted by the Center for Political Studies at the University of Michigan; the General Social Survey, 1973–1996, conducted by the National Opinion Research Center, University of Chicago; and data from Princeton Survey Research Associates.

93. Alan Wolfe, "The Homosexual Exception," *New York Times Sunday Magazine*, 8 February 1998, 46.

should be noted, though, that disapproval rates regarding gays and lesbians, while still high, have been declining sharply in the 1990s.[94] And, far more importantly, *national public support for gay and lesbian rights is actually quite strong and climbing*. "In 1996, fifty percent more Americans (84%) think gay people should have equal rights in terms of job opportunities than in 1977, when 56% thought so." Similarly, "Eighty percent of the American people think there should be 'equal rights for gays in terms of housing.'" These data are quite similar to the polling results for the Colorado public discussed in chapter 5. Sherrill and Yang summarize the best available data as follows: "The American people's attitudes toward the rights of lesbians and gay men can be characterized as a combination of a distaste for homosexuality per se, a dislike of homosexuals as a group, along with an evolving tolerance for the rights of lesbians, gay men and bisexuals."[95]

So public support for the rights of gays and lesbians goes well beyond their cold "feeling thermometers" regarding gays and lesbians as a group.[96] There is substantial public support for protecting the basic rights of all Americans, including gays and lesbians. This is why the current class-based equal protection jurisprudence has created such political and legal problems for gays and lesbians. Given the public's cold attitudes toward gays and lesbians, we would hardly expect the public, or a similarly socialized judiciary, to support suspect-class status for gays and lesbians as a group. But a rights-based jurisprudence would allow courts to enforce gay and lesbian rights without making gays and lesbians a "special class." The public's current attitudes toward gay and lesbian rights are far more subtle and nuanced than is the Supreme Court's equal protection doctrine. Using a rights-based balancing approach in equal competitive opportunity cases could help close that gap.

Again, it should be emphasized that the balancing approach would not be some sort of all-purpose test. Courts would apply it only to laws affecting specifically defined rights of economic opportunity such as equal edu-

---

94. Sherrill and Yang, "Public Opinion."

95. *Ibid.*

96. This complexity of public opinion mirrors the findings of Paul Sniderman and Thomas Piazza regarding race, affirmative action, civil rights, and other race-related issues. People's attitudes toward programs designed to benefit African Americans appear to be more highly correlated with attitudes regarding such issues as government spending in general than with their abstract feelings toward African Americans. Paul M. Sniderman and Thomas Piazza, *The Scar of Race* (Cambridge: Harvard University Press, Belknap Press, 1993). Thus, it is not so surprising that negative feeling thermometer scores regarding gays and lesbians can coexist with strong support for protecting their rights to fair job and employment opportunities.

cation and job opportunities. In other areas, especially in areas of economic equality such as welfare policy, the courts would be more deferential to the legislative will. This is discussed in the next section.

Economic Equality

Wilkinson argues that the Court should be least aggressive in promoting economic equality. Rights falling within this category would receive the lowest level of judicial protection. Economic-equality rights can be divided into three basic categories: "requir[ing] states to distribute welfare benefits more evenhandedly among the poor, [relieving] the poor from payment of selected public fees or for selected services, or, in its more advanced stages, [undertaking] some affirmative steps to satisfy the indigent's 'just wants' or most basic needs."[97] Wilkinson argues that the Court should avoid attempting to promote economic equality in any of these ways: "The argument here is not that greater equality of wealth is somehow undesirable or even unachievable, but that it is not the place of the judiciary to attempt it."[98] Unless the denial of economic equality directly infringes political equality or equality of competitive opportunity, the Court should generally defer to the legislature.

It is true that denial of welfare benefits may have substantial indirect effects on political and opportunity equality. Nonetheless, the Court should be highly reluctant to interfere with legislative judgment in this area: "[T]he dangers of intervention are apparent. One is that, in voiding public welfare classifications, courts engage in what is undisputedly the most basic of all legislative functions—from whom and to whom to raise and distribute revenue. For the very essence of politics is often simply a matter of who gets and who pays."[99]

Of course some economic equality cases *do* directly affect political equality and / or equality of competitive opportunity. The poll tax in *Harper v. Virginia State Board of Elections*[100] is one obvious example of this. But the Court should be cautious about finding such a direct connection in most economic inequality cases. "Constitutional adjudication with its imprimatur of permanence seems a poor technique with which to approach the redress of economic inequality, where knowledge is in such a developing and conflicting state."[101]

97. Wilkinson, "Three Faces of Constitutional Equality," 998–99 (citations omitted).
98. *Ibid.,* 1005.
99. *Ibid.,* 1010.
100. 383 U.S. 663 (1966).
101. Wilkinson, "Three Faces of Constitutional Equality," 1013.

This discussion of a rights-based system is just an outline of what one such system might look like, and it no doubt fails to answer many questions about how it might work in practice. But the goal here is not to lay out a detailed blueprint. The goal is merely to show that the class-based system is not the only feasible way to enforce the equal protection clause. The approach discussed above sketches one possible alternative that may avoid the pitfalls of the current approach while also avoiding the difficulties of the other alternatives discussed in this chapter. This discussion makes no pretense to answer all, or even most, questions about how such a rights-based approach would work in practice. But if it presents an idea engaging enough to stimulate future debate, the goal will have been achieved.

How Might the Rights-Based Approach Apply to Amendment 2?

To recap, I propose replacing the class-based system with a rights-based system. Rights that relate to political equality would receive the highest level of protection, something akin to strict scrutiny. Rights relating to equality of competitive opportunity would be protected at an intermediate level—the state interest would be balanced against the nature and the degree of the right deprivation. Economic equality rights would receive the least protection.

It is not clear that Amendment 2 would have resulted in actionable injury to gays' and lesbians' rights to political equality. As discussed in chapter 6, the courts often uphold provisions that cause political disadvantage to some group, such as state constitutional provisions that prevent Mormons (primarily) from seeking legislative approval for bigamy, or provisions that deny convicted felons the right to hold office. (Moreover, Amendment 2 would probably have survived Wilkinson's more stringent inquiry as well, for it could have been repealed with only a bare majority vote.) During the argument before the Supreme Court, Jean Dubofsky tried to distinguish Amendment 2 from such lawful provisions denying political rights; she argued that the amendment was unique because it created an *across-the-board* denial of rights to gays and lesbians. But what if a state passed a law prohibiting gays and lesbians from running for office, attending public schools, or holding government jobs? The argument that Amendment 2 is unconstitutional solely because of its breadth leaves gays and lesbians unprotected from discrimination in all these areas.

Regardless of whether Amendment 2 could be construed to deny gays and lesbians the right to political equality, at a minimum Amendment 2 would have deprived gays and lesbians of the right to equal competitive opportunity. It would have nullified protections against job discrimination and discrimination by the Colorado University system. Supporters

of Amendment 2 might respond that Amendment 2 did not directly command any public official or private actor to deny jobs or educational
opportunities to gays and lesbians. But the amendment did put the imprimatur of the government on such discrimination. The Supreme Court has
recognized that such an imprimatur is itself a powerful form of state discrimination. In *Reitman v. Mulkey*, the Supreme Court struck down an
amendment to the California constitution that stated, "Neither the State
nor any subdivision or agency thereof shall deny, limit or abridge, directly
or indirectly, the right of any person, who is willing or desires to sell, lease
or rent any part or all of his real property, to decline to sell, lease or rent such
property to such person or persons as he, in his absolute discretion,
chooses."[102] The Court concluded that the design and intent of the amendment was to overturn state laws prohibiting racial discrimination by private sellers of real estate. The Court struck down the amendment for
reasons that have obvious bearing on Amendment 2:

> [Under the amendment p]rivate discriminations in housing were
> now not only free from [antidiscrimination laws] but they also en-
> joyed a far different status than was true before the passage of
> those statutes. The right to discriminate, including the right to
> discriminate on racial grounds, was now embodied in the State's
> basic charter, immune from legislative, executive, or judicial regu-
> lation at any level of the state government. Those practicing racial
> discriminations need no longer rely solely on their personal
> choice. They could now invoke express constitutional authority,
> free from censure or interference of any kind from official
> sources.[103]

This logic applies with even greater force to Amendment 2. As with the
California amendment, the right to discriminate would have been embod-
ied in the state's basic charter. Further, Amendment 2 specifically singled
out gays, lesbians, and bisexuals, stigmatizing them as uniquely vulnerable targets for discrimination. Thus Amendment 2 represented a
significant abridgement of gays' and lesbians' right to equal competitive
opportunity.

Under the proposed system, this deprivation must be balanced against
the state interest in the law. As discussed in chapter 6, Colorado has enu-
merated several state interests that may be advanced by Amendment 2.
The promotion of public morality is one such interest. In *Bowers v. Hardwick*, the Supreme Court held that antigay sodomy laws survive a due

102. 387 U.S. 369, 371 (1966).
103. *Reitman*, 387 U.S. at 377.

process challenge because of the state interest in promoting public morality; the majority opinion stated that laws are "constantly based on notions
of morality."[104]

However, even if a ban on homosexual sodomy could be justified on the
basis of public morality, this does not mean that Amendment 2 can be justified on the same basis. When society enacts its moral judgments and makes
them part of the criminal code, there are several powerful barriers that
shield the individual from the moral judgment of the state. The district attorney's office must decide that violations of the antisodomy law are worth
prosecuting. A judge must decide that the law is one that is regularly enforced and not selectively prosecuted. A jury must be convinced that the
defendant has done something worth punishing. Guilt must be proved beyond a reasonable doubt according to strict rules of evidence. Rumor, in-
nuendo, stereotypes, and gossip are barred from the courtroom. The jury is
strictly forbidden from assuming that the defendant broke the law simply
because the defendant admits to being gay or lesbian. Defendants cannot
be forced to testify against themselves.

Thus, while it is true that the criminal law codifies moral judgment, in-
numerable safeguards are in place to protect the individual from abusive
or baseless punishment. None of these safeguards would have existed
with respect to Amendment 2. By specifically repealing only those civil
rights laws that protect gays, lesbians, and bisexuals, Amendment 2 deprived gays and lesbians of equal opportunity for jobs and education. As
discussed above, its scope might have gone so far as to authorize discrimination by the government in the provision of public services.[105] As a result
of Amendment 2, a person can be fired for merely stating that he or she is
gay or for being seen holding hands with a same-sex partner. Further, under Amendment 2 gays and lesbians are prevented from even "voting with
their feet" by moving to communities within Colorado that do not wish to
tolerate discrimination against them.

Also, it is far from clear that Amendment 2 represents the judgment of
Colorado citizens that homosexuality is an affront to majority morality. Indeed, Colorado was among the first states in the nation to repeal its ban on
sodomy.[106] As discussed in chapter 4, many citizens voted for Amendment
2 in order to assure that gays and lesbians did not receive the benefits of af-

---

104. *Bowers v. Hardwick*, 478 U.S. 186, 196 (1986).
105. See the reference above to the question Justice O'Connor posed during oral argument in *Romer*.
106. Bransford, *Gay Politics vs. Colorado*, 2.

firmative action quotas or preferences. Yet Amendment 2 was hopelessly overbroad in terms of achieving this goal.

Other possible state interests furthered by Amendment 2 are discussed extensively in chapter 6. While these interests are not "irrational," they are quite tenuous. The state expressed concern that adding sexual orientation to the list of protected characteristics would dilute protection for other groups. But as discussed in chapter 6, the trial court found no empirical basis for this concern. The interest is purely speculative. A speculative concern is not irrational, but under the proposed rights-based system of equal protection, Amendment 2 would be held to a higher standard (although not as high as strict scrutiny) because it denies equality of competitive opportunity to gays and lesbians.

Thus, Amendment 2 probably could not survive the balancing test advocated above. This is not to say that the citizens of Colorado are not entitled to attempt to find other means to address their concerns. However, whatever means they choose must not single out any group of individuals as legally vulnerable targets of discrimination.

While the approach laid out in this chapter is only an outline of what a fully developed rights-based system of equal protection would look like, I believe that this is the right direction for the Court to move in. While no approach to equal protection can predict how courts will answer constitutional questions, a rights-based approach would focus the courts on the right questions. Under the current class-based system, the courts have confused both themselves and the public. In trying to determine the constitutionality of Amendment 2, the trial court asked whether gays and lesbians are a discrete and insular minority. The Supreme Court asked whether the voters of Colorado were motivated by animus. Both these questions have shed more heat than light on the issues posed by Amendment 2.

A rights-based approach would focus the Court's attention on the harm done to gays and lesbians by Amendment 2. I believe that this approach would be less politically balkanizing because all classes of people would receive the same level of constitutional protection. There would be no issues of "special rights" or "minority status." It would also begin the arduous process of restoring some sense of coherence to a constitutional doctrine that has lost its way.

The debate over gay and lesbian rights is taking place against a background of a fear of loss of control. This is equally true of the Supreme Court and of the general public. The Court fears that, if it holds that gays and lesbians are a suspect or quasi-suspect class, it will lose control over its own agenda. It will have to apply a heightened level of scrutiny to issues as diverse as the ban on gay and lesbian service members and family law issues such as gay and lesbian adoption. Yet if the Court simply deferred to the voting majority, this would also represent a loss of control by the Court over the issue of gay rights. Thus, the Court maximizes its control by reserving the right to sometimes raise the level of rational-basis scrutiny without explicitly saying so. In this way, the Court could strike down Amendment 2 without obligating itself to apply a heightened level of scrutiny to any other law disadvantaging gays and lesbians. The cost of this strategy, however, is a loss of judicial accountability, doctrinal coherence, and, most importantly, truly equal protection of the laws.

Similarly, there are strong indications that passage of Amendment 2 was largely motivated by the Colorado public's fear of loss of control over the issue of gay and lesbian rights. They feared that, if gays and lesbians were considered a protected class, gays and lesbians would benefit from "special rights." The Court has contributed to this fear through its construction of a class-based jurisprudence that reinforces the idea that oppressed and powerless minorities deserve across-the-board protection from the democratic process.

All of these concerns are exacerbated by the perception of legal and constitutional rights as special protections for certain groups rather than general protections from discrimination. Certainly, many civil rights laws eschew the class-based approach and protect all persons from discrimination on the basis of certain characteristics such as race and gender. Yet the controversy over affirmative action, along with the Supreme Court's creation of suspect classes, has undermined the distinction between this type of protection and class-based protection.

The Court's decision in *Romer v. Evans* indicates that the Court has no inclination to wean itself from the class-based three-tiered framework. Indeed, the Court is now in a comfortable position. It can strike down laws it considers unfair as "irrational" while not obligating itself to extend to gays and lesbians the same protection it has extended to other groups. Thus, while this book focuses on the Supreme Court and on constitutional doctrine, it may be that state and federal legislatures will have to take the lead in moving us away from group-based legal protections.

There are some indications that this is already taking place. In fact, even before the controversy over Amendment 2, the Colorado legislature passed a law prohibiting employers from firing an employee as a result of any legal off-duty activity.[107] Such a law may well protect an employee

107. Colo. Rev. Stat. § 24-34-402.5(1) (Supp. 1996).

from being fired on account of his or her sexual orientation. A Colorado appellate court recently held that it did. The decision was reversed by the Colorado Supreme Court on the technical ground that the trial judge failed to use a proper jury instruction, but the supreme court did not rule out the possibility of applying the statute to protect gays and lesbians.[108] Thus, such a law can protect gays and lesbians from discrimination without making them vulnerable to the charge that they are seeking or benefiting from special rights.

At English common law, protections from discrimination were broader than they are today. Innkeepers, smiths, and others who "made a profession of public employment" were prohibited from refusing to serve *any* person without good reason.[109] This common law protection, and the Colorado statute mentioned above, can serve as a model for legislation that would move us away from the "gay rights" debate toward a discussion of what type of rights we all should benefit from.

Any attempt to change the direction of a major area of the law can only be the beginning of a long and difficult process. Yet all solutions must begin with a recognition of the problem. We must recognize the costs of the current approach in terms of the law's lack of fairness and coherence and the way that it has undermined the public's support for protections against discrimination for any group.

The debate over gay and lesbian rights, although important in and of itself, reveals far-reaching contradictions and difficulties with how we conceive of constitutional and civil rights. The question now is whether we respond to these difficulties by accusing one another of bigotry or of seeking special rights, or whether we work together to create a nation in which we can all live together under the equal protection of the laws.

108. *Borquez v. Ozer*, 923 P.2d 166 (Colo. Ct. App. 1996), *reversed*, 940 P.2d 371 (Colo. 1997).
109. See *Hurley v. Irish-American Gay, Lesbian and Bisexual Group of Boston*, 515 U.S. 557 (1995).

Ackerman, Bruce A. "Beyond *Carolene Products.*" *Harvard Law Review* 98 (1985): 713–46.

Adamany, David. "The Supreme Court." In *The American Courts: A Critical Assessment,* edited by John B. Gates and Charles A. Johnson. Washington, D.C.: Congressional Quarterly Press, 1991.

Adamany, David, and Joel B. Grossman. "Support for the Supreme Court as a National Policymaker." *Law & Policy Quarterly* 5 (1983): 405–37.

Afzelius, B. A. "Inheritance of Randomness." *Medical Hypotheses* 47 (1996): 23.

Allport, Gordon W. *The Nature of Prejudice.* Garden City, N.Y.: Doubleday, 1958.

Arkes, Hadley. "Gay Marriage and the Courts: *Roe v. Wade II?*" *Weekly Standard,* 20 November 1995, 38–39.

Baer, Judith. "The Fruitless Search for Original Intent." In *Judging the Constitution: Critical Essays on Judicial Lawmaking,* edited by Michael W. McCann and Gerald L. Houseman. Glenview, Ill.: Scott Foresman, 1989.

———. "Reverse Discrimination: The Danger of Hardened Categories." *Law & Policy Quarterly* 1 (1982): 71–94.

Bagnall, Robert G. "Burdens on Gay Litigants and Bias in the Court System: Homosexual Panic, Child Custody, and Anonymous Parties." *Harvard Civil Rights–Civil Liberties Law Review* 19 (1984): 497–559.

Bass, Larry R. "The Constitution as Symbol: Patterns of Meaning." *American Politics Quarterly* 8 (1980): 237–56.

———. "The Constitution as Symbol: The Interpersonal Sources of Meaning of a Secondary Symbol." *American Journal of Political Science* 23 (1979): 101–20.

Bass, Larry R., and Dan Thomas. "The Supreme Court and Policy Legitimation: Experimental Tests." *American Politics Quarterly* 12 (1984): 335–60.

Baum, Lawrence. *The Puzzle of Judicial Behavior.* Ann Arbor: University of Michigan Press, 1997.

———. "Courts and Policy Innovation." In *The American Courts: A Critical Assessment,* edited by John B. Gates and Charles A. Johnson. Washington, D.C.: Congressional Quarterly Press, 1991.

Bawer, Bruce. "Notes on Stonewall." *New Republic,* 13 June 1994, 24–30.

Becker, Theodore L., and Malcolm M. Feeley, eds. *The Impact of Supreme Court Decisions: Empirical Studies.* 2d ed. New York: Oxford University Press, 1973.

Berger, Raoul. *Government by Judiciary: The Transformation of the Fourteenth Amendment.* Cambridge: Harvard University Press, 1977.

Berkson, Larry C. *The Supreme Court and Its Publics: The Communication of Policy Decisions.* Lexington, Mass.: Lexington Books, 1978.

Bickel, Alexander M. "The Original Understanding and the Segregation Decision."
    Harvard Law Review 69 (1955): 1–65.
Bickel, Alexander M., and Harry H. Wellington. "Legislative Purpose and the Judi-
    cial Process: The *Lincoln Mills* Case." *Harvard Law Review* 71 (1957): 1. Cited in
    Michael J. Klarman, "An Interpretive History of Modern Equal Protection,"
    Michigan Law Review 90 (1991): 248 n. 62.
Black, Charles L. "The Lawfulness of the Segregation Decisions." *Yale Law Journal*
    69 (1960): 421–30. Cited in Michael J. Klarman, "An Interpretive History of
    Modern Equal Protection," *Michigan Law Review* 90 (1991): 255 n. 190.
Bork, Robert H. *The Tempting of America: The Political Seduction of the Law*. New York:
    Free Press, 1990.
Boyum, Keith O., and Lynn Mather, eds. *Empirical Theories about Courts*. New York:
    Longman, 1983.
Bransford, Stephen. *Gay Politics vs. Colorado: The Inside Story of Amendment 2*. Cas-
    cade, Colo.: Sardis Press, 1994.
Browne, Kingsley. "Title VII as Censorship: Hostile Environment Harassment and
    the First Amendment." *Ohio State Law Journal* 52 (1991): 481–550.
Cain, Maureen, and Christine B. Harrington. *Lawyers in a Postmodern World: Trans-
    lation and Transgression*. New York: New York University Press, 1994.
Cain, Patricia A. "Litigating for Lesbian and Gay Rights: A Legal History." *Univer-
    sity of Virginia Law Review* 79 (1993): 1551–641.
Caldeira, Gregory A. "Courts and Public Opinion." In *The American Courts: A Crit-
    ical Assessment*, edited by John B. Gates and Charles A. Johnson. Washington,
    D.C.: Congressional Quarterly Press, 1991.
———. "Neither the Purse nor the Sword: Dynamics of Public Confidence in the
    Supreme Court." *American Political Science Review* 80 (1986): 1209–26.
———. "Children's Images of the Supreme Court: A Preliminary Mapping." *Law &
    Society Review* 11 (1977): 851–71.
Canon, Bradley C. "The Supreme Court as a Cheerleader in Politico-Moral Dis-
    putes." *Journal of Politics* 54 (1992): 637–53.
———. "Courts and Policy: Compliance, Implementation, and Impact." In *The
    American Courts: A Critical Assessment*, edited by John B. Gates and Charles A.
    Johnson. Washington, D.C.: Congressional Quarterly Press, 1991.
Cardozo, Benjamin N. *The Nature of the Judicial Process*. New Haven: Yale University
    Press, 1921.
Carter, Robert L. "The Warren Court and Desegregation." *Michigan Law Review* 67
    (1968): 237–48.
Cathey, Karen C. "Note: Refining the Methods of Middle-Tier Scrutiny: A New Pro-
    posal for Equal Protection." *Texas Law Review* 61 (1983): 1501–55.
Chaitin, Ellen, and V. Roy Lefcourt. "Is Gay Suspect?" *Lincoln Law Review* 8 (1973):
    24–54.
Chang, David. "Discriminatory Impact, Affirmative Action, and Innocent Victims:
    Judicial Conservatism or Conservative Justices?" *Columbia Law Review* 91
    (1991): 790–844.
Choper, Jesse H. *Judicial Review and the National Political Process: A Functional Recon-
    sideration of the Role of the Supreme Court*. Chicago: University of Chicago Press,
    1980.
Comstock, Gary D. "Dismantling the Homosexual Panic Defense." *Law & Sexuality*
    2 (1992): 81–102.

"The Constitutional Status of Sexual Orientation: Homosexuality as a Suspect Classification." *Harvard Law Review* 98 (1985): 1285–1309.

Courrie, David P. *The Constitution and the Supreme Court*. 2 vols. Chicago: University of Chicago Press, 1985, 1988.

D'Emilio, John, and Estelle B. Freedman. *Intimate Matters: A History of Sexuality in America*. New York: Harper & Row, 1988.

"Developments in the Law—Equal Protection." *Harvard Law Review* 82 (1969): 1065–1192.

Downs, Donald A. *Nazis in Skokie: Freedom, Community, and the First Amendment*. Notre Dame, Ind.: University of Notre Dame Press, 1985.

Dubay, William H. *Gay Identity: The Self under Ban*. Jefferson, N.C.: McFarland & Co., 1987.

Dworkin, Ronald M. *Taking Rights Seriously*. Cambridge: Harvard University Press, 1977.

Editors of the Harvard Law Review. *Sexual Orientation and the Law*. Cambridge: Harvard University Press, 1990.

Ely, John Hart. *Democracy and Distrust: A Theory of Judicial Review*. Cambridge: Harvard University Press, 1980.

———. "Flag Desecration: A Case Study in the Roles of Categorization and Balancing in First Amendment Analysis." *Harvard Law Review* 88 (1975): 1482–508.

Epstein, Lee, ed. *Contemplating Courts*. Washington, D.C.: Congressional Quarterly Press, 1995.

———. "Courts and Interest Groups." In *The American Courts: A Critical Assessment*, edited by John B. Gates and Charles A. Johnson. Washington, D.C.: Congressional Quarterly Press, 1991.

Epstein, Lee, and Joseph L. Kobylka. *The Supreme Court and Legal Change*. Chapel Hill: University of North Carolina Press, 1992.

"Equal Protection: A Closer Look at Closer Scrutiny." *Michigan Law Review* 76 (1978): 771–891.

Ferguson, T. "Alternative Sexualities and Evolution." *Evolutionary Theory* 11 (1995): 55.

Fielding, Richard. "Fundamental Personal Rights: Another Approach to Equal Protection." *University of Chicago Law Review* 40 (1973): 807–31.

Fiss, Owen. "Groups and the Equal Protection Clause." *Philosophy and Public Affairs* 5 (1976): 108–77.

———. "Racial Imbalance in the Public Schools: The Constitutional Concepts." *Harvard Law Review* 78 (1965): 564–617. Cited in Michael J. Klarman, "An Interpretive History of Modern Equal Protection," *Michigan Law Review* 90 (1991): 255 n. 191.

Foucault, Michel. *The History of Sexuality, Volume One*. New York: Vintage Books, 1980.

Franklin, Charles H., and Liane C. Kosaki. "Media, Knowledge, and Public Evaluations of the Supreme Court." In *Contemplating Courts*, edited by Lee Epstein. Washington, D.C.: Congressional Quarterly Press, 1995.

———. "Republican Schoolmaster: The U.S. Supreme Court, Public Opinion, and Abortion." *American Political Science Review* 83 (1989): 751–71.

Galanter, Marc. "The Radiating Effects of Courts." In *Empirical Theories about Courts*, edited by Keith O. Boyum and Lynn Mather. New York: Longman, 1983.

Galloway, Russell. *Justice for All? The Rich and Poor in Supreme Court History, 1790–1990.* Durham, N.C.: Carolina Academic Press, 1991.

Gardiner, John A., ed. *Public Law and Public Policy.* New York: Praeger, 1977.

Gates, John B., and Charles A. Johnson, eds. *The American Courts: A Critical Assessment.* Washington, D.C.: Congressional Quarterly Press, 1991.

George, Tracey E., and Lee Epstein. "On the Nature of Supreme Court Decision Making." *American Political Science Review* 86 (1992): 323–37.

Gilbert, Arthur N. "Conceptions of Homosexuality and Sodomy in Western History." *Journal of Homosexuality* 6 (1981): 57–89.

Goldman, Sheldon, and Austin Sarat, eds. *American Court Systems: Readings in Judicial Process and Behavior.* San Francisco: W. H. Freeman, 1978.

Goldstein, Anne B. "Comment: History, Homosexuality, and Political Values: Searching for the Hidden Determinants of *Bowers v. Hardwick.*" *Yale Law Journal* 97 (1988): 1073–1103.

Gottlieb, Stephen, E., ed. *Public Values in Constitutional Law.* Ann Arbor: University of Michigan Press, 1993.

Gray, John C. Jr., and David Rudovsky. "The Court Acknowledges the Illegitimate." *University of Pennsylvania Law Review* 118 (1969): 1–39. Cited in Karen C. Cathey, "Note: Refining the Methods of Middle-Tier Scrutiny: A New Proposal for Equal Protection," *Texas Law Review* 61 (1983): 1507–8 n. 29.

Gunther, Gerald. "In Search of Judicial Quality on a Changing Court: The Case of Justice Powell." *Stanford Law Review* 24 (1972): 1001–35.

———. "Foreword: In Search of Evolving Doctrine on a Changing Court: A Model for a Newer Equal Protection." *Harvard Law Review* 86 (1972): 1–48.

Halley, Janet E. "The Politics of the Closet: Towards Equal Protection for Gay, Lesbian, and Bisexual Identity." *UCLA Law Review* 36 (1989): 915–76.

———. "Sexual Orientation and the Politics of Biology: A Critique of the Argument from Immutability." *Stanford Law Review* 46 (1994): 503–68.

Harris, Angela. "Race and Essentialism in Feminist Legal Theory." *Stanford Law Review* 42 (1990): 581–608.

Hart, H. L. A. *Law, Liberty, and Morality.* New York: Vintage Books, 1963.

———. *The Concept of Law.* Oxford: Clarendon Press, 1961.

Hart, Henry M. "The Supreme Court, 1958 Term—Foreword: The Time Chart of the Justices," *Harvard Law Review* 73 (1959): 84. Cited in Michael J. Klarman, "An Interpretive History of Modern Equal Protection," *Michigan Law Review* 90 (1991): 248 n. 162.

Herek, Gregory M., Jared B. Jobe, and Ralph M. Carney. *Out in Force: Sexual Orientation and the Military.* Chicago: University of Chicago Press, 1996.

Hirsch, Harry N. *A Theory of Liberty: The Constitution and Minorities.* New York: Routledge, 1992.

Hoekstra, Valerie J. "The Supreme Court and Opinion Change: An Experimental Study of the Court's Ability to Change Opinion." *American Politics Quarterly* 23 (1995): 109–29.

Hutchinson, Denis J. "Unanimity and Desegregation: Decision Making in the Supreme Court, 1948–58." *Georgetown Law Journal* 68 (1979): 1–87.

Johnson, Charles A. "The Implementation and Impact of Judicial Policies: A Heuristic Model." In *Public Law and Public Policy,* edited by John Gardiner. New York: Praeger, 1977.

Johnson, Charles A., and Bradley C. Canon. *Judicial Policies: Implementation and Impact*. Washington, D.C.: Congressional Quarterly Press, 1984.

Jones, Franklin D., and Ronald J. Koshes. "Homosexuality and the Military." *American Journal of Psychiatry* 152 (1995): 1–21.

Kahn, Ronald. *The Supreme Court and Constitutional Theory, 1953–1993*. Lawrence: University of Kansas Press, 1994.

Karst, Kenneth L. *Belonging to America: Equal Citizenship and the Constitution*. New Haven: Yale University Press, 1989.

———. "The Freedom of Intimate Association." *Yale Law Journal* 89 (1980): 624–92.

Klarman, Michael J. "An Interpretive History of Modern Equal Protection." *Michigan Law Review* 90 (1991): 213–318.

Koegal, Paul. "Lessons Learned from the Experience of Domestic Police and Fire Departments." In *Out in Force: Sexual Orientation and the Military*, edited by Gregory M. Herek, Jared B. Jobe, and Ralph M. Carney. Chicago: University of Chicago Press, 1996.

Kluger, Richard. *Simple Justice: The History of* Brown v. Board of Education *and Black America's Struggle for Equality*. New York: Knopf, 1976.

Krause, Harry D. "Legitimate and Illegitimate Off-Spring of *Levy v. Louiana*— First Decisions on Equal Protection and Paternity." *University of Chicago Law Review* 36 (1969): 338–63. Cited in Karen C. Cathey, "Note: Refining the Methods of Middle-Tier Scrutiny: A New Proposal for Equal Protection," *Texas Law Review* 61 (1983): 1507–8 n. 29.

Lewis, Neil. "Court Upholds Clinton Policy on Gay Troops." *New York Times*, 6 April 1996, p. 1, col. 5.

Locke, Don. "The Trivializability of Universality." *Philosophy Review* 77 (1968): 25. Cited in Peter Westen, "The Empty Idea of Equality," *Harvard Law Review* 95 (1982): 547 n. 30.

Lockhart, William B., et al. *Constitutional Law: Cases, Comments, Questions*. 7th ed. St. Paul, Minn.: West, 1991.

Lusky, Louis. "Footnote Redux: A *Carolene Products* Reminiscence." *Columbia Law Review* 82 (1982): 1093–1105.

Marcosson, Samuel A. "The Special Rights Canard in the Debate over Lesbian and Gay Civil Rights." *Notre Dame Journal of Law, Ethics and Public Policy* 9 (1995): 137–183.

Marshall, Thomas R. *Public Opinion and the Supreme Court*. Boston: Unwin Hyman, 1989.

———. "The Supreme Court as an Opinion Leader: Court Decisions and the Mass Public." *American Politics Quarterly* 15 (1987): 147–68.

McNollgast. "Politics and the Courts: A Positive Theory of Judicial Doctrine and the Rule of Law." *Southern California Law Review* 68 (1995): 1631–89.

Minstrom, Michael. "Why Efforts to Equalize School Funding Have Failed: Towards a Positive Theory." *Political Research Quarterly* 46 (1993): 847.

Mishler, William, and Reginald S. Sheehan. "Response: Popular Influence on Supreme Court Decisions." *American Political Science Review* 88 (1994): 716–24.

Mison, Robert B. "Homophobia in Manslaughter: The Homosexual Advance as Insufficient Provocation." *California Law Review* 80 (1992): 133–78.

Mohr, Richard D. *Gays/Justice: A Study of Ethics, Society, and Law*. New York: Columbia University Press, 1988.

Moltenbre, M. J. "Alternative Models of Equal Protection Analysis: *Plyler v. Doe.*" *Boston College Law Review* 24 (1983): 1363–97.

Mondak, Jeffery J. "Institutional Legitimacy, Policy Legitimacy, and the Supreme Court." *American Politics Quarterly* 20 (1992): 457–77.

———. "Perceived Legitimacy of Supreme Court Decisions: Three Functions of Source Credibility." *Political Behavior* 12 (1990): 363–84.

Moreshead, Craig D. "*Evans v. Romer* and Amendment 2: Homosexuality and the Constitutional Dilemma." *Capital University Law Review* 24 (1995): 485–505.

Moskos, Charles. "From Citizens' Army to Social Laboratory." *Wilson Quarterly* 17 (1993): 83–94.

Mueller, Gerhard O. W. *Sexual Conduct and the Law.* New York: Oceana Publications, 1980.

Murphy, Walter F., Joseph Tanenhaus, and Daniel L. Kastner. "Public Evaluations of Constitutional Courts: Alternative Explanations." In *American Court Systems: Readings in Judicial Process and Behavior,* edited by Sheldon Goldman and Austin Sarat. San Francisco: W. H. Freeman, 1978.

Nelson, William E. "The Changing Meaning of Equality in Twentieth Century Constitutional Law." *Washington and Lee Law Review* 52 (1995): 3.

Neubauer, David W. *Judicial Process: Law, Courts, and Politics in the United States.* 2d ed. Fort Worth, Tex.: Harcourt Brace College Publishers, 1997.

Niblock, John F. "Anti-Gay Initiatives: A Call for Heightened Judicial Scrutiny." *UCLA Law Review* 41 (1993): 153–98.

Norpath, Helmut, and Jeffrey Segal. "Comment: Popular Influence on Supreme Court Decisions." *American Political Science Review* 88 (1994): 711–16.

Note, *Texas Law Review* 47 (1969): 326. Cited in Karen C. Cathey, "Note: Refining the Methods of Middle-Tier Scrutiny: A New Proposal for Equal Protection," *Texas Law Review* 61 (1983): 1507–8 n. 29.

Ortiz, Daniel R. "The Myth of Intent in Equal Protection." *Stanford Law Review* 41 (1989): 1105–51.

Page, Benjamin I., Robert Y. Shapiro, and Glenn R. Dempsey. "What Moves Public Opinion?" *American Political Science Review* 81 (1987): 23–43.

Paglia, Camille. *Sex, Art, and American Culture: Essays.* New York: Vintage Books, 1992.

Petrick, Michael J. "The Supreme Court and Authority Acceptance." *Western Political Quarterly* 21 (1968): 5–19.

Pollack, Louis H. "Racial Discrimination and Judicial Integrity: A Reply to Professor Wechsler." *University of Pennsylvania Law Review* 108 (1959): 1–34. Cited in Michael J. Klarman, "An Interpretive History of Modern Equal Protection," *Michigan Law Review* 90 (1991): 255 n. 190.

Posner, Richard A. *Sex and Reason.* Cambridge: Harvard University Press, 1992.

Radin, Margaret J. "Reconsidering the Rule of Law." *Boston University Law Review* 69 (1989): 781–819.

Roper, W. G. "The Etiology of Male Homosexuality." *Medical Hypotheses* 46 (1996): 85.

Rosen, Jeffrey. "Disoriented." *New Republic,* 23 October 1995, 24–26.

———. "Sodom and Demurrer." *New Republic,* 29 November 1993, 16–19.

Rosenberg, Gerald N. *The Hollow Hope: Can Courts Bring About Social Change?* Chicago: University of Chicago Press, 1991.

Rubenfeld, Jed. "The Right of Privacy." *Harvard Law Review* 102 (1989): 737–807.

Rubenstein, William B. "Since When is the 14th Amendment Our Route to Equality: Some Reflections on the Construction of the Hate Speech Debate from a Lesbian / Gay Perspective." *Law and Sexuality* 2 (1992): 19–27.

———, ed. *Lesbians, Gay Men, and the Law.* New York: New Press, 1996.

Sanders, Francine. "*Brown v. Board of Education:* An Empirical Examination of its Effects on Federal District Courts." *Law & Society Review* 29 (1995): 731–47.

Scales-Trent, Judy. *Notes of a White Black Woman: Race, Color, and Community.* University Park: Pennsylvania State University Press, 1995.

Schacter, Jane S. "The Gay Civil Rights Debate in the States: Decoding the Discourse of Equivalents." *Harvard Civil Rights–Civil Liberties Law Review* 29 (1994): 283–317.

Scheingold, Stuart A. *The Politics of Rights: Lawyers, Public Policy, and Political Change.* New Haven: Yale University Press, 1974.

Schwartz, Bernard. *A History of the Supreme Court.* New York: Oxford University Press, 1993.

———. *The Ascent of Pragmatism: The Burger Court in Action.* Reading, Mass.: Addison-Wesley Publishing Co., 1990.

Schwartz, Herman. "The 1986 and 1987 Affirmative Action Cases: It's All Over but the Shouting." *University of Michigan Law Review* 86 (1987): 524–76.

Segal, Jeffrey A., and Harold J. Spaeth. *The Supreme Court and the Attitudinal Model.* New York: Cambridge University Press, 1993.

Sheppard, Annamay T. "Lesbian Mothers II: Long Night's Journey into Day." *Women's Rights Law Reporter* 8 (1985): 219–46.

Sherman, Jeffrey G. "Undue Influence and the Homosexual Testator." *University of Pittsburgh Law Review* 42 (1981): 225–67.

Sherrill, Kenneth, and Stephen Yang. "Public Opinion toward Lesbian and Gay Rights." In *The Encyclopedia of Homosexuality,* edited by George Haggerty. Binghamton, N.Y.: Haworth Press, in press.

Shiffrin, Steven H., and Jesse H. Choper. *The First Amendment: Cases—Comments—Questions.* St. Paul, Minn.: West, 1991.

Slovenko, Ralph. "The Homosexual and Society: A Historical Perspective." *University of Dayton Law Review* 10 (1985): 445–57.

Sniderman, Paul M., and Thomas Piazza. *The Scar of Race.* Cambridge: Harvard University Press, Belknap Press, 1993.

Songer, Donald R. "The Circuit Courts of Appeals." In *The American Courts: A Critical Assessment,* edited by John B. Gates and Charles A. Johnson. Washington, D.C.: Congressional Quarterly Press, 1991.

Songer, Donald R., Jeffrey A. Segal, and Charles M. Cameron. "The Hierarchy of Justice: Testing a Principal-Agent Perspective on Supreme Court–Circuit Court Interactions." *American Journal of Political Science* 38 (1994): 673.

Sullivan, Andrew. "Undone by Don't Ask, Don't Tell." *New York Times,* 9 April 1998, op-ed page.

Sullivan, Kathleen M. "Categorization, Balancing, and Governmental Interests." In *Public Values in Constitutional Law,* edited by Stephen E. Gottlieb. Ann Arbor: University of Michigan Press, 1993.

Sunstein, Cass R. "Homosexuality and the Constitution." *Indiana Law Journal* 70 (1994): 1–28.

————. "Sexual Orientation and the Constitution: A Note on the Relationship between Due Process and Equal Protection." *University of Chicago Law Review* 55 (1988): 1161–79.

Tarr, G. Alan, and Russell S. Harrison. "School Finance and Inequality in New Jersey." In *Constitutional Politics in the States: Contemporary Controversies and Historical Patterns*, edited by G. Alan Tarr. Westport, Conn.: Greenwood Press, 1996.

Tate, C. Neal. "The Methodology of Judicial Behavior Research: A Review and Critique." *Political Behavior* 5 (1983): 51–82.

Thomas, Kendall. "Beyond the Privacy Principle." *Columbia Law Review* 92 (1992): 1431–516.

Tribe, Laurence H. *American Constitutional Law*. 2d ed. Mineola, N.Y.: Foundation Press, 1988.

————. *Constitutional Choices*. Cambridge: Harvard University Press, 1985.

————. "The Puzzling Persistence of Process-Based Constitutional Theories." *Yale Law Journal* 89 (1980): 1063–80.

————. *American Constitutional Law*. Mineola, N.Y.: Foundation Press, 1978.

Tyler, Tom R., and Kenneth Rasinski. "Procedural Justice, Institutional Legitimacy, and the Acceptance of Unpopular U.S. Supreme Court Decisions: A Reply to Gibson." *Law & Society Review* 25 (1991): 621–29.

Ulmer, Sidney S. "Earl Warren and the *Brown* Decision." *Journal of Politics* 33 (1971): 689–702.

Volokh, Eugene. "Freedom of Speech and Workplace Harassment." *UCLA Law Review* 39 (1992): 1791–872.

Weber, Max. *Law in Economy and Society*. Translated by Max Rheinstein. New York: Simon & Schuster, 1967.

Wechsler, Herbert. "Toward Neutral Principles of Constitutional Law." *Harvard Law Review* 73 (1959): 1–35.

Welch, Don. "Legitimate Government Purposes and State Enforcement of Morality." *University of Illinois Law Review* 1993: 67–103.

Wellington, Harry H. *Interpreting the Constitution: The Supreme Court and the Process of Adjudication*. New Haven: Yale University Press, 1990.

Westen, Peter. "The Empty Idea of Equality." *Harvard Law Review* 95 (1982): 537–96.

Wilkinson, J. Harvie, III. "The Supreme Court, the Equal Protection Clause, and the Three Faces of Constitutional Equality." *Virginia Law Review* 61 (1975): 945–1018.

Wolfe, Alan. "The Homosexual Exception." *New York Times Sunday Magazine*, 8 February 1998, 46–47.